Peiper had been an SS officer. Thirty years later his past came back to haunt him. . . .

Peiper sent his wife and teenage daughter away from the house. . . . Later that evening he telephoned Ernst Ruthe in Bresigau, told him about the impending attack, and repeated that he was ready for all comers. The friend later said that Peiper seemed excited as he talked over the telephone and sounded as though he were preparing for a military action similar to those in which he had participated during World War II.

Police believe that Peiper took his shotgun and revolver and went out onto the balcony of the house. His two guard dogs sat beside him as he waited. . . .

The gunfire was heard in the district and the flames of the burning Peiper house lighted the entire countryside. Peiper was dead. There was a gaping wound in his chest and his body was burned badly. One leg and one arm were missing. As evidence of his resistance, Peiper's shotgun was empty and there was only one shell remaining in the revolver.

SECRETS OF THE SS

GLENN B. INFIELD

JOVE BOOKS, NEW YORK

This Jove book contains the complete
text of the original hardcover edition.
It has been completely reset in a typeface
designed for easy reading, and was printed
from new film.

SECRETS OF THE SS

A Jove Book / published by arrangement with
Stein and Day, Inc.

PRINTING HISTORY
Stein and Day edition published in 1982
Jove edition / February 1990

ISBN: 0-515-10246-6

Jove Books are published by The Berkley Publishing Group,
200 Madison Avenue, New York, New York 10016.

PRINTED IN THE UNITED STATES OF AMERICA

10 9 8 7 6 5 4 3 2

For Braden

Contents

A section of photographs follows page 148.

Introduction

When Justice Michael A. Musmanno, President Judge of Tribunal II of the War Crimes trials at Nuremberg, looked at the twenty-four SS defendants in his courtroom on September 29, 1947, the opening day of their trial, he said to an acquaintance: "Never has there been brought before a tribunal such a collection of refined cutthroats, intellectual assassins, world disturbers, and malignant egoists."

His statement describes the controversial nature of the Nordic "supermen" who manned the Nazi elite *Schutzstaffel* (literally, Protection Detachment; abbreviated, SS) organization. They were refined, intelligent, confident, and handsome; they were also cutthroats, murderers, assassins, and rapists. The SS was the "show-biz" organization of the Nazi party, the main attraction next to the Führer himself at every rally and parade. With their black uniforms, shining boots, gleaming daggers, and death's-head rings, the SS officers were the pride of the Third Reich, the image of the NSDAP (National Socialist German Workers' Party) that Hitler wanted projected to the world. But their purpose was not to entertain. These same tall blond giants were the largest group of murderers ever assembled.

This regression from elitist to thug is the mystery of the SS. The SS had two faces—simulated respectability and programmed brutality. Its members had a set of values that resulted in despair, anguish, and death for millions. The normal, accepted rules of morality were forgotten. Crimes were committed under the assumption that they were justified in achieving goals set by the Führer. Hitler had the power; the SS kept that power intact.

The inhumanity of the SS was first discovered immediately after the end of World War II when the world learned about the gas chambers, the crematoria, the mobile death squads, and the torturous medical experiments. These revelations created horror and disbelief, but they were only the beginning. As the curtain of secrecy was opened further during the ensuing years, the revealed atrocities increased in number and barbarity. Secret practices of the SS, straining the boundaries of human emotions, have been disclosed by the recent declassification of secret documents in the United States and Europe, practices that still have a serious consequence for mankind thirty-five years after the SS was disbanded.

Or was it really disbanded when the Third Reich collapsed? New evidence gathered from various areas around the world indicates that the SS, far from being disbanded, is alive and thriving. Operating under the guise of such names as *Die Spinne* (The Spider), the Bormann Brotherhood, Odessa, and various neopolitical parties, former SS members are well organized, still uphold the basic principles of Adolf Hitler, protect their members still sought for war crimes committed during the Third Reich, and hope to establish their brutal authority again in the future.

The SS was a secret Reich within Nazi Germany that threatened to supersede Hitler's Third Reich and came very close to doing so by its secret practices. This book exposes those practices and the men and women who directed them—practices that Hitler initially encouraged and abetted. Later, facing reality, he discovered he had created a monster over which he had lost control.

Acknowledgments

It was very difficult and painful for those who suffered at the hands of the SS during the Third Reich to relate these experiences to me because it brought back into sharp focus the tragic incidents that had been somewhat muted by the passing of time. To these persons, who willingly made this sacrifice so that I could get a better understanding of the SS, I am greatly indebted.

Among many others who helped me with my research and to whom I am grateful are: Lieutenant General Arthur G. Trudeau (Ret.); Donald Spencer of the Justice Department; Thomas F. Conley of the U.S. Army Intelligence and Security Command; Daniel P. Simon of the Berlin Document Center; Captain Miles C. Wiley III of the USAF; Dr. Milton O. Gustafson, John E. Taylor, Timothy P. Mulligan, and Gerald K. Haines, all of the National Archives in Washington, D.C.; Blair P. Hall and Irene Piechowicz of the Department of State; and Louis E. Foster of the Defense Intelligence Agency. All photos not otherwise attributed are from the National Archives.

Julius Mader of East Berlin gave me valuable information about SS officers in eastern Europe after the collapse of the Third Reich, as did several SS survivors whom I interviewed at Potsdam but who go unnamed at their request. Otto Skorzeny, whom I met in Madrid prior to his death in 1975, provided me with information that otherwise would not have been available. Stewart F. Alexander, today a physician well known in New Jersey, turned his secret Bari files over to me after the U.S. Army decided the details of the 1943 poison gas incident were still too controversial to be made public.

My years of association with the late Justice Michael A. Musmanno enabled me to read and study his voluminous Third Reich files, especially those on the SS and the *Einsatzgruppen* (Task Forces) killers.

Tom Johnson of Geneva College translated all German documents for me as he had during the writing of my previous books. Judi Billingsley did an excellent job of handling research in Washington, D.C., while my wife Peggy aided me in Europe.

I must admit that not all SS men were cooperative. I was rebuffed and threatened in Berchtesgaden, Berlin, and Munich when my questions became too personal for those who have never been tried for their crimes. These threats helped me understand the feelings of those who feared the SS during the Third Reich and, I hope, give the book an added dimension it otherwise would not have had.

SECRETS OF THE SS

1

"No One Can Hate That Much!"

The tall straight-backed man with the short-cropped white hair, a vivid contrast to his tanned face, smiled as he faced the store clerk in the village of Vesoul in southeastern France. "I need chicken wire to build a pen for my two dogs," he said.

Paul Cacheu, the clerk, stared at the customer for a few seconds, through his horn-rimmed glasses, before answering. Finally he pointed to the roll of chicken wire at the rear of the store. "Measure what you need."

Cacheu watched the man as he cut the required length of wire from the roll. It was 1975, thirty years after the end of World War II, but Cacheu had never forgotten the five years he had lived under the German boot. How could he ever forget the atrocities of the Nazis, especially the hated SS (*Schutzstaffel*: Protection Detachment)? There was something about the stranger purchasing the chicken wire that brought memories of those days more sharply into focus. When the man walked back to the counter, Cacheu said, "If you want the wire delivered, I'll have to have your name and address."

Without any hesitation, the customer took the proferred pen and wrote: "Joachim Peiper, Traves."

Cacheu watched Peiper until he had disappeared down the road leading to the village of Traves, then went directly to the back of the store and got a book from the top shelf. It was a copy of the Brown Book, a publication of the East German Communist party that contained the names of all alleged Nazi war criminals. Leafing through the book, he soon found what he was hunting. Former SS officer Joachim Peiper's name and alleged crimes were listed on page 103 of the book. He immediately notified his comrades.

Who was Joachim Peiper and why did his presence in France three decades after the Third Reich had collapsed cause such an outcry? Primarily because he had once been a member of the SS. The reputation of the SS, Hitler's mysterious and sinister secret society, as the brutal killers responsible for millions of deaths during the Third Reich has not diminished in the slightest over the postwar years. The suffering, humiliation, and death that resulted from the actions of the black-uniformed Nazi terrorists are a stain on the character of every German who belonged to the SS. Their treatment of the Jews and Communists especially is a universal reminder of humankind's inhumanity. By the time Paris was occupied on June 14, 1940, approximately 300,000 Jews in France were under Nazi control and it was the beginning of the end for them. The Gestapo, the secret state police arm of the SS, began rounding them up and interning them in a camp at Drancy. Shortly afterward, the deportations from Drancy to Auschwitz, the extermination camp in Poland, began. Only a small percentage of those Jews ever saw France again.

Peiper was not a member of the Gestapo. Even Cacheu knew that. Peiper was a decorated officer of the Waffen-SS, the military arm of the SS, an organization with a controversial history. Supposedly the Waffen-SS was the Nazi "army," the party counterpart of the Wehrmacht (German army). At its peak the Waffen-SS provided 40 divisions to fight at the side of the Wehrmacht, and its battle record was distinguished. Yet, one of the units of the Waffen-SS was the *SS-Totenkopfverbände* (SSTV; Death's Head Formations), which became infamous for providing the guards for the concentration camps and death camps and for the murders and tortures perpetrated by these guards. Even the Nazis had difficulty in deciding how to rate the Waffen-SS. In a 1942 report to Heinrich Himmler, Reichsführer of the SS, from Bruno Streckenbach, an officer of the *Sicherheitsdienst* (SD; the Security Service of the SS), this variance in opinion was pointed out. "Basically it may be stated that by its achievements the Waffen-SS had won its place in the popular esteem. Special reference is made to the fine comradeship and excellent cooperation among officers, NCOs, and men. Critical voices, however, are heard saying that the Waffen-SS is a kind of military watchdog, that SS men are trained to be brutal and ruthless so they can be used against other German formations if required. The overall impression is that the Waffen-SS is the most ruthless force; it takes no prisoners but totally annihilates its enemy."

Joachim Peiper had followed the Waffen-SS practice to the letter.

Peiper noticed the expression of the face of Paul Cacheu, the clerk, when he bought the chicken wire. When Ernst Ruthe, a former NCO in the Waffen-SS and a friend of Peiper, visited with him a week later, he mentioned his trip to the store. "Joachim was apprehensive when I visited him. He told me he thought he was being watched and was considering going to the police. I told him it was probably just his imagination. After all, who could still hate after thirty years? I misjudged the depth of the emotions of the Frenchmen in the area."

Ruthe stayed with Peiper in the house Peiper had built with his own hands. It was located near the River Saône in a grove of trees which partially hid it from view. It had taken Peiper several years to complete the house and during that time no one in Traves or Vesoul, the nearest town of any size, had bothered him. The local villagers and farmers had asked no questions and he had not volunteered any personal information. When he completed the house in 1972, he applied for a French residence permit in his own name and it was routinely granted with no objections registered.

Pierre Durand, a reporter for *L'Humanité*, was alerted by the French Communists about the possibility that a former SS member accused of war crimes was living near Traves. Cacheu's information had reached him within days after the clerk's encounter with Peiper. Durand began a detailed investigation; piece by piece he compiled a revealing dossier on Peiper.

Peiper, born January 30, 1915, in Berlin, had an excellent military background. His father had been a Prussian army officer. He had enrolled his son in the SS officer cadet school shortly after Hitler came to power and by 1936, Peiper was a lieutenant in the SS. Two years later he was an aide to Himmler, the leader of the SS, a prestige position that made him the envy of his comrades. Tall, slim, and good-looking, with a disciplined attitude that exemplified the basic tenets of the SS, Peiper was earmarked for greater things. His courage made him an ideal choice for a command in the Waffen-SS and he proved himself many times during World War II. At Kharkov he rescued the trapped German 320th Infantry Division; fought brilliantly in France and Poland; and by 1944 was a lieutenant colonel in command of the 1st SS Panzer Regiment. He was awarded the Knight's Cross and was a media star for Dr. Joseph Goebbels, the Nazi party's propaganda chief. Even the jealous Wehrmacht commanders admitted that Peiper was an outstanding military leader, but they tempered their praise because of a flaw they detected in him. Peiper accepted Hitler's ideological fantasies without demur and would go to any extreme to carry the Führer's orders.

The flaw the Wehrmacht officers felt was unacceptable was Peiper's violation of the rules of "honorable" warfare. It had first been displayed in September 1943 when Peiper was fighting in Italy. When two of his men were captured by Italian partisans in the village of Boves in northeastern Italy, Peiper seized two of the village elders as hostages and demanded the release of his SS men. He threatened to wipe out the entire village of 4,000 if there was any delay in responding to his demand. There wasn't. Less than one hour later the two SS men were released and back with Peiper's unit, safe and uninjured. According to Durand's investigation, however, Peiper was not satisfied. He ordered every house and building in Boves burned to the ground. During the conflagration, thirty-four civilians died. The OKW (*Oberkommando der Wachmacht*; High Command) disapproved of his action. Hitler approved.

But it was another action of Peiper's fifteen months later in Belgium that made him a marked man for the Allies and resulted in his indictment as a war criminal after the fall of Hitler and the Third Reich.

Even while Durand's investigation was still under way and his final report still pending, the harassment of Peiper began.

Strangers constantly reconnoitered his house, stoned his two dogs. He had an unlisted telephone number but he received calls often, most of the calls threatening him. He was advised to leave France while he was still able, called a murderer of women and children, and told that he would die in the flames of his home just as the thirty-four citizens of Boves had died. Peiper, however, had lost none of his personal courage, misdirected or not, and he refused to be cowed by his French enemies. Slowly the battle of the seventies, like the battle of the forties, developed into a stalemate between the SS represented by Peiper and the SS victims represented by a French guerrilla group named the Avengers. At a press conference held in the Grand Hotel in Paris, members of the Avengers, all wearing white hoods over their faces to conceal their identity, vowed to kill the "assassin of Malmédy."

The Malmédy massacre emphasized the overall dedication of the SS to Hitler's "close your hearts to pity" and "act brutally" policy. Each section of the SS tried to outdo the other, tried to gain more power and influence with Hitler by actions approved by the ruthless Führer. Malmédy, a village in Belgium, figured prominently in Hitler's last offensive of World War II, his final gamble in a winner-take-all struggle that started on December 16, 1944. Hitler's implicit faith in his own military genius, despite the defeats his forces had experienced in 1944, led him to believe he could change the course of the war by a single military stroke. Always a devotee of Frederick the Great—a portrait of the ruler hung behind his desk in his study and the oath taken by SS officer candidates was based on the Frederician oath to the flag—Hitler was convinced he could duplicate Frederick's feat of snatching victory from defeat in the Seven Years War. The ruler had faced superior forces closing in on his kingdom from all points of the compass. At Rossbach and Leuthen he had taken a great risk but he had defeated armies twice as large as his own. The victory had enabled Frederick to hang on until he was able to split those allied against Prussia and obtain a satisfactory peace. As Hitler paraphrased Frederick's own words: "The damned enemies got too tired to fight any longer."

Hitler's Rossbach and Leuthen were Liège and Antwerp. He ordered a quick thrust by German forces to Antwerp through Liège. That, he planned, would isolate not only the British 21st Army Group but also the U.S. Ninth Army and most of the U.S. First Army. He decided that such an action, if successful, would lead the British and Americans to agree to a separate peace.

"A blow there will strike a seam between the British and Americans and lead to political as well as military disharmony between the Allies," Hitler stated. "It will also erase the enemy ground threat to the Ruhr."

Against the advice of his generals, who told him they lacked both the manpower and equipment needed for such a thrust, Hitler ordered the operation, known officially as the Ardennes Offensive and informally as the Battle of the Bulge, to get under way early on the morning of December 16. One of the commanders in whom he had complete trust was Joachim Peiper.

Peiper's lst SS Panzer Regiment was augmented by several other SS units, forming a *Kampfgruppe* (Combat Group)). It was a tough, seasoned group of SS officers and men who had survived the ice and snow of Russia and the hedgerows of France, men who asked for no mercy and gave no quarter. When Peiper was ordered to lead the group from Honsfeld to Trois Ponts by way of Baugney, Ligneuville, and Stavelot, he didn't ask how. He just nodded his head and started out shortly before daylight on December 16.

Peiper's *Kampfgruppe* was supposed to follow the 12th Volks Grenadier Division through the lines of the American 99th Infantry Division. He soon discovered, however, to his disgust, that the lead German division had stopped northwest of Losheim because of a blown bridge. Rather than wait for the bridge to be repaired, Peiper turned his group ninety degrees to the west and headed for the bridge at Lanzerath. However, at Lanzerath he was again delayed when the 3rd Parachute Battalion hesitated to attack the American lines. Peiper personally took an infantry battalion, positioned two of his Panther tanks at the point, and launched an attack toward Honsfeld. Breaking through the thin lines of the American forces, he captured Honsfeld easily.

But the extra maneuvering of his *Kampfgruppe* had not

only cost Peiper hours of time but much extra fuel. His tanks, armored vehicles, and trucks were nearly out of gasoline and there were no German supply lines in the area. When he learned from his advance detachment that there was an American gasoline storage depot at nearby Büllingen, Peiper immediately changed his plans. Instead of following his prescribed route to Schoppen, over a muddy, nearly impassable road, Peiper moved his *Kampfgruppe* to a paved road which led to Schoppen through Büllingen. This was the road the 12th Volks Grenadier Division was supposed to use but it hadn't arrived on the scene yet. Speeding up the paved road, Peiper's group surprised the small contingent of Americans at Büllingen and with a minimum of losses was soon in control of the fuel depot. The Germans forced the Americans to fill the tanks of their vehicles from the 50,000 gallons available. In addition, Peiper's SS troops destroyed 12 liaison aircraft at the Büllingen airfield and looted the depot of materials they needed. By the time American artillery units on the outskirts of Büllingen were alerted and began shelling the village, Peiper's *Kampfgruppe* had moved out on its way to Ligneuville.

Between noon and one o'clock on December 17, as the Germans moved from Modersheid toward Ligneuville, Peiper's SS troops ran headlong into an American truck convoy of Battery B of the 285th Field Artillery Observation Battalion coming from Malmédy. The point men of the SS unit immediately opened fire on the trucks and the Americans scrambled out of the vehicles and took to the woods and ditches. The main body of the *Kampfgruppe* following the point men rounded up the dazed and wounded Americans and marched them into a field at Malmédy. Initially it appeared that the SS men intended to treat the Americans as prisoners of war under the normal rules of warfare. They permitted them to keep their wallet photographs and cigarettes and even refrained from taking their wristwatches. The apprehensive Americans began to relax, but at that moment a young SS private later identified as Georg Fleps raised his pistol and aimed it at the prisoners. Virgil Lary, a second lieutenant who was standing in the front row of the group of prisoners, stared in disbelief at the German. Before he could protest at the SS private's action, however, Fleps pulled the trigger on the pistol and shot Lary. A moment later the other SS men opened fire with machine guns and pistols. At least eighty-six Americans were shot down and killed. A few escaped by pretending to be dead. Lary survived despite his serious wound. After Peiper's men moved on, laughing and joking about the massacre, Lary climbed a fence and hid in a nearby shed until rescued late that afternoon by a patrol of the 291st Engineer Combat Battalion.

Later it was discovered that Peiper's SS troops had also murdered nineteen American prisoners at Honsfeld and fifty at the gasoline depot at Büllingen before meeting the ill-fated men of the 285th Field Artillery Observation Battalion. By December 20, Peiper's command was accused of murdering approximately 350 prisoners of war and at least 100 unarmed Belgian civilians at twelve different locations along his route.

Peiper was arrested in Austria shortly after the end of World War II. He was one German whom the American authorities definitely wanted to put on trial, and they wasted little time in doing so. His trial started May 14, 1946, at Dachau, where he faced a nine-man U.S. military court. Peiper used the same defense at Dachau that he was to use a quarter of a century later at Traves—he was only following orders. The court refused to accept such logic, citing Article 47 of the German Military Penal Code:

> If through the execution of an order pertaining to the service a penal law is violated, then the superior giving the order is alone responsible. However, the obeying subordinate shall be punished as an accomplice:
>
> (1) if he went beyond the order given him, or
>
> (2) if he knew that the order of the superior concerned an act which aimed at a civil or military crime or offense.

On July 11, 1946, Peiper was ordered hanged for the shooting of the American prisoners at Malmédy. His only comment to the court was a request to be shot rather than hanged, and it was granted. Peiper was taken to Landsberg Prison to await his execution, but in 1951, five years after being sentenced, he was still waiting. By that time the SS officers and men who had survived the Third Reich were regrouped and exerting considerable influence in Germany. Otto Skorzeny, Hitler's commando chief, who was acquitted of war crimes and became a dominant force behind *Die Spinne* (The Spider), the leading postwar SS organization, revealed the leverage the former SS men had when he gave an interview to a journalist in Spain. "If Peiper dies it is all over. In good faith, even with a certain amount of enthusiasm, we have put ourselves at the disposal of the Americans. Yet, I repeat in the name of all German officers who are working for the future victory of the West, if Peiper dies we will no longer lift a finger to help but will yield to the opposing point of view."

This threat by a former intimate associate of Adolf Hitler, and a man who had been accused of war crimes, was evidence of the strength of *Die Spinne* only six years after the fall of the Third Reich and four years after the International Military Tribunal at Nuremberg had branded the SS an "army of outlaws."

How had the former SS members gained such power? The Cold War! While the Allies had demobilized their military forces after the end of World War II, the Soviets had not. When the warm relationship between the Russians and the West that existed during the war turned to icy enmity during the postwar years, the West discovered it had neither the manpower nor industrial capability in Europe to resist the relentless takeover of occupied countries by the Soviets. During this critical period, the thousands of SS officers and men available, men who were experienced fighters and who despised the Russians, volunteered to fill the gap. Key SS men and industrialists who were in prison were released or their sentences reduced so they could help the West. But in return Skorzeny and *Die Spinne* expected—and received—certain considerations. One was the release of Peiper from prison. In December 1956, he was paroled.

Life for the released SS commander was relatively quiet for a while. With the help of *Die Spinne* and other neo-Nazi groups, he obtained a position in Stuttgart with Porsche, but when his identity became known—Peiper refused to change his name—he was dismissed because of union protests. A stint with Volkswagen ended in the same manner, only this time the protesters were Italian workers who remembered the massacre at Boves.

The Dachau trial had not mentioned the Boves accusation but in 1964, at the insistence of Italy, an investigation into the Boves incident was ordered by West German officials. It dragged on for years but finally the case was dismissed. *Die Spinne* made certain of the verdict. It was after this investigation that Peiper went to France seeking a place where his action with the Waffen-SS during the Third Reich would be ignored, hoping that the French would let bygones be bygones.

He didn't understand that the atrocities of the SS would never be forgotten.

Durand, the reporter for *L'Humanité*, completed his investigation of Peiper in mid-June, 1976, and the results left no doubt that the man living on the banks of the River Saône was Joachim Peiper. The details of his findings were published in *L'Humanité*, and l'affaire Peiper headed for a climax. On the road leading into Traves his enemies used white paint to write "Peiper SS" in three-foot-high letters. Others handed out information sheets to passersby that stated: "Citizens of Traves, a war criminal, SS Joachim Peiper, is among you." Strangers kept his house under surveillance day and night and he received innumerable death threats. The mayor of Traves, Ernest Rigoulot, who had routinely signed Peiper's French residence permit in 1972, encouraged him to leave Traves before it was too late. Peiper refused. He had decided to stay and settle the matter once and for all.

The residents of the area were divided in their opinions about Peiper living in their midst. Some were willing to forgive; others thought that his prison term erased his guilt; some were neutral. But there were many who saw Peiper as a symbol of the organization that could never be forgotten or forgiven.

As the harassment increased Peiper prepared for the worst. He made certain that his weapons—a shotgun and a revolver—were in good condition and that he had an ample supply of ammunition. Each night he unfastened the leashes from his dogs and allowed them to run loose. Their barking always warned him when intruders were in the area. The anonymous telephone calls telling him to leave France before Bastille Day on July 14 became more frequent. The local police paid him a visit and insisted that he leave the area and suggested he return to West Germany, but Peiper refused to budge. Why he didn't return to his homeland, where he would have had the protection of *Die Spinne* and the other neo-Nazi groups, is not known. According to one visitor, Peiper was determined to show the French and the world that he and all other former SS members had the same rights as any other citizen. "Moral principles are not the question," he stated. "It is whether I am now a law-abiding citizen or not. I cannot continually pay for what happened in the past."

He was wrong. As the Bastille Day deadline approached, l'affaire Peiper became much larger than one man's personal battle. *France-Soir*, France's most widely distributed newspaper, published a list of names of high-ranking ex-Nazis who were prominent in West Germany, emphasizing that several hundred Nazis condemned to death *in absentia* in France were those named. German newspapers retaliated by stating the harassment of SS officer Joachim Peiper was the start of a campaign against the West German government. One German magazine reminded the French of the atrocities committed by French troops in Algeria.

Shortly after 6:00 P.M. on the eve of Bastille Day, Peiper received a final anonymous telephone threat. "We're coming for you tonight."

"Fine. I'm ready for you."

Peiper sent his wife and teenage daughter away from the house after the call. His family never lived at the house in Traves but often visited Peiper from their permanent home in Munich. Now that l'affaire Peiper was reaching a climax, he wanted them out of the way. Later that evening he telephoned Ernst Ruthe in Bresigau, told him about the impending attack, and repeated that he was ready for all comers. The friend said later that Peiper seemed excited as he talked over the telephone and sounded as though he were preparing for a military action similar to those in which he had participated during World War II.

Police, reconstructing the SS-Avenger battle at Traves on the night of July 13/14, believe that Peiper took his shotgun and revolver and went out onto the balcony of the house. His two guard dogs sat beside him as he waited for the attackers. There was a full moon that night so Peiper probably saw the death squad park on a nearby side road, probably watched quietly and patiently as they climbed over the barbed wire fence surrounding his property. When they were close enough, he fired.

"Joachim would take the offensive," Ruthe insists. "He was never one to allow the other man to hit first if he could help it."

The gunfire was heard in the district and the flames of the burning Peiper house lighted the entire countryside. By the time the local police arrived on the scene, the attackers had disappeared. Peiper was dead. There was a gaping wound in his chest and his body was burned badly. One leg and one arm was missing. As evidence of his resistance, Peiper's shotgun was empty and there was only one shell remaining in the revolver.

Even in death controversy surrounded Peiper. Some persons still believe that Peiper killed one of his attackers with his shotgun and drove the others off. They think he then hacked off the leg and arm of the victim because they did not have the scars of his war wounds and set fire to his own house, burning the corpse in the resulting flames. Evidence produced by investigators during the months after the incident, however, doesn't support this theory.

Peiper's death in 1976, three decades after his trial at Dachau, brought into focus once again the never-ending debate about the role played by the SS during the Third Reich. Peiper has become a symbol for the veterans of the SS, a dangerous symbol for a powerful and influential group still loyal to the memory of Adolf Hitler. This look at the secret practices of the SS during the Third Reich, based on recently declassified information in the United States and Europe, answers the question asked by Peiper shortly before his death:

"How can anyone hate that much after thirty years?"

2

The Mysterious Super-Nazis

On April 13, 1945, Sergeant Bruce Jacobs of the United States 3rd Armored Division walked into the concentration camp at Nordhausen and the sight that met his eyes stunned him. As the Army Signal Corps later reported about that day: "The bodies of hundreds of slave laborers of many nationalities were found in conditions almost unrecognizable as human. All were little more than skeletons; the dead lay beside the sick and dying in the same beds; filth and human excrement covered the floors. No attempt had been made to alleviate the diseases and gangrene that had spread unchecked among the prisoners. Most of the men were dead when the camp was taken. The few still alive were removed to hospitals where all possible is being done to save their lives."

Jacobs and those accompanying him that April day were sickened at the sight. These were soldiers who had experienced the horrors of the battlefield, hardened military men.

That same day British troops entered the camp at Belsen and a British army review stated: "Deaths were averaging 500 per day. More than half the total inmates needed immediate hospital treatment. Ten thousand unburied bodies, typhus-infested, many in an advanced stage of decomposition, lay about the camp. There had been neither food nor water for five days. A great many of the internees were little more than living skeletons."

Benjamin B. Ferencz, and American soldier who later became a prosecutor at the war crimes trials at Nuremberg after the war, recalled that when he entered Buchenwald, it was the carts loaded with skeletons and the mounds of emaciated bodies covered with lye, piled like cordwood before the crematoria, that affected him most.

Yet despite the eyewitness testimony of men such as Jacobs and Ferencz and thousands of other American, British, French, and German soldiers and civilians, people were reluctant for many years after the collapse of the Third Reich to believe that 11 million persons, among them 6 million Jews, were deliberately murdered by the Nazis. There are many reasons for this. A normal person is horrified by the murder of a close friend or relative, but when the victims total in the millions the enormity of the crime is incomprehensible. One feels inadequate and avoids becoming involved if at all possible. Photographs and films shown to well-fed citizens living in homes untouched by enemy bombers and enemy troops and several thousand miles from the death camps brought gasps of dismay and sympathy and angry comments. But unless there was a personal connection, the business of forgetting the war and reestablishing a civilian career, welcoming home loved ones from the combat zones, visiting those who were in veterans hospitals recovering from the rigors of the battlefield, and a hundred other activities, often pushed the death camp scenes aside. It wasn't a lack of sympathy, but a lack of empathy in the United States. It was an "out-of-sight, out-of-mind" syndrome that lasted for years.

Another reason for this seeming indifference was the lack of unity among the Allies and among the American public, in particular on the issue of whether any of the Nazis should be brought to trial for crimes against humanity. It was understandable that the Germans who faced the International Military Tribunal would contest the justice of such trials. Admiral Karl Dönitz, sentenced to ten years in prison by the IMT, argued that there was no moral foundation for such a proceeding. August von Knieriem, who was acquitted, agreed with Dönitz. But criticism from Americans such as Hugh Baille, a former president of United Press, who stated that the law was used at Nuremberg for the purpose of hanging as many of the Nazis as possible, and from Senator Robert H. Taft, who vowed that the IMT proceedings were a blot on the American record, introduced considerable doubt into the minds of many persons without first-hand knowledge of Nazi atrocities. Who is telling the truth? many wondered. Were the photographs faked? Perhaps the camp inmates died from disease or Allied bombing attacks or lack of food? What's the big fuss? People die in every war.

Gradually, however, as the truth about the atrocities became known, the world began to accept the fact that what Hitler had "wrought" would forever affect the lives of everyone who had survived, and their offspring as well. The horrors of Nazi Germany didn't die with the Führer but have been relived throughout the world during the postwar years. The terrorism developed to a high degree of sophistication and effectiveness during the Third Reich is now standard operating procedure around the globe. The lack of compassion, the violation of human rights, man's inhumanity to man, and the absence of moral principles—all Hitlerian characteristics—are the norm. And when these Nazi tactics began touching the lives of those who previously had paid little notice to them, the demand for further information about the secret practices of Hitler's staff of murderers became a clamor. During the three and a half decades since the end of World War II, new facts have been uncovered about the elite killers of the Third Reich, facts that have unraveled the fate of millions.

The tall, well-proportioned black-uniformed SS men march in perfect alignment in Leni Riefenstahl's famous Nazi film *Triumph of the Will*, the movie made of the party's 1934 rally at Nuremberg. Even today, it is difficult to realize they were Hitler's murderers. No scene in *Triumph of the Will* is more memorable than the outdoor review of the SS held in the vast Luitpold Arena. The cameras sweep the area, showing thousands of SS men grouped together like so many black squares on a white field. Hitler, accompanied by Himmler and Viktor Lutze, walks between the groups to a cenotaph where he places a wreath in honor of SS members who have died. This impressive ceremony projected the image of a well-disciplined organization of elite Nazis that would establish the Third Reich as the millenial epoch. As Hitler stated later: "I do not doubt for a moment, despite certain people's skepticism, that within a hundred years or so from now all the German elite will be a product of the SS."

How then did Hitler's "German elite" develop into what the IMT called "an army of outlaws"?

In 1925, when Hitler was still facing great obstacles in his uphill battle to become ruler of Germany, he decided that he needed a bodyguard of party members to protect him from his opponents at public meetings and rallies. As he explained it in 1942: "I told myself that I needed a bodyguard, even a very restricted one, but made up of men who would be enlisted unconditionally, ready even to march against their own brothers. I'd rather have a mere twenty men per city whom I could count on absolutely than an unreliable mass."

Hitler asked Julius Schreck, an old comrade and at that time his chauffeur, to form the new unit. Schreck took his new position very seriously, insisting that this new headquarters bodyguard organization would be composed of only specially qualified men. Restrictive guidelines included age limits between twenty-three and thirty-five; recommendations from at least two sponsors; a police registration stating that the applicant had been in good standing during the previous five years; and the candidate had to be physically strong and healthy. No habitual drunkards, gossipmongers, or other delinquents were accepted. Since Schreck made the final decision on applicants and he himself could not meet these standards, it was miraculous that he succeeded in forming the reliable and proficient headquarters unit that he did. He made certain that all applicants also understood what was expected of them if they became members of the new organization: "Protection of meetings in their area, recruitment of subscribers and advertisers for the [Nazi party newspaper] *Völkischer Beobachter*, and recruitment of party members. We carry the death's head on our black cap as a warning to our enemies and an indication to our Führer that we will sacrifice our lives for his concept."

Hitler made certain that the SS was not merely an extension of the *Sturmabteilung* (SA; Storm Detachment) but a completely separate organization. He had a very good reason for this. He had discovered that if he were ever going to reach the zenith of power in Germany, he was going to have to divorce himself from the street-fighting rough-necks who composed the SA. The image projected by these old comrades frightened the average German citizen and indirectly hurt his own chances of gaining power and winning elections. Looking into the future, Hitler decided that he needed a more sophisticated personal protection unit that could eventually replace the SA or at least dominate it. So when Schreck discovered that a party member in Munich had formed an SS unit composed entirely of ex-SA members, he ordered it disbanded immediately, stating: "The SS is an organization laboriously built upon sound foundations and its image must not be tarnished by imitation copies."

This animosity between the leader of the new SS and the members of the old established SA set the stage for a struggle that lasted as long as the Third Reich existed. Characterized by party members and the Wehrmacht as the battle of the brownshirts (SA) versus the blackshirts (SS), this internal conflict led to many of the excesses of the SS in later years. At the beginning, however, the desire of Hitler and Schreck was to form a unit that would far outshine the SA and would result in an elite group of men who would be a great asset not only to the Nazi party and the Führer but also the regime they had molded. In fact, the new SS even outgrew its initial leader, Schreck. He was replaced in April 1926 by Joseph Berchtold, a businessman who held the number-two spot in the Nazi party treasury office. He was much more dynamic and forceful a leader than Shreck, who was gradually losing control of the SS members as the organization became larger. But Berchtold discovered that not only did the SS face a formidable adversary in the SA but that his organization had other opponents, in the Nazi party bosses. Hitler told him to operate under the guidelines that the party was not to interfere in the internal affairs of the SS, emphasizing that the SS was a completely independent organization within the Nazi movement.

The Nazi party bosses publicly agreed with Hitler, but it soon became evident to Berchtold that down at the Gau level (Nazi party territorial district), the Gauleiters had no intentions of permitting a strong, influential SS unit to operate outside their rigid control of the area. The constant in-fighting got the best of Berchtold and in March 1927 he resigned, and his deputy Erhard Heiden took over the reins of the organization. Heiden decided that, since the number of SS members was limited to 10 percent of that of the hated SA, there was no way they could outshout their opponents and verbal opposition was useless. He therefore issued an order stating: "The SS will never take part in discussions at meetings. SS men will attend discussions for the purpose of political instruction only. The SS man and SS commander will remain silent and will never become involved in matters concerning party or SA members which do not concern him." The SS adopted the slogan: "The aristocracy keeps its mouth shut." This unique attitude puzzled both the Nazi party bosses and SA leaders and established a mysterious aura around the arrogant SS members that remained intact through the years of the Third Reich.

On January 6, 1929, the SS changed leaders again. Heinrich Himmler, a deceptively weak-looking man who had a receding chin, wore wire-rimmed glasses, and had small, always perfectly manicured hands, became the new Reichsfürer-SS. Behind this outward appearance, however, was an inward determination to make the SS the master of the Third Reich, and Himmler never wavered from this ambition to his dying hour. The Nazi party members were elated at Hitler's appointment of Himmler to lead the SS, as were the SA leaders, because they thought Himmler was a man they could easily dominate. This was the same mistake the industrialists made four years later when they supported Adolf Hitler for chancellor. No one dominated Hitler; and only Hitler himself was able to dominate the ineffective-appearing Himmler. Even the Führer had problems doing so in the last years of the Reich. Many of those party and SA members who wrote Himmler off as an indecisive ex-chicken farmer of no real substance died at the hands of his SS not long afterward.

Yet his critics—and even his admirers—could be excused for their error in underestimating Himmler because he was a very dichotomous man. He was raised a strict Catholic, yet he subsequently forced thousands of SS members to leave the Church and even publicly supported the assassination of the Pope. Himmler was a married man who insisted on approving the women his SS members wished to marry so that he could be certain that they would be suitable additions to the SS family. He personally created a strict marriage ceremony each member was forced to follow. Yet Himmler himself had a mistress and children out of wedlock. He pampered his legitimate daughter Gudrun yet showed no remorse for having ordered hundreds of thousands of small children executed with their parents. He lived rather modestly in a home in Bavaria for which he had to borrow money from Hitler's secretary, Martin Bormann. But as Reichsführer-SS, he set up headquarters in Wewelsburg, a Westphalian castle, that by the end of the war had cost 13 million marks. He devoted his every waking hour to his idol Adolf Hitler, seriously considered Hitler the greatest man alive, but periodically joined in attempts to overthrow the Führer or betray the Third Reich to the Allies by signing a separate peace. Consequently, those who knew Himmler in the flesh had problems trying to forecast his next move; those who knew him only by reputation were completely confused about the man.

Himmler, of course, knew precisely what sort of organization he wanted to build. As he said in a speech during the war: "We went about it like a nursery gardener trying to reproduce a good old strain which has been mixed and debased; we started from the principles of plant selection and then proceeded, quite unashamedly, to weed out the men whom we did not think we could use for the buildup of the SS." To aid in selecting only a master-race type for SS membership, Himmler asked the help of Professor Bruno K. Schultz. Schultz set up the criteria that all SS applicants had to pass prior to being accepted. These criteria were of three sorts, but related: racial appearance, general bearing, and physical condition. Under racial appearance the professor, with Himmler's blessing, had a scale that included five categories. In order to obtain a five-star rating an applicant had to be "pure Nordic." From this top rating down, the scale ran "predominantly Nordic," "harmonious bastard with slight Alpine, Dinaric, or Mediterranean characteristics," "bastards of East-Baltic or Alpine origin," and "bastards of extra-European origin." Only those who rated three stars or better were accepted because Himmler was convinced that these three types would assure his reaching his goal of a pure-blooded Nordic German population within a century. Besides the racial appearance, Himmler took great pride in the physical bearing of his men. He wanted tall men, for example, but the overall height had to be distributed properly between the legs and the body. Schultz had nine categories in the physical-bearing requirements, but only the top four—ideal, excellent, very good, and good—permitted the applicant to receive his black uniform.

These rigid requirements eliminated from candidacy for the SS many men who were acceptable to the SA. This, of course, increased the bitterness between the two groups. Himmler continuously impressed on his men that they were better, physically and mentally, than their counterparts in the SA, and in most instances this was true. Many of the new SS members were academics whose careers had been ruined by the economic situation and there were many dissatisfied professional men, as well. These men disliked the image of the SA and didn't want to be classed as street-fighters and bullies. The sophistication of the SS was more to their liking and gave them status and prestige among their acquaintances. The SS grew so rapidly that even the regular Nazi party bosses were unable to stop the expansion. Hitler, however, who had earlier wanted to keep the organization small, was delighted at the success of his "bodyguard" unit, so delighted that he dealt the SA a blow. While he forebade Himmler to canvass the SA for recruits, Hitler, in one of his many double-talk decisions, ordered the SA to provide "selected personnel" for the SS. The most far-reaching decision, however, was Hitler's decree to the Nazi party in November 1930 stating "the task of the SS is primarily to carry out police duties within the party." Before the collapse of the Reich, Himmler's SS had become the most dreaded police force in history.

One of the reasons Hitler decided to use the SS in this fashion was that he had discovered that he had created a monster in the SA—one that he could not control. As the SS grew in size and its budget increased, SA leaders became more and more suspicious of Hitler's motives. Walther Stennes, the senior SA commander in eastern Germany, became the main agitator since he was convinced that Hitler, in his fight for the chancellorship, had decided that the rough-and-tumble SA was more of a liability than an asset. As the Reichstag elections of September 1930 approached, Stennes sent an ultimatum to NSDAP headquarters in Munich demanding authorization for SA commanders to enter parliament, less power for the Gauleiters in SA matters, and payment to SA units whenever they were used to keep order at Nazi functions. Hitler ignored the delegation Stennes sent as well as the ultimatum.

At the same time, Goebbels, in the midst of his election campaign on behalf of the party, had scheduled a mass gathering at the Sports Palace in Berlin. Goebbels was depending upon the SA to maintain order. When Stennes heard about the SA delegation's rebuff in Munich, he withdrew all his SA men from the Sports Palace, leaving the Nazi party members at the mercy of the Communists and other anti-Hitler groups. It appeared that the outnumbered party members were going to be waylaid by their enemies, but at the last moment Himmler rushed the Berlin SS into the breach and restored order. Although Stennes and Hitler were later reconciled, the SA never forgot what happened that September night at the Sports Palace—and neither did Adolf Hitler. He knew that Stennes might turn against him again at the slightest provocation, that the SA was more interested in its own future than the future of Hitler and the Nazi party. The SS, on the other hand, was composed of men who had sworn allegiance to him personally: "I swear to thee, Adolf Hitler, obedience until death." Hitler, determined to safeguard his own future, decided that the SS had to be built up to a point where it could dominate the SA. At every opportunity he bragged about the SS and said less and less about the achievements of the SA.

Hitler made two other moves at this time. First, he brought back an old friend from Bolivia, Ernst Röhm, to take charge of the SA, thinking he could trust and influence Röhm in his handling of the brownshirts. Second, he gave Himmler orders to devote more time investigating enemies of the party, both inside the NSDAP and outside. Himmler quickly set up intelligence units in every SS district and fed all the reports to Hitler's headquarters. It was an excellent secret pipeline and enabled Hitler to avoid many pitfalls during the following three years as he struggled to reach the pinnacle of power in Germany. But it was obvious, mostly through Himmler's intelligence units, that Röhm and the SA were on a collision course with Hitler and the SS. Röhm was a Bavarian swashbuckler who enjoyed fighting more than he did eating. There was only one action he enjoyed as much as fighting, and that was going to bed with young men. However, when Himmler attempted to blackmail Röhm over his homosexual activities, the squat, bullet-scarred SA commander just laughed at him, saying that most people were aware of his sexual preference anyway. Röhm's organizational ability far exceeded Himmler's at that time. By the beginning of 1933, Röhm had increased the membership of the SA to 300,000 while Himmler's SS totaled only 50,000. Although Himmler bragged that his men were the elite of Germany, there was real concern in Hitler's headquarters about the growth of the SA under Röhm. And this concern was increased immeasurably when Himmler's secret reports indicated that Röhm, like Stennes, had his doubts about Hitler's future policies regarding the SA.

Hitler assumed the chancellorship of Germany on January 30, 1933. It was a great day for the NSDAP in general but for Himmler and the SS it was a disappointment, because their expectations had been so high. Himmler had been confident that once Hitler became chancellor, he himself would be given a very important position in the government and that the Führer's favoritism for the SS would be allowed to manifest itself more fully to Röhm and the SA. Instead, Himmler was ignored during the takeover of the government. After a period of depression and inactivity, Himmler awakened to the fact that if he were going to better his position, it was going to be up to him alone. Hitler wasn't going to hand him anything on a silver platter.

His initial plan to attract Chancellor Hitler's attention was clever. Himmler was aware that Hitler constantly worried that he would be assassinated. Consequently, Himmler began a series of arrests—making certain that he gained as much publicity from each as possible. First he arrested Count Arco-Valley, whom he accused of planning a coup against Hitler. Following this arrest he revealed that Russian agents had placed a time bomb near the Richard Wagner memorial—a device which was to be exploded as Hitler's car passed. One warning after another, often unsubstantiated, was relayed to Hitler by the Reichsführer-SS until Hitler became a nervous wreck. He even became suspicious of the sentries at the Reich Chancellery, which were provided by the Army, because he didn't trust the generals. In desperation he turned to Himmler, the one man who seemed to be as concerned about the Führer's life as the Führer himself. He ordered Himmler to form a new and special "Headquarters Guard." This new unit consisted of 120 select SS men who formed a triple human fence around the Reich Chancellery through which all visitors had to pass. Hitler was so pleased with this new SS guard that in September 1933, at the Nuremberg party rally, he renamed the unit the *Leibstandarte-SS Adolf Hitler* (SS bodyguard bearing Hitler's personal flag) and suggested General Josef (Sepp) Dietrich, one of the most brutal of men, as commander. Himmler now had the beginnings of a military unit that was to grow in strength until it was in competition with the German army. At the same time, the new unit was available for a more immediate operation—attacking the SA.

By the end of 1933, Röhm's SA numbered more than 3,000,000 and constituted a threat to both the SS and the Reichswehr. The German generals were determined never to allow any military unit except the Reichswehr to be the official armed force of the country, but now they faced a serious challenge in Röhm. When, in early February of 1934, Röhm sent a memorandum to General Werner von Blomberg, Minister of Defense, demanding a more influential role in military matters for himself and a status for his SA more equal to that of the army, Blomberg was furious. He turned the matter over to Hitler immediately, leaving no question in Hitler's mind that the Reichswehr was definitely opposed to such a move. This placed Hitler in a predicament. He needed the support of the generals and the armed forces. Yet, Röhm was a friend from the early days when the NSDAP was considered to be a mere handful of radicals with no future. At many of the early meetings, it was Röhm and his men who kept Hitler from receiving a physical beating and who maintained order so that Hitler could get his message across to the audience. Röhm had definitely helped him obtain the chancellorship, and now the burly SA leader expected his reward.

Caught between the General Staff and Röhm, Hitler tried desperately to find a solution that would allow him to maintain the support of both factions. On the last day of February he invited Blomberg and Röhm to meet with him at the War Ministry, where he convinced them to sign an agreement specifying the responsibilities of the Reichswehr and the SA. The Reichswehr was given the right to bear arms and handle all military operations; the SA was placed in charge of some aspects of training. Röhm signed his name to the agreement merely to escape from the room. He had no intention of abiding by it and he didn't. Himmler, whose SS was still considerably smaller in number than Röhm's SA, learned within hours through the secret police units of the SS that the SA leader was calling Hitler a traitor and vowing to overthrow him. Himmler and Röhm were old friends, too. In fact the older Röhm had been Himmler's mentor when the Reichsführer-SS was a mere cadet, and after his graduation the two of them had made speeches together, often dined together, and worked as a team to promote the NSDAP and Hitler. But now the time had come to weigh friendship against opportunism—and friendship lost. Himmler saw the conflict between the generals and the SA leader as an excellent opportunity for the SS to move to the top of the Third Reich power hierarchy.

Himmler's plan was as simple as it was ruthless: Get rid of Röhm. He ordered his associates to collect information that would convince Hitler that Röhm was plotting treason against the NSDAP and the Reich. Since Hitler had already given Himmler orders after the Stennes revolt to set up SS intelligence units to investigate enemies of the party, Himmler knew Hitler would approve of his spying. Yet, his investigation provided little substantive evidence to show Hitler. Röhm was convinced that Hitler would eventually come to his senses and understand that the SA was his best guarantee of continued power, that Hitler would gradually conform to the demands of the SA. Consequently, Röhm waged a verbal war of nerves but did little to foment an actual revolt. Himmler, by June 1934, was ready to abandon his idea of convincing Hitler that Röhm had to be eliminated when an unexpected opportunity presented itself. On June 17 Franz von Papen, who was Hitler's vice-chancellor but also a leader of a group of influential bourgeois opposed to many of Hitler's policies, made a speech at Marburg University during which he attacked "the characterless arrogance and vulgarity concealed under the cloak of the German revolution." The speech was praised throughout Germany. Himmler took his cue from the acceptance of the von Papen speech. He hinted to Hitler that if the von Papen bourgeois and the SA joined forces, as reports from the SS secret police indicated was imminent, it would be catastrophic for the Führer.

Hitler agreed but was not yet convinced that such an alliance against him was contemplated. However, Blomberg arrived at the Chancellery the following day and informed Hitler that President Paul von Hindenburg was very upset over the differences between Hitler and von Papen and insisted that he wanted a strong and united government for Germany. Blomberg left no doubt in Hitler's mind that the German armed forces would carry out Hindenburg's wishes and if Hitler wanted the support of the military against the von Papen group, he would have to downgrade the Reichswehr nemesis, the SA. Hitler didn't hesitate. He agreed that Röhm had to go. To quiet any of Röhm's suspicions and to disable the SA leadership so that resistance to the planned purge would be at a minimum, Hitler ordered the SA to take a month's leave starting July 1. Röhm was delighted and immediately made reservations at the hotel in Bad Wiesse, intending to spend a month of hard drinking and sexual orgy at the spa.

He did neither. On June 30 Hitler made his move. Supported by SS members of Sepp Dietrich's *Leibstandarte-SS Adolf Hitler*, the Führer arrived at the hotel in Bad Wiesse and personally directed the arrest of his old friend Röhm. The only concession Hitler made was to order Röhm taken to Stadelheim Prison in Munich unharmed; most of Röhm's associates who were at Bad Wiesse were executed on the spot. For two days, Hitler fluctuated between exiling his old friend or executing him. Finally he decided that Röhm, if permitted to live, would never change his ways, that he would never conform to the new image Hitler wanted to project for his Third Reich. Nor would the generals ever accept the SA commander in their ranks—and Hitler needed the generals on his side. Himmler, of course, favored killing his rival despite the fact that they had once been close companions. On June 2 Hitler gave Sepp Dietrich the order to execute Röhm. The Führer made one concession to his old friend—he gave him a chance to die the "honorable" way. He ordered a pistol put in Röhm's cell and the SA commander left alone for ten minutes. Röhm refused the offer and Dietrich's SS guards

3

September Conspiracy

The loud ringing of the telephone in the hotel room in Gleiwitz, Germany, at 4:00 P.M. on August 31, 1939, startled the SS major, who had been studying a map. He picked up the receiver and heard a high-pitched voice he recognized immediately as that of Reinhard Heydrich, head of the Reich Security Service (*Sicherheitsdienst*, or SD).

"Call back," the voice said.

Major Alfred Naujocks cradled the telephone for a few seconds and then called the SD office in Berlin. A moment later he heard Heydrich's voice again. "Grandmama dead!"

No answer was needed. Naujocks, a former engineering student at Kiel University who did much more brawling than studying, understood the secret code words perfectly. Grabbing his cap, he hurried from the hotel room, strode down the hall to a room at the far end, and knocked twice. When the door opened, he nodded to the five men waiting inside. "It's time to go."

The six men went immediately to the lobby of the hotel where Naujocks stopped long enough to make one more telephone call. He called Heinrich Müller, chief of the Gestapo, and told him to have the "canned goods" at the radio transmitter a short distance from Gleiwitz on the back road leading to Tarnowitz by 8:20 P.M. As soon as he had delivered the message and made certain Müller understood and would comply, Naujocks led his small group of SS men to a truck and motioned for them to get in. Pointing down the Tarnowitz road, he told the driver: "Take us to the radio station."

World War II was about to start.

It is appropriate that history reveal that World War II began as a result of a diabolical ruse instigated and carried out by the SS, since this organization caused so much tragedy throughout the conflict. The Gleiwitz raid, often known as "Operation Himmler," involved two men whose names were synonymous with terror and death: Reinhard Heydrich and Alfred Naujocks. Heydrich planned the operation; Naujocks carried it out. The SS as a whole obtained credit for the success of the secret raid which meant, of course, that Himmler's esteem in the eyes of Hitler was raised to new heights. In the five years after Röhm's death, Himmler had come a long way, so far that Hitler had entrusted him with the important assignment of giving the German army an excuse to march into Poland.

Himmler could not have pulled off the Gleiwitz raid himself. He had neither the imagination to visualize such a brutal yet clever plan nor the courage to present it to Hitler if, by some miracle, he had planned it. That took a man of the caliber and complexity of Reinhard Heydrich. Slim and handsome, with a long, sharp face, and blond hair, he had opposing characteristics that baffled even his closest friends. He was a gifted violinist with long sensitive fingers that could coax soft love tunes from his instrument, yet he was also known as the "Man with the Iron Heart" because of his sadism. As a naval cadet he handled the men aboard ship and the women on land with the same gentle finesse, but as head of the SD, the intelligence branch of the SS, he had only contempt for human life. His winning ways with women caused him trouble with a daughter of a German industrialist who thought he was going to marry her. This led to the end of his naval career. The jilted girl's father was a friend of Admiral Erich Raeder, commander in chief of the German navy, and when Heydrich continued to shun her despite Raeder's insistence that he marry her, Heydrich was cashiered by the board of officers. Fortunately, he was already in love with Lina Mathilde von Osten, another lovely blonde, and she arranged an interview for her out-of-work fiance with Himmler through her friendship with a member of Himmler's staff.

The two men, who developed a love-hate relationship that lasted as long as they both lived, met at Waldtrudering, where Himmler was recovering from an illness. It was June 4, 1931, a time when Himmler was still trying desperately to upgrade the SS. Less than a year earlier, during the Stennes revolt against Hitler, Himmler had been given "investigative powers" by the Führer, but prior to his meeting with Heydrich his efforts along these lines had not been very successful. Heydrich's Nordic appearance immediately impressed Himmler but since he did not know the man's background, he decided to give Heydrich a written examination. He ordered Heydrich to outline his plans for developing a secret intelligence unit within the SS and gave him thirty minutes to do so. If he thought he would stump Heydrich, he was badly mistaken. Within twenty minutes Heydrich handed Himmler his plan, one so satisfying to the Reichsführer-SS that he offered Heydrich a position on his headquarters staff at once. It was one of the most effective moves Himmler made during his career.

Heydrich moved rapidly up the SS command ladder as the organization grew in size and influence. By the holiday season of 1931 he was a major, and during the early part of 1932 was deeply involved in secret police investigations. He started a file system that collected the life history of individuals within and outside the Nazi party. Initially Himmler protested Heydrich's collecting details about the lives of Nazi party members, reminding his chief of secret police that his job was to investigate *enemies* of the party. Heydrich was the type of man who always agreed with his superior when he was criticized but followed up this agreement with subtle arguments of his own that eventually swung the superior to his own way of thinking. This is exactly what he did with Himmler when his files were criticized by the Reichsführer-SS. Carefully and with great tact he showed Himmler how the secret files containing facts about his Nazi associates, facts which were not public knowledge and many of which were defamatory, could be used as a weapon. Blackmail, he gently insisted, could be a valuable tool in building the SS and helping Himmler struggle through the maze of intrigue that surrounded the Nazi hierarchy. It didn't take the Reichsführer-SS long to see the light and give Heydrich the go-ahead to build the files into the most feared asset of the secret police. Even Hitler was concerned about his own personal file although Himmler assured the Führer time and time again that the SS would not dare maintain such a file on the chancellor of Germany.

In 1936 Heydrich was made chief of all secret-police organizations in the Third Reich—Gestapo, Criminal Police, Security Service. This didn't satisfy the ambitious and energetic Heydrich. He began to expand his secret police activities outside the Third Reich despite the protests of Admiral Wilhelm Canaris, director of the Abwehr, the counterintelligence department of the headquarters of the armed forces. The fact that Heydrich and his wife, Lina, lived in the same Dölle-Strasse area of Berlin as Canaris and his wife, Erika, and had regular social contacts with them, made no difference to Heydrich. He tried in every way possible to undermine Canaris and his agents, hoping that he could pull off an intelligence coup that would convince Hitler to give the additional responsibility of intelligence operations in foreign countries to the SS. His opportunity came in late 1936 when Heydrich heard from SD agents that resistance groups were being formed in the Soviet Union to oppose Stalin.

If one characteristic of Heydrich stood out above even his brutality, it was his creative planning talents. He never was satisfied with "standard operating procedures" if he could devise a scheme he thought might be more successful. When he heard that the leader of the resistance group was Marshal Mikhail Tukhachevsky, Heydrich began a drawer-by-drawer search of official documents dealing with German-Russian negotiations immediately after World War I. He decided that if he could find some documents with the signatures of Tukhachevsky and other prominent generals, he would have the contents of the documents changed by forgery and delivered to Stalin. Heydrich figured that the resulting purge of Red Army generals would disrupt the Soviet Union and weaken that country. The necessary documents of the immediate post-World War I era were found and within a week Heydrich had his forgeries completed. He then had Colonel Hermann Behrends, SD commander in the east, take the forged documents to Prague, Czechoslovakia, and hand them over to Eduard

Benes, the president, who "leaked" word to Moscow that he had some papers of interest to them. Stalin sent a representative to Prague who purchased the documents for 3,250,000 rubles.

Canaris, of course, was completely unaware of Heydrich's plan. On June 11, 1937, when he heard that Tukhachevsky and seven other Soviet army generals had been sentenced to death for having "maintained treasonable relationships with leading military circles of a foreign power which is pursuing a policy hostile to the Soviet Union," he was taken by surprise. Nor did the purge stop with Tukhachevsky and his associates. Thirty-five thousand officers, including 90 percent of the Soviet army's generals and 80 percent of its colonels, were affected. Heydrich was delighted. Canaris was puzzled and concerned. He knew that the condemned Soviet generals certainly had not established any treasonable relationship with the Abwehr and he had no answers to give his headquarters, the *Okerkommando der Wachmacht*; so the OKW could not keep Hitler informed on the developments.

It wasn't until later that Canaris discovered that Hitler was well aware of what had happened. One of Canaris' officers, Lieutenant Colonel Dr. Karl Spalcke, discovered during his investigation of the Tukhachevsky affair that Heydrich was bragging about his SD coup in Russia. Canaris set up a meeting with Heydrich during which Heydrich admitted that he had instigated the plot that led to the downfall of the Soviet general. Canaris was furious. "Why in heaven's name did you play such a game?"

Heydrich's answer: "The Russian armed forces had to be decimated at the top and weakened in consequence. The whole thing is a gambit on the Führer's part—it fits into his overall plan for the next few years."

Until the Tukhachevsky affair Canaris had not taken very seriously the SD's intrusion into the Abwehr's area of responsibility. Now that attitude changed abruptly. Upon investigating he learned that he had been outflanked by Heydrich. Already Heydrich's SD headquarters on Berlin's Wilhelmstrasse had a staff of 3,000, who handled the information received from more than 50,000 informants. The Tukhachevsky affair had delighted Hitler and more and more he relied upon the unusual talents of Heydrich as he led Germany along the road to war. The road led through the Austrian Anschluss on March 13, 1938, the Munich agreement and occupation of the Sudetenland on October 1, 1938, the take-over of the remainder of Czechoslovakia on March 15, 1939, and the military pact between Germany and Italy on May 22, 1939. By this time Hitler was confident that neither France nor Great Britain was ready or able to stop his plan to take Poland. He began his campaign to take over the Polish nation by demanding the return of the Free City of Danzig, a city that, along with a narrow corridor of Polish territory, separated East Prussia from the remainder of the Reich. Both Danzig and the corridor had been severed from Germany at the end of World War I. During a Berlin meeting between Hitler and Polish Foreign Minister Józef Beck on January 5, 1939, Hitler had bluntly told Beck that he considered Danzig a German city and that sooner or later it had to be returned to German sovereignty. Beck had replied that the Danzig question was a very difficult problem.

Hitler decided that if the "difficult problem" could not be solved peacefully, he would solve it through force. On April 3, 1939, he gave the OKW some specific directives regarding plans to invade Poland:

1. Preparations must be made in such a way that the operation can be carried out at any time from September 1, 1939, onward.
2. The High Command of the Armed Forces had been directed to draw up a precise timetable for "Fall Weiss" [Case White] and to arrange by conferences the synchronized timings among the three branches of the armed forces.
3. The plans of the branches of the armed forces and the details for the timetable must be submitted by the OKW by May 1, 1939.

However, Hitler failed to inform the OKW that he had a secret operation in the planning stage at this time, a plan that had been devised by the same man who pulled off the Tukhachevsky affair. Heydrich, knowing Hitler needed a frontier incident of some sort to justify his attack on Poland, had come up with a double-barreled scheme this time. He proposed that SD agents, masquerading as Polish rebels, should attack the German radio station at Gleiwitz, broadcast a defamatory statement against Germany, and escape. At the same time, Polish-speaking Germans from Upper Silesia wearing Polish army uniforms should seize the German customs post near Hochlinden and stage a mock battle with SS troops stationed there in an effort to lure real Polish troops into the skirmish. Heydrich even had a Polish army defector primed to lead the Polish troops into the fray. To add realism to both incidents, he arranged to have Heinrich Müller scatter corpses from the Dachau concentration camp around the customs post and the radio station. The corpses, of course, were to be wearing Polish uniforms.

The plan was approved by Hitler in early July but was kept secret from the OKW. Canaris first became suspicious in late July when Colonel Heinz Jost, chief of the SD's foreign intelligence service, visited him and told Canaris that Hitler had ordered the Abwehr to assist the SD in carrying out a secret operation. Jost gave Canaris a list that included 150 Polish army uniforms, sidearms and paybooks to go with them, and 364 men to be placed on temporary duty with the SD. He gave no details of the secret operation to Canaris, who was upset by the request. The conservative Canaris knew that if his agents were forced to wear Polish uniforms and sent into foreign territory they would be violating international law and he didn't like the idea. He delayed providing the uniforms and even contacted the OKW to protest the SD's request. Field Marshal Wilhelm Keitel, chief of staff of the OKW, not in on the secret operation himself, merely shook his head and told Canaris he certainly couldn't countermand the Führer's order. "Say you don't have any Polish uniforms," was Keitel's only suggestion, one which Canaris ignored because Hitler would know it was a lie. Canaris didn't want Germany involved in a war with the Western powers but he now feared Hitler was determined to take Poland at any cost.

It there was any doubt in his mind or in the minds of the German generals, Hitler's meeting with them at the Berghof on August 22 eliminated it. Even the scenario for the meeting was unusual. Hitler requested that his senior commanders attending the meeting should wear civilian clothes, not uniforms. This attire on well-known generals and Nazi associates of Hitler attracted more attention from the citizens of nearby Berchtesgaden than the uniforms would have attracted. No news of the meeting was leaked to the press. The only man attending the meeting who violated the "plainclothes" order was the flamboyant, heavy-set Luftwaffe commander Hermann Göring. He was dressed in a "green leather jerkin with thick yellow buttons over a white silk blouse, grey knickerbockers, and long grey stockings. He had a gold dagger dangling at his side." Hitler glared at him for a moment after he entered the conference hall, then ignored the gaudy costume. Standing by the grand piano in the room, he bluntly told those attending the meeting that "White," the invasion of Poland, would start within a few days.

> "It was clear to me that a conflict with Poland had to come sooner or later. I had already made this decision in the spring but I thought I would first turn to the West for a few years and only afterwards against the East. But the sequence cannot be fixed. One cannot close one's eyes before a threatening situation. I wanted to establish an acceptable relationship with Poland in order to fight first against the West. But this plan, which was agreeable to me, could not be executed since essential points have changed."

The speech lasted nearly two hours, during which Hitler emphasized that the present time was ideal for invading Poland, that he did not fear intervention on behalf of Poland by Great Britain and France, and that the recent negotiations with Stalin indicated that Russia would side with Germany. (The Non-Aggression Pact between Germany and the Soviet Union was signed the next day.) Toward the end of the speech he hinted about Heydrich's forthcoming SD operation:

> "I shall give a propagandistic cause for starting the war—never mind whether it be plausible or not. In starting and making a war, not the right is what matters but victory."

The British and French governments were issuing warnings to Hitler by then that if he attacked Poland their countries would not stand idly by. The United States, while not committed to come to the aid of Poland as were the French and British, was nevertheless pressuring the German government to settle the Danzig problem peacefully. On August 14 New York's Congressman Hamilton Fish, in 1939 president of the

U.S. delegation to the Interparliamentary Union Congress conference at Oslo, stopped in Germany to meet with Joachim von Ribbentrop, the German foreign minister. Fish was a vocal isolationist and an opponent of President Franklin D. Roosevelt. The congressman advocated better relations with Germany and hoped to solve the Danzig question during the August 15-19 conference in Norway.

> "I met with von Ribbentrop in Salzburg but our meeting was delayed from 10:00 A.M. in the morning until 4:00 P.M. I was angry but when von Ribbentrop promised to fly me all the way to Oslo in his own aircraft if I waited until 4:00 P.M. for the meeting I agreed. At 3:30 P.M. an automobile picked me up at the hotel and took me to von Ribbentrop's villa near Lake Fuschel. I was impressed by the foreign minister's appearance. He was 45 years of age, handsome, and a very gracious host. However, he quickly told me that Germany had now come to the end of her patience and unless Danzig was restored to Germany war would break out. He ignored my proposals for a peaceful settlement of the Polish dispute and would offer no suggestions as to how to preserve peace through any action that might be initiated at the Interparliamentary Union Congress conference at Oslo."

Von Ribbentrop made certain he introduced the Nazi propaganda line into his conversation with Fish.

> "He presented me with considerable data about the maltreatment and attacks on Germans in Poland, much of which I thought then and still think was sheer propaganda. He spoke of a half a dozen German boys who had been castrated in Poland and said he feared to publish the facts as they would arouse the German people to immediate revenge."

Ribbentrop was a member of the SS by this time and he was well aware of the Heydrich plan to provide an excuse for the German army to march into Poland. Of course he didn't mention the SD plan to Fish. Nor did Hitler leak any information about the plan to Sir Nevile Henderson, the British ambassador to Germany, when Henderson flew to Berchtesgaden on August 23 to deliver a message to the Führer from Prime Minister Neville Chamberlain. Hitler read the letter, which stressed the British determination to fulfill their obligation to Poland, the British government's readiness to discuss the problem, and the desire to see an immediate resumption of direct discussion between Germany and Poland. Hitler dismissed the letter as unrealistic. His reply, given to Henderson later that day, stated that while Germany did not seek conflict with England, his nation was determined to solve the Polish question promptly. His letter to Chamberlain also included statements meant to lend credibility to the border incident Heydrich had planned.

> "The unconditional assurance given by England to Poland that she would render assistance to that country in all circumstances, regardless of the causes from which a conflict might spring, could only be interpreted in that country as an encouragement thenceforward to unloosen, under cover of such a charter, a wave of appalling terrorism against the one and a half million German inhabitants living in Poland. The atrocities which since then have been taking place in that country are terrible for the victims but intolerable for a Great Power such as the German Reich which is expected to remain a passive onlooker during these happenings."

Heydrich had already selected his man to lead the simulated attack on the Gleiwitz radio station. He was Alfred Helmut Naujocks, a charter member of the SD who had helped him in several earlier escapades. Naujocks ranked with Otto Skorzeny as one of the most publicized adventurers of the Third Reich, but in 1939 he was just at the initial stage of his career. He wasn't an intelligent leader and lacked the mental capacity for creating plans such as those that Heydrich invented, but he was an expert in carrying out an operation once it was explained to him. He had helped Heydrich with the Tukhachevsky affair and had staged some bombings in Slovakia which were blamed on Slovak nationalists. This latter terrorist attack had convinced President Emil Hácha to dismiss the Slovak provincial leadership on the night of March 9, 1939, creating a Czech governmental crisis on which Hitler quickly took advantage. So Naujocks was not a newcomer to subterfuge and terror when Heydrich gave him the all-important assignment which started World War II.

By August 10, Naujocks and his companions were holed up in the hotel in Gleiwitz waiting for Heydrich's signal to start the operation. It was a long and tense wait as Hitler wavered between invading Poland immediately and waiting until he was more certain of the reaction to be expected from the governments of France and England. Early on August 23, Hitler decided that the invasion would begin at 4:30 A.M. on August 26. At 3:00 P.M. on August 25, he verified the timing and issued his final order. Heydrich promptly notified Naujocks to stand by for the "attack" on the radio station, ordered the Polish-speaking Germans from Upper Silesia wearing Polish army uniforms, whom he had placed under the command of Obersturmbannführer-SS Ottfried Hellwig, to start their march toward the Hochlinden customs post, and told Müller to transport the corpses from the Dachau concentration camp to the general area in his trucks.

Late in the afternoon of August 25, however, Hitler had a change of heart. He received a letter from the British government that reaffirmed the British intention to help Poland if Germany invaded that country, and that a mutual assistance program between England and Poland had been worked out in detail.

"Stop everything at once," Hitler ordered Keitel. "I need time for negotiations."

This presented Heydrich with a serious problem. He was able to contact Naujocks, who was still awaiting a call from Berlin in his Gleiwitz hotel room; and he succeeded in recalling Müller's trucks loaded with the Dachau concentration camp corpses. He was, unable, however, to stop Hellwig's men, who had already crossed the border into Poland and were preparing their mock attack on the German customs station, an attack designed to lure regular Polish troops into the fray and create an "incident" justifying the German invasion of Poland. Hellwig, assured that the personnel at the customs station had been alerted that a mock attack was under way, received a rude surprise when his men came under fire. Because of Hitler's change of mind, the cautionary notice had never reached the customs station and the border guards there were under the impression they were under attack by regular Polish troops. Before Heydrich could get the battle stopped several German soldiers were killed.

During the next few days various orders, some conflicting with others, were issued from Hitler's headquarters. On the afternoon of August 27, all communication between Berlin and London and Paris was cut off for several hours. A Nazi celebration at Tannenberg which Hitler planned to attend was canceled, as was a party rally scheduled at Nuremberg. German airports were closed; all naval, army, and air attachés in Berlin were confined to the city limits. At 10:30 P.M. August 28, British ambassador Sir Nevile Henderson met with Hitler at the Chancellery in Berlin to deliver another letter from the British government. "Hitler was once again friendly and reasonable and appeared to be not dissatisfied with the answer which I had brought him. Our conversation lasted for well over an hour."

Hitler gave no hint that he had Heydrich waiting in the wings to start the deception that would result in the invasion of Poland. But Henderson's reception on August 29 when he appeared at the Chancellery at 7:15 P.M. to receive Hitler's reply to the British government's letter was different. His reception outside the building was the same as always: guard of honor at the main door, roll of drums announcing his arrival, greeting by Otto Meissner, chief of the Chancellery, at the door. Inside the Chancellery, however, it was another matter. "I immediately sensed a more uncompromising attitude than the previous evening on Hitler's part." Hitler's reply to the British government's letter was just as uncompromising, summing up the situation by stating the Danzig problem must be settled on German terms peacefully by the next day or he would use force. As Henderson left the Chancellery he noticed the anteroom was filled with German army officers.

Hitler waited no longer. On August 31 he gave the order to invade Poland at 4:45 A.M. on September 1. At 4:00 P.M. on August 31, Heydrich alerted Naujocks in Gleiwitz.

Naujocks was ordered to be at the Gleiwitz radio station at 7:45 P.M. that evening and Müller's trucks with the Dachau concentration camp corpses were expected to arrive approximately one-half hour later to scatter the dead "Polish soldiers" around the station. The Germans arrived at the six-foot-high wire fence surrounding the station right on time, finding both the station and the two attached buildings used for living quarters unguarded. The German personnel operating the station were not in on the Heydrich plan, so when an engineer named Foitzik saw Naujocks and his companions walk into the station, he wondered what was happening. As they started up the steps leading to the broadcasting studios, he called to them, asking where they thought they were going. His answer was the muzzle of a revolver aimed at a spot between his eyes.

When they reached the broadcasting studios, Naujocks and his men began making as much noise as possible, hoping to give the impression that a large Polish insurgent force had the station under attack. Several shots were fired through the ceiling of the studio to add to the bedlam and to scare the radio personnel, who had by this time decided that resistance to the strangers was futile. The personnel of the station were handcuffed and taken to the basement of the building. Naujocks, meanwhile, discovered a flaw in his plan. None of his men knew how to operate the radio equipment! Flipping switches and turning dials, the SS men finally found the storm switch which would permit them to interrupt the program in progress. (Normally this switch was used to inform listeners that bad weather was interfering with their reception.) During the next five minutes, Naujocks' Polish-speaking "announcers" broadcast anti-German statements to the background accompaniment of shots fired by other SS men. When Naujocks decided they had convinced listeners that the German radio station was under attack by armed Poles, he and his men withdrew. As they left the station, he noticed one of the Dachau concentration camp corpses sprawled near the entrance, deposited there by Müller.

Heydrich's SS detachment also made a successful mock attack on the German customs station at Hochlinden where Müller scattered additional concentration camp corpses wearing Polish uniforms. The fact that the dead inmates' bodies were rigid because of the time of their death many hours previously was of little importance to the SS leaders. Their assignments had been carried out, Hitler had his "justification" for invading Poland, and the Polish military forces and civilian police would not be able to investigate the bodies at Gleiwitz and Hochlinden to determine just when death occurred.

In fact Hitler's soldiers and tanks were on the move before the SS men had returned to their bases. The Nazi newspaper

4

The Intellectual Killer

The forty-year-old former SS general didn't have an ounce of fat on his body. His delicate features, excellently modulated voice, and self-confident attitude accented his lean, muscular physique as he sat on the witness stand at Nuremberg in September 1947. But his words shocked those listening to him in the courtroom.

"There is nothing worse for people spiritually than to have to shoot defenseless populations."

Prosecutor James E. Heath stared at him unsmiling. "There is nothing worse than to be shot when you are defenseless."

But the calm SS killer facing Heath didn't agree. "I can imagine worse things. For example, to starve."

There was absolute silence in the courtroom for several seconds as everyone stared in disbelief at the defendant. It took a suggestion from the presiding judge, Michael A. Musmanno, to get the questioning under way again.

Who was this man who passed off so lightly the accusation that he had killed ninety thousand people. His name was Otto Ohlendorf, one of the most remarkable men of the SS, a prime example of the Jekyll-and-Hyde personalities that composed the membership of that organization. A Hannoverian farmer born in 1907, Ohlendorf had a career in the SS that went from one extreme to another, from reformer to killer, without the flicker of an eyelash. He was both a lawyer and an economist, a graduate of Leipzig and Göttingen universities, and a well-known lecturer, when he decided his future was at Hitler's side. He joined the party early but soon discovered that he didn't agree with many of its policies. While a member of the Institute for World Economics in Kiel, he became convinced that the Nazi party had collective socialist tendencies and he spoke out against this flaw. Unfortunately for him, he spoke his mind once too often and the Gestapo arrested him. It was his first experience with the secret police procedures of the Nazis, and by the time the Gestapo interrogation experts had finished with him, he had no desire to speak against party policies any longer.

"I am shattered," he wrote his wife after his release from prison. "I no longer have the old, carefree assurance about National Socialism."

Ohlendorf was certain that his days with the Nazi party were ended, but during his hunt for a new job he was sent by a friend to see Professor Reinhard Höhn in Berlin. Höhn, who was in charge of an SD section, was in need of an economic advisor, and Ohlendorf's qualifications were perfect. He was hired on the spot and quickly found himself back in the thick of the Nazi party movement. He collected a staff of economists from all over Germany and continually analyzed the economic health of the Third Reich.When he became convinced that Hitler's rearmament policies were causing excessive strain on other aspects of the economy, Ohlendorf didn't hesitate to issue a report saying so. The Führer, of course, ignored the report. This didn't discourage the young lawyer-economist or even slow him down. He expanded his activities to include reporting on culture, science, education, law, administration, and even the party and the state.

The reports weren't taken very seriously by Hitler or Himmler at the beginning, but as the documents became more and more critical of the situation, the customary Nazi intrigue intervened. Himmler began to call Ohlendorf "Nazism's Knight of the Holy Grail" and when he felt the "Knight" had overstepped his bounds once too often, he summoned him to his office. In no uncertain terms he explained to the SD would-be reformer that his reports were illegal and unwanted, that from that moment on he was to stick with economics as he had previously, and that even the economic reports were to be less critical in the future. Ohlendorf immediately offered his resignation from the SD but Himmler ignored the request. He wanted to retain Ohlendorf's expertise in economics. Finally, however, in 1938 Ohlendorf was permitted to transfer to the Reich Commerce Group, a Nazi party organization, but even then Himmler forced him to work at least two hours a day for the SD at the Wilhelmstrasse offices.

While Ohlendorf concentrated on criticizing certain actions of the Nazi party, there is no indication that his criticism included the treatment of the Jews. True, he did not agree with the Kristallnacht pogrom of November 9, 1938. That night 101 synagogues and 7,500 Jewish-owned stores and other buildings were destroyed. But Ohlendorf said little and did nothing in protest. Nor is there any record of "Nazism's Knight of the Holy Grail" speaking out against the atrocities that began in Poland within hours after the Gleiwitz incident at the radio station. From the very first moment of the invasion of Polish territory, the German army, the SS, and the Gestapo began a systematic execution of segments of the civilian population. Hitler had told his generals prior to the invasion that certain actions would be taken in Poland that might not meet their approval, so he would have the SS handle these operations. The Führer's plan was simple: Himmler was to form task groups that were to follow the German troops into Poland and liquidate the upper classes. The SD task groups, wearing the uniform of the *SS-Verfugungstruppe* (the early military arm of the SS) with the SD diamond on the left sleeve, did their job well. They rounded up previously designated teachers, priests, businessmen, doctors, and politicians, herded them into "reception camps" that usually ended up being execution camps, and quickly sentenced them to death. Twenty-seven days after the German troops first crossed into Poland, Heydrich was able to announce: "Of the Polish upper classes in the occupied territories only a maximum of three percent is still present."

Ohlendorf, at the time chief of the Inland (Internal) SD, concentrated on his "spheres of life" reports and ignored the actions being taken in Poland by other sections of the SD. Economics and legal matters were more important to him than the treatment of the Jews and the Polish upper class. He spent much of his time lecturing to German businessmen, especially the *Freundeskreis Heinrich Himmler* (Heinrich

Himmler Friendship Circle), a group of wealthy and influential industrialists who supported the activities of the SS. His reputation as a Nazi administrator who was logical, intelligent, and humane spread throughout the Third Reich. While some of the Nazi hierarchy were wary of him because he often criticized the regime, even his enemies agreed that he was a stabilizing influence among the more radical elements of the party. Even his closest SD associates at that period never dreamed he would change in attitude and action so dramatically in 1941.

While Ohlendorf was climbing up through the ranks of the SS, a small man with a cherubic face highlighted by wavy gray hair was developing his own law career in and around Pittsburgh, Pennsylvania, many thousands of miles from the turmoil in Europe. Michael A. Musmanno was one of a family of eight children who discovered early in life that he had to fight for everything he wanted. At fourteen years of age he was a coal miner; at sixteen, a steelworker; and at seventeen, although under draft age, he joined the naval militia during World War I. When that war ended, he began accumulating academic degrees: a Bachelor of Arts and a Master of Arts from George Washington University, a law degree from Georgetown University, and a Doctor of Laws degree from the University of Rome. Shortly after setting up his law office in Pittsburgh, Musmanno began a lifelong battle against injustice in any form, a battle that was to lead him to a head-to-head confrontation with Ohlendorf during the biggest murder trial in history, the trial of Ohlendorf and twenty-two companions who led death teams responsible for exterminating over a million people.

Musmanno's first nationally known battle against injustice was his effort in behalf of Nicola Sacco and Bartolomeo Vanzetti, two Italians accused of murdering two payroll guards at Braintree, Massachusetts, in 1920. From 1921 until 1927, when the pair was finally executed, the names Sacco and Vanzetti were household words on six continents. Musmanno, like many others, including H. G. Wells, Albert Einstein, Madame Curie, Alfred Dreyfus, and Ramsey MacDonald, felt that the two men were convicted less because of evidence that they committed the murders than because of their record as labor radicals. Sleeping on the floor at the Sacco-Vanzetti headquarters because he had no money for a hotel room, Musmanno fought to save the pair when all others had given up the battle. When the lights dimmed as the executioner threw the electric chair switch at midnight on August 22, 1927, he was still trying to get the governor to issue a stay until the U.S. Supreme Court had time to review the case again. This case left a lasting impression on Musmanno, one that made him fight that much harder when he felt that human rights were being violated.

After the Sacco-Vanzetti ordeal, he took on the infamous coal and iron police, the private armies of the coal and steel companies whose brutal actions gave Musmanno a preview of the Ohlendorf tactics he would judge years later. This battle raged until 1935, when the coal and iron police were abolished by law. During that long fight, Musmanno took time out to debate the famous criminal lawyer Clarence Darrow on the subject "Does Man Live Again?" holding his own with the silver-tongued Chicago lawyer before a packed house in Pittsburgh's Carnegie Hall. By this time Musmanno was a judge of the Court of Common Pleas with a national reputation as "The Great Dissenter," but as soon as World War II was declared, he took off his robes and joined the U.S. Navy as a lieutenant-commander. After six months in the Judge Advocate General's office in Washington, D.C., Musmanno finally got his wish—he was ordered into combat. Ohlendorf had had plenty of experience in the combat zone by this time, but Musmanno was on his way to get the experience that helped convince President Harry S. Truman to appoint him a Nuremberg trial judge at the end of the war. He was wounded twice; his ship was sunk at sea; he was trapped in a volcanic eruption at Mt. Vesuvius; he evacuated the populace of an Italian town from a battle zone; and he served as military governor of Italy's Sorrentine Peninsula—before he faced Ohlendorf across the bench.

Musmanno's appearance was deceptive and fooled many persons both on the battlefield and in the courtroom. A British general in Italy soon discovered that he had tackled the wrong man when he tried to give Musmanno orders without authorization. At the time Musmanno was aide to General Mark Clark, commander of the U.S. Fifth Army, who had assigned him the task of providing a villa for the famed Italian philosopher Benedetto Croce, designated to head the new Italian government. Musmanno found the Italian a fine villa and moved him in. A short time later, however, a British general arrived at the villa, jauntily walked to the door carrying his walking stick, and looked at the small-statured Musmanno standing in the doorway.

"Yank, I will give you half an hour to move your belongings and your men from this villa. I am taking it over for my personal use."

Musmanno just grinned. "Pick yourself another villa, general. This villa belongs to Benedetto Croce, the next Italian head of state. We can't oust him."

The British general shook his walking stick under Musmanno's nose. "Thirty minutes is all you have."

There was no time to contact General Mark Clark and Musmanno's aides advised moving Croce immediately. Musmanno refused.

In exactly one half hour, the British general was back, once again striding up the walk to the front entrance to the villa as though he owned the place. Behind him his aides carried his bags and other personal belongings. He was almost at the front entrance of the villa before he noticed Musmanno leaning nonchalantly against the doorjamb.

"I told you to . . ." The British general's lips kept moving but there was no sound as he stared at the .45 caliber automatic Musmanno had pointed at his midriff. Finally the general found his voice. "You'll hear about this, Yank."

Musmanno never did hear any more about the incident and Croce stayed in the villa. It was a toughness he was to show later when he faced Ohlendorf, the SS killer with whom he was already on a collison course.

Otto Ohlendorf's life of economics and law changed abruptly when Adolf Eichmann became the administrator of the whole genocide operation. Eichmann, despite his later statements to the contrary, appeared to be born for the job that both brought him to the exercise of great power during the Third Reich and to the hangman's noose in Israel in 1962. Born in Solingen, Germany, in 1906, his whole life was entwined with Jews and Jewish affairs. He played with Jewish children, learning their customs, traditions, and ambitions, and even learning some Yiddish and Hebrew. After he joined the Nazi party he was sent to Palestine in 1937, primarily to set up an espionage organization, but during his stay he learned a great deal more about world Jewry. At the time, the British controlled Palestine; when they discovered Eichmann's purpose in the country, he was asked to leave. On the way back to Germany he visited with the Grand Mufti of Jerusalem to discuss the harassment of Jews in Arab areas.

Eichmann was soon recognized by Himmler and Heydrich as the resident Nazi expert on the Jews. Himmler appointed him director of the Jewish Museum with the responsibility of collecting and collating data on all aspects of Jewish history and, particularly, modern-day holdings of Jews in Germany. His card file on Jews became so extensive and complete that Hitler soon became aware of him and selected Eichmann to head the most gigantic murder organization in the history of the world. Prior to Eichmann's taking over the operation that became known as the Final Solution, the extermination program was in near-shambles. Transportation problems alone were complex. Men, women, and children designated by the Nazi conquerors to die had to be moved to the death camps, causing a logistical logjam. Such a movement required guards, engineers, firemen, interpreters, and other personnel. Trains that were needed to carry troops and supplies to the front had to be used instead to carry the doomed Jews to their death. With the invasion of the Soviet Union planned for the near future, the problems would multiply because of the greater number of Jews to be rounded up, the longer distances required to reach the established death camps, and the increased number of personnel required for the exterminating program.

Eichmann was brought in to bring order out of chaos. The fact that he was dealing with human lives meant nothing to him. The improvement of the system was his goal and he did his job efficiently. One of his first innovations was to change the entire concept of the murders. If the doomed Jews could not be taken to the executioners, why not take the executioners to the doomed Jews? He submitted his suggestion to Himmler who, after consultation with Heydrich and, it is assumed, with Hitler (since all such important matters had to be discussed and approved or disapproved by the Führer), gave Eichmann the signal to go ahead with his plan. He immediately formed four *Einsatzgruppen* (Special Mobile Task Forces) to follow the German armies into eastern Europe, especially the Ukraine and Russia. Initially, Eichmann and his superiors feared that the OKW would attempt to control the *Einsatzgruppen*, knowing this would seriously hamper their plans to exterminate the eastern European Jews. The German army adhered to international law more closely than the SS, a trait that the SS considered detrimental to the best interests of the Third Reich, but in 1941 Himmler's organization was not in a position to challenge the German generals. However, in April 1941 the SS and the OKW came to an agreement which stated, in part, that "the *Einsatzgruppen* are authorized, within the framework of their task and on their own responsibility, to take executive measures affecting the civilian population." This clause in the agreement opened the way for the mobil death squads to operate freely.

The four *Einsatzgruppen* were: *Einsatzgruppe* A, assigned to operate in Latvia, Lithuania, and Estonia, commanded by Walter Stahlecker; *Einsatzgruppe* B, assigned the area between the Baltic states and the Ukraine, commanded by Arthur Nebe; *Einsatzgruppe* C, operating in the Ukraine south of Nebe's group, under the command of Otto Rasch; and *Einsatzgruppe* D, taking care of the remainder of the Ukraine, commanded by "Nazism's Knight of the Holy Grail," Otto Ohlendorf.

How did the lawyer-economist with such high ideals that he was once ostracized by the Nazi party become commander of a mobile murder group that ultimately was charged with killing hundreds of thousands of innocent victims? This is another of the mysteries of the SS and its effect on the men who became its members. Nebe, for instance, testified that he volunteered to command one of the task forces in hopes that he would be awarded the Iron Cross, First Class, and be promoted by Heydrich. Stahlecker had been chastised by Heydrich for past actions and transferred to the foreign ministry. He was convinced that if he did a good job in the east he would once again bask in the favor of Heydrich. Rasch wanted a position in Berlin and thought that if he distinguished himself in his new command he would be justified in requesting such an assignment. And Ohlendorf? Long considered one of the most intelligent members of the SS and not at all a believer in excesses, he nevertheless accepted the assignment as commander of *Einsatzgruppe* D without complaint. But even after accepting the command he had ample opportunity to either find a way to be relieved of the assignment or to avoid being involved in the mass murders. The original commander of *Einsatzgruppe* A, for example, was Heinz Jost, but he managed to discover a loophole in the assignment and find himself another position prior to the start of the killings. Ohlendorf, on the other hand, ultimately became an expert on human extermination. He sat impassive in the castle of Pretsch and without a word of protest listened to Heydrich declare that "Communists, Jews, gypsies, saboteurs, and agents must basically be regarded as persons who, by their very existence, endanger the security of the troops and are therefore to be executed without further ado." When asked later why he didn't go on record as protesting the concept, he said, "I felt it was my duty to obey the orders of my government no matter whether I regarded them as moral or immoral."

Within three days after the German troops invaded Soviet territory, Ohlendorf's *Einsatzgruppe* D headed eastward, 500 men strong. His course of action had been outlined for him very clearly by Eichmann. At each city Ohlendorf or one of his officers was to summon the most prominent Jews of the area to his headquarters and explain to them that for the safety of all Jews they were to be resettled in a non-combat zone. Many such Judenräte or "Councils of Jewish Elders" established by the Germans knew they had no choice in the matter. The Council was required to list all the Jews in the area and, at the order of *Einsatzgruppe* personnel was to notify the victims to appear at a designated assembly point at a certain time with all their possessions. Once the Jews were assembled, their personal belongings were quickly confiscated by Ohlendorf's men, they were forced into trucks, and driven to secluded wooded areas where firing squads were waiting. The Council members, now aware that they had unwittingly helped lure their friends to their deaths, were often forced to watch the executions and then were shot themselves. (For a fuller treatment of this very complex issue, read Isaiah Trunk's books *Judenrat* and *Jewish Responses to Nazi Persecution*.)

Gypsies, of course, were much easier to round up. Their gaily colored clothing, tents, violins, and gold bracelets and earrings made them conspicuous. Ohlendorf's men merely announced to the gypsies that it was necessary they be moved from the battle area. Rarely did the gypsies protest because they were accustomed to being on the move all the time anyway. Their belongings were loaded onto the German trucks and their wagons were escorted to the new "settlement area"—a quiet spot in the woods where a deep ditch had already been dug. They were carefully lined up on the edge of the ditch so that when they were shot their bodies would topple over into it. This saved the *Einsatzgruppe* D men the effort of dragging their corpses to the ditch before burying them.

How did a man of Ohlendorf's intellect stand up under the strain of such wholesale killing? The records indicate that he was just as precise and thorough in his extermination of human beings as he had been previously when analyzing the financial affairs of the German economy. When he discovered a Crimean sect known as the Krimchaks he was unable to determine their origin. However, he didn't bypass them and keep going. Ohlendorf was much too thorough for that. Although he learned that the Krimchaks stemmed from a southern Mediterranean country and spoke the Turkish language, he wanted to make certain that they might not have at least a little Jewish blood in their veins. He sent a radio query back to Eichmann, who assigned his staff to investigate. The staff members couldn't determine whether the Krimchaks had any Jewish blood or not but to be on the safe side told Eichmann there was a possibility they did. That was enough for Eichmann and Ohlendorf. The Krimchaks were executed.

When Ohlendorf discovered that the farm providing milk for a German military hospital in the Ukraine wasn't able to send a large enough daily supply, he investigated. He learned that the farm was operated by the mental patients of a large asylum and that much of the milk was kept for the use of those mental patients. As one of his subordinate officers reported later: "A way out of this difficulty was found by deciding that the execution of 565 incurables should be carried out in the course of the next few days under the pretext that these patients were being removed to a better asylum in Charkow."

Ohlendorf kept exact score of his murders. None of his financial reports of earlier years was more precise or better prepared than were the reports of his daily activities with the mobile murder squads. By the winter of 1941-42 Ohlendorf's *Einsatzgruppe* D had liquidated 92,000 Jews—and Ohlendorf was still going strong. The other *Einsatzgruppen* commanders, however, were feeling the effects of the murders. Rasch went on leave and never returned to the murder squads. Nebe was a mere shadow of himself and on the verge of a nervous breakdown. Many of the lower-ranking SS officers had broken under the strain of the constant slaughter and had to be replaced. Others were exhausted. Ohlendorf, however, became more fanatical, an SS idealist who considered himself in a class far above the ordinary member of the elite organization. It was Ohlendorf and other SS officers like him whom Himmler addressed at Posen on October 4, 1943, when he said (in part): "Most of you must know what it means when a hundred corpses are lying side by side, or five hundred or a thousand. To have stuck it out and at the same time, apart from exceptions caused by human weakness, to have remained decent fellows, that is what has made us so hard. This is a page of glory in our history which has never been written and will never be written."

Decent fellow? Musmanno, the feisty American naval officer who by 1943 had two rows of ribbons on his dress uniform and was moving up the Italian peninsula with the U.S. Fifth Army toward Germany, would ask that question of Ohlendorf at Nuremberg three years later.

5

The SS Penguin Defense

Otto Ohlendorf sat in the front row of the twenty-three SS defendants when the largest murder trial in history opened at Nuremberg on September 29, 1947. The damage to the city's historic Palace of Justice caused by American and British bombers during the war had been repaired. The stone floors were carpeted, microphones and amplifiers installed, a glass enclosure for the required interpreters constructed, and a judge's bench and defendant's dock built. Ohlendorf and his associates sat on two long wooden benches against the east wall facing Michael Musmanno, the judge, whose bench was along the west wall.

The two men—Musmanno and Ohlendorf—had reached the main courtroom at the Palace of Justice along separate paths after the war ended. When Hitler's suicide in the Berlin bunker was reported on April 30, 1945, Ohlendorf traveled by automobile to Flensburg, where Himmler had established a temporary headquarters. Himmler had been trying to arrange surrender terms with the Allies on his own initiative and he had failed. The Reichsführer-SS was both angry and disappointed that Hitler had appointed Admiral Karl Dönitz to succeed him as head of the German government. Himmler vowed to Ohlendorf that he would establish his own SS government in Schleswig-Holstein. On May 6, however, Dönitz made his feelings very clear regarding any further association with Himmler:

Dear Herr Reich Minister:

In view of the present situation, I have decided to dispense with your further assistance as Reich Minister of the interior and member of the Reich government, as Commander in Chief of the Reserve Army, and as chief of the police. I now regard all your offices as abolished. I thank you for your service which you have given to the Reich.

Dönitz also issued an order forbidding further resistance by the diehard SS members. Ohlendorf, convinced the days of the SS were ended, advised Himmler to surrender to the Allies and defend the actions of the SS against the accusations being made. Himmler refused. On May 10, with Ohlendorf at his side, Himmler set out for the east coast of Schleswig-Holstein. When they reached the Elbe they paid a boatman 500 marks to ferry them across the river with other refugees. On May 21 Himmler and Ohlendorf reached Bremervörde, 100 miles from Flensburg. No one recognized them; they had removed all traces of rank and insignia from their uniforms and carried forged identification papers. Himmler even wore a patch over his eye, had shaved off his mustache, and taken off his glasses. At Bremervörde, however, Ohlendorf discovered that they needed additional travel documents in order to get through the British checkpoint established at the outskirts of the city. He sent Josef Kiermaier, Himmler's bodyguard, to the British authorities to apply for the required travel permits only to learn than any SS member was automatically subject to immediate arrest. Kiermaier was taken prisoner and Ohlendorf, Himmler, and their entourage tried to escape. While crossing a bridge on the east side of the city, however, they fumbled into another British checkpoint and were taken into custody.

At this point Ohlendorf and Himmler made the wrong move. Instead of trying to remain inconspicuous, they demanded that they see the British commanding officer of the area at once. Captain Tom Selvester, who was in command of 031 Civilian Interrogation Camp, was notified about the two German prisoners. He was interested because most German prisoners were quiet, well-behaved, and friendly in hopes of better treatment. Selvester told his aide he wanted to see the men one at a time. Himmler, still the Reichsführer-SS in his own mind, went into the interrogation room first. Within minutes his vanity overcame his discretion. He removed the patch from his eye, put on his wire-rimmed glasses, and announced haughtily that he was Heinrich Himmler. Instead of being treated as a visiting dignitary as his warped mind had led him to expect, Himmler was ordered to undress and was searched for weapons, documents, and poison. One brass case with a glass vial inside was taken from him but a second brass case was empty. Himmler had hidden the vial containing cyanide in his mouth. Later that night, while being subjected to a second search, he crushed the glass vial between his teeth and despite prompt medical attention died.

Ohlendorf learned of Himmler's suicide within minutes. He, too, was undressed and searched but he had no intention of committing suicide. He was convinced that he could justify every one of his actions during the Third Reich and looked forward to the opportunity to do so. It came at Nuremberg in 1947.

Two days before Dönitz dismissed Himmler from all further duties and six days before Ohlendorf and Himmler departed from Flensburg in an effort to escape the Allies, Musmanno was at General Clark's side when Clark accepted the surrender of the German armies in Italy. After the surrender ceremonies, the gregarious Musmanno talked with several German generals and discovered that despite the official announcement from Dönitz's headquarters that Hitler had committed suicide in the Berlin bunker, they did not believe it. They were convinced Hitler was alive and would return to power in a new Germany in the future. As this rumor became more prevalent, Musmanno recommended to the U.S. Navy that the facts of Hitler's death should be investigated closely and, in late May 1945, he was given permission to do so along with his other duties. He interviewed more than two hundred persons who had known and associated intimately with Hitler during the twelve years of the Third Reich—from cooks to high-ranking Nazi officials. This investigation, while not turning up any evidence that documented Hitler's suicide or escape, gave Musmanno a background of secret German activity not previously made public. When General Clark was named American High Commissioner of Austria, Musmanno accompanied him to Vienna. Later Clark appointed him president of the U.S. Board of Forcible Repatriation, which administered the Soviet demand that Russian refugees be returned to the Soviet Union whether they so desired or not. In this position, Musmanno saved thousands of refugees from certain death by refusing to repatriate them.

Musmanno was then selected for a three-man board to review the cases of Dönitz and Raeder, who were tried in 1946 before the Nuremberg International Military Tribunal. This report was so well received by American authorities that President Harry S. Truman appointed Musmanno to the War Crimes Tribunal of the U.S. government. He sat on the bench during the trials of Field Marshal Erhard Milch, the Luftwaffe's senior officer after Göring, and Oswald Pohl, the concentration camp administrator. After those trials ended, General Lucius D. Clay, military governor of the U.S. Zone of Occupation, selected him as President Judge of Tribunal II to try the *Einsatzgruppen* members. Consequently, Musmanno was well-prepared for his confrontation with Ohlendorf, whom he later described as "the most remarkable person I ever faced in a courtroom."

The indictments against Ohlendorf and his *Einsatzgruppen* comrades numbered four:

Count One. Common Plan or Conspiracy: Conspiring to acquire totalitarian control over Germany, mobilizing the German economy for war, to construct a huge military machine for conquest and to commit war crimes and crimes against humanity.

Count Two. Crimes Against Peace: Waging aggressive war against Poland, Great Britain, France, Denmark, Norway, Belgium, Netherlands, Luxembourg, Yugoslavia, Greece, the Soviet Union and the United States.

Count Three. War Crimes: Violating laws and customs of war, specifying the murder and ill-treatment of millions of civilians in the German-occupied countries, deportation of other millions to slave labor, murder and ill-treatment of prisoners of war, killing of hostages, plunder and looting and unjustified devastation.

Count Four. Crimes Against Humanity: Crimes which included atrocities, murders, other offenses and persecution on racial or religious grounds.

The reading of the indictment, with special emphasis on count four because of the documented evidence against the *Einsatzgruppen*, left Ohlendorf unmoved. He dismissed the allegations as a waste of everyone's time, explaining to Musmanno and the tribunal that they just didn't understand the actions of the SS. When the tribunal charged his *Einsatzgruppe* D with averaging 340 killings a day and peaking at 700 per day for as long as 30 days at a time, the mathematically inclined Ohlendorf, to the horror of those in the courtroom, showed that he was proud of the figures. He told Musmanno that he did his duty as best he could at all times. Asked if he killed others than Jews, Ohlendorf admitted he did: gypsies.

"On what basis did you kill gypsies?"

"It is the same as for Jews," he replied.

"Racial? Blood?"

Ohlendorf avoided a direct answer to the question and instead talked about Jews until Musmanno ordered him to reply to the prosecutor's query. Ohlendorf shrugged his shoulders. "There was no difference between gypsies and Jews."

Pressed for a further explanation, the suave, confident SS officer referred back to a minor incident of the Thirty Years War of 1618-1648 in which gypsies became involved. Musmanno and the prosecution refused to permit him to rely upon such an ancient alibi and insisted he give his motive for the killings.

"Self-defense," he finally said. "The Jews posed a continuous danger for the German occupation troops. Moreover, some day they could attack Germany proper if permitted to live."

"And the Jewish and gypsy children? What conceivable threat were the children?"

Reverting to the sharp tone of voice he had used as an SS general, Ohlendorf replied that it wasn't his responsibility to determine the basis for the order to kill all Jews, including children, but to carry out the order. Musmanno, however, was persistent and continued to question Ohlendorf about the execution of the children until finally the SS general lost his composure.

"I believe that it is very simple to explain, if one starts with the fact that this order did not only try to achieve a temporary security (for Germany) but also a permanent security. For that reason, the children were people who would grow up and surely, being the children of parents who had been killed, would constitute a danger no smaller than that of the parents."

Musmanno, who had made certain that the Italian children under his command when he was U.S. military governor of the Sorrentine Peninsula had care as fine as was possible under the circumstances, shook his head as he summed up Ohlendorf's explanation. "The witness has stated the reason these children under five, under four, under three, down to conception I imagine, were killed is that they were a possible threat to Germany in the future years."

Ohlendorf did not object to Musmanno's explanation but he did insist on explaining to the tribunal that the execution of children was an assignment some of his SS men did not like. According to the SS general, his riflemen often thought about their own children at home as they centered their sights on the victims. This emotional problem made their aim bad and quite often they had to finish off the writhing, crying children with a revolver. Ohlendorf tried to convince the tribunal that the SS riflemen deserved sympathy due to the task they had been asked to accomplish. He completely ignored the fact that the real victims were the children.

When Ohlendorf was asked point blank whether he considered the order to kill Jews morally right, he evaded the question. "I asked him if the question of morality didn't enter his mind when he ordered defenseless people executed," Musmanno said later. "I inquired what he would've done if he had been ordered to kill a member of his own family. Would he have carried out the order."

Ohlendorf countered the question of morality by reminding the tribunal that many German civilians, including women and children, were killed during the American and British bombing attacks on German cities. The comparison, however, was too slight and left the tribunal cold. The prosecution again referred to Ohlendorf's family, which consisted of his wife, five children, a sister, and two brothers. "If you had received an order from Adolf Hitler to kill your own flesh and blood, would you have executed the order or not?"

Ohlendorf was trapped. If he admitted he would kill a member of his own family if ordered to do so by the Führer, he knew that he would be considered inhuman. If he admitted he would not follow such an order his entire defense of "I was just following orders" would collapse. His attorney recognized the dilemma and objected to the question. The tribunal conferred and decided to overrule the objection. Ohlendorf was ordered to answer the question. As Musmanno explained when overruling the objection: "You will admit that in normal times such a proposition would be incredible and intolerable but you claim the circumstances were not normal. Now suppose that in the discharge of your duty during these abnormal times you had been confronted with the necessity of deciding whether to kill, among hundreds of unknown people, one whom you knew very well."

Ohlendorf hesitated, then admitted he would follow orders and kill the acquaintance as well as the strangers. It was an admission that the Führer's order took preference over any blood ties or friendship. "But I never hated an opponent or an enemy and I still do not do so today."

Why then, he was asked, if he had no animosity toward the Jews and gypsies, did he continue to order them killed? Why, for instance, didn't he do as other *Einsatzgruppen* commanders did—avoid this duty by claiming illness? Or, if as documented evidence proved, he had problems with the Eleventh German Army commander to whom *Einsatzgruppe* D was attached, why didn't he ask for a transfer back to Berlin?

The question insulted Ohlendorf. "I would have betrayed my men if I had left the command. I considered my duty and I still consider it today, as much more valuable than the cheap applause which I could have won if I had at that betrayed my men by simulating illness."

He wanted the world to know that he was no quitter. "You must understand that I look at events of war in a different way than you do."

That was the understatement of the trial.

Despite the enormity of his murder operation and his inhumane personal actions, the details of which made listeners in the courtroom shudder, Ohlendorf managed to raise some controversial issues. One was his contention that a nation that had used the atom bomb should not condemn others. "The fact that individual men killed civilians face to face is looked upon as terrible," he said, "and is pictured as specially gruesome because the order was clearly given to kill these people. I cannot morally evaluate a deed which made it possible by pushing a button to kill a much larger number of civilians, men and women and children, any better. This hurt them for generations."

Musmanno responded by pointing out that as deplorable as dropping an atom bomb on a city was, the one and only purpose of the bombing was to weaken the enemy and bring the war to a close. As soon as the war ended the bombing was halted. The execution of the Jews, on the other hand, did not weaken the military forces of the enemy nor was there any assurance that once the fighting stopped the executions would be discontinued. The role of the *Einsatzgruppen* had little or no bearing on the military issues. Musmanno also reminded Ohlendorf about the use of the V-1 and V-2 weapons against London, weapons which were aimed at a city, not a military target, because of the lack of precise guidance equipment. These weapons were the responsibility of the SS during the closing months of the war.

Ohlendorf countered the V-1 and V-2 weapon accusations by calling the tribunal's attention to the British bombing of Dresden on the nights of February 18 and 19, 1945. "I cannot imagine that these planes, which systematically covered a city, square meter by square meter, with incendiaries and explosives and again with phosphorous bombs, could possibly not hope to kill civilians, including children."

The devastating air attack on Dresden was one of the most controversial military actions of the war and many others besides Ohlendorf had condemned the bombing. The atom bomb dropped on Hiroshima killed 71,379 persons and the fire bomb raids on Tokyo killed 83,793. But after the British Lancaster heavy bombers released 650,000 incendiary bombs on Dresden, the city burned for seven days and nights; the flames could be seen 200 miles away. A total of 135,000 persons died. Ohlendorf brought silence to the courtroom with his comments about the Dresden attack. Musmanno answered the charge by stating that the horror of Dresden pointed out the futility, savagery, and uselessness of war but at the same time reminded Ohlendorf: "I can't forget who started the war and made such attacks necessary if the tyranny of the Third Reich, as exemplified by the *Einsatzgruppen*, was to be stopped."

It became apparent that Ohlendorf had lost this portion of the exchange, so he changed tactics. He attempted to justify his actions by insisting that there were far too many Jews in high positions in comparison to the total Jewish population. He told the tribunal that it was his duty to eliminate this dangerous segment of the population to guarantee the security of Germany. It was a desperate effort to justify his actions, one that fell on deaf ears. With this testimony he rested his defense.

A few of the other SS defendants spoke before the tribunal in Ohlendorf's behalf. SS Lieutenant Heinz Schubert, Ohlendorf's adjutant from October 1941 until July 1942, tried to prove that they were only doing the duty assigned them, but while trying to help Ohlendorf he revealed the details of one of Ohlendorf's most reprehensible mass murders. As Christmas 1941 neared, the SS general received orders that the Jews and gypsies in Simferopol, a city in the Crimea, were to be liquidated before the holiday season. What irritated and worried Ohlendorf when he received the order was not that the approaching holiday season was supposed to be filled with joy and good will toward men but that he and his *Einsatzgruppe* D had a manpower shortage. Like any good manager, he knew this would slow down his production–and in this case his product was executed Jews and gypsies. He assigned the task to SS Colonel Werner Braune, commander of *Einsatzkommando* 11b, and told him to do the best he could under the circumstances. But then Ohlendorf came up with an idea to help accomplish the executions by the deadline—borrow trucks, rifles, ammunition, and men from the nearby German Eleventh Army.

No sooner had he solved the manpower problem than he faced another obstacle. The Jewish registration list in Simferopol was not very accurate and many suspected Jews were claiming that they were not Jews. Ohlendorf immediately contacted Heydrich and asked for a quick answer since Christmas was only a short time off. Heydrich replied within hours:

> Many of the Jews listed in your register are already known for continually trying to deny that they belong to the Jewish race by all possible and impossible reasons. It is, on the whole, in the nature of the matter that half-breeds of the first degree in particular try at every opportunity to deny that they are Jews. You will agree that in the third year of the war there are matters of more importance for the war effort than worrying about the wailing of Jews, making tedious investigations and keeping so many of my co-workers from other much more important tasks.

This was clear enough for Ohlendorf. If in doubt, kill. He did. The official documentation of the Simferopol massacre verified that 300 more Jews were killed than there were Jews registered in the city. Yet Schubert wanted the tribunal to know that Ohlendorf completed the task in as gentle and kindly a manner as possible. "I know that it was of the greatest importance to Ohlendorf to have the persons who were to be shot killed in the most humane and military manner because otherwise it would have been a strain too great for the execution squad. I made certain the condemned persons were not beaten while the loading was going on and there was no violence when their personal belongings were taken from them."

SS Captain Felix Rühl also had a "good" word for his superior Ohlendorf. When he was asked by the tribunal if a fellow SS officer was quite often drunk and unable to perform his share of the executions, Rühl became indignant. "I can assure you that if such a thing had occurred even once Herr Ohlendorf wouldn't have stood for it. That would have been the end of his career as a Kommando leader, insofar as I got to know Herr Ohlendorf." It was obvious from Rühl's testimony that Ohlendorf expected the executions carried out on schedule and would not have put up with a drunken officer who interfered with the schedule.

Musmanno allowed the defense lawyers to present every shred of evidence they could gather in Ohlendorf's behalf. In fact, his "Penguin Rule" was used throughout this and other war crimes trials and became known the world over among lawyers. This rule came about when the defense introduced testimony in an effort to show that the members of the extermination squads were normal citizens and had been forced into the assignments with the *Einsatzgruppen*, that they were victims of a police state. The prosecution protested to Musmanno that the introduction of such testimony regarding the home life of the accused in pre-Nazi days was irrelevant. Musmanno overruled the objection. "The defense can introduce any evidence short of describing the lives of the penguins in the Antarctic," he said, "and if the defense can convince me the habits of the penguins are relevant evidence to the case, then the lives and times of the white-fronted creatures can also be admitted as evidence."

After the trial the defense lawyers, in appreciation of his fairness, presented Musmanno with a model of the Antarctic bird.

After all the evidence was submitted and the witnesses had testified, Ohlendorf, in accordance with European courtroom practice, was permitted to address the bench with a final statement. He neither asked for mercy nor exoneration but made one last effort to convince the tribunal that he acted for the betterment of mankind and for his country, that there had been nothing personal about his duty with *Einsatzgruppe* D. He was then taken back to prison to await the verdict of the tribunal.

On April 10, 1948, an elevator brought Ohlendorf from the basement of the Palace of Justice directly to the dock of the courtroom. A sliding panel in the wall of the courtroom was opened and the SS general stepped forward. He bowed politely, put on the earphones handed him, and looked directly at the bench.

Musmanno nodded to him. "Otto Ohlendorf, you have been found guilty on all counts which charged you with crimes against humanity, war crimes, and membership in criminal organizations. The court sentences you to death by hanging."

Ohlendorf didn't change expression. He carefully took off

the earphones, gave them back to the guard, and stepped back through the open panel into the elevator.

On June 8, 1951, after all appeals had been heard, Otto Ohlendorf, lawyer-economist turned murderer, was hanged at Landsberg Prison, the same prison where Hitler had been held after the Beer Hall Putsch of 1923 and where the Führer had written *Mein Kampf*.

On October 12, 1968, Michael A. Musmanno, then a justice of the Pennsylvania Supreme Court, died of a massive cerebral hemorrhage and was buried in Arlington National Cemetery with full military honors. At the time of his death the model penguin presented to him by the defense lawyers at Nuremberg twenty years earlier still occupied a prominent place in his Pittsburgh judicial chambers.

6

Death Camp King

Despite such dedicated murderers as Ohlendorf, the shootings of Jews and others whom the Nazis considered enemies came to be considered much too slow a method. Moreover, the executioners' morale often sank after several long months of such massacres. Himmler personally traveled to Minsk to encourage his executioners, but when he attended the shooting of 200 Jews he nearly collapsed. Shortly after this visit he told Nebe that another method of killing had to be developed. It was this remark that led to the construction of the gas vans and gas chambers.

The gas vans were suggested by a Dr. Becker, an Untersturmführer-SS who was assigned to Ohlendorf's *Einsatzgruppe*. In a report to Himmler's headquarters Becker said that he had developed a Series I van and a Series II van. The first could be used in all types of weather but the second, not constructed as well as the first, could only be used in absolutely dry weather. The transmissions and clutches on the Series II vans were not as sturdy and, if the backwoods area where the executions took place were muddy, the vans would fail mechanically. He explained that he had equipped both series of vans with window shutters to camouflage them but unfortunately the modification was not successful. The Jews still called them "death vans." One reason he couldn't keep the purpose of his vans secret was the fact that the rough ground and mudholes over which the vans had to travel jarred loose the rivets and caulking, allowing much of the gas to leak out. This was dangerous to the SS men operating the vans. He had other problems, too.

> I should like to take this opportunity to bring the following to your attention: several commands, after the gassing is completed, have had the bodies unloaded by their own men. There is great danger that this will lead to their health being affected, if not immediately, at least later on. The commanders do not want to countermand these orders as they fear that if the prisoners were employed they would find some opportunity to escape.
>
> The application of gas is not always carried out in the correct manner. In order to get the job finished as quickly as possible, the driver presses the accelerator down to the fullest extent. Thereby the victims suffer death by suffocation and not by dozing off as was intended. By correct adjustment of the levers death comes faster and the prisoners fall asleep peacefully. Previously the victims' faces and other signs showed that they died in agony.

Initially those to be gassed had been marched to a secluded area where the vans were parked; the victims were then forced into the vans. But this, Becker said, made them nervous and restless. He recommended that the intended victims be loaded on the vans in the villages and driven to the spot where they were to be executed. Ohlendorf agreed, suggesting that the waiting Jews be told that they were being taken to a safer area. As soon as the unsuspecting passengers were aboard the van and the doors closed and locked, the driver would start the flow of carbon monoxide into the rear compartment. By the time the van reached the outlying district where a long deep ditch had been dug, the victims were dead. Within a few minutes they were buried and the van was on its way back to the village for a new load.

Becker tried to keep the entire operation on a business-like basis. If there were not enough vans on a particular day to fill all the requests, he made certain that the available vans went to the SS commander with the largest number of prospects. All bills, invoices, letters, and requisitions were kept in filing cabinets, such as the request from the Security Police and Security Service Ostland to Amt IV, B4, dated June 15, 1942, that asked for the immediate shipment of one five-ton van and twenty gas hoses with holes. When Becker sent his letter complaining that the drivers were not using the proper procedure when gassing the victims, Eichmann promptly set up a training school for the drivers to teach them the correct method.

As effective as the gas vans were in comparison with the previous bloody and slow method of shooting, there were still problems. The corpses had to be removed from the vans and buried. While this was being done traces of the gas often sickened the drivers. A physician was assigned to each *Einsatzgruppe* to oversee the health of the SS men involved with the van operations, but many of the SS men had to be hospitalized or reassigned for medical reasons. Becker had, of course, received considerable acclaim for his development of the gas vans and praise from Himmler himself. Other SS members wanting to bask in the warmth of Himmler's esteem and enjoy the benefits that derived from such glory tried to outdo Becker. One such man was Christian Wirth, a former Stuttgart police officer. Wirth had been loaned to Operation Euthanasia by Himmler and was an expert in all three phases of the program: incurables, direct extermination by special treatment, and experiments in mass sterilization. He did such an efficient job that when Dr. Ernst Grawitz, the SS medical officer in chief, heard Himmler complain that a better method had to be found to execute Polish Jews than the gas vans, he suggested that Wirth might be the man for the task. Himmler immediately assigned Wirth to Poland with instructions to find a fast and efficient method of liquidating one million Polish Jews.

Wirth was an egotist without a conscience. He scoffed at the method being used by Hauptsturmführer-SS Lange, the officer in charge of executing Jews when Wirth arrived in Poland. Lange was using gas vans such as had been used in Russia but he had set up a procedure entirely different from Becker's. He had taken over an old mansion 40 miles northwest of Lodz and used it as a staging station for his murder operation. Jews were brought by train to Kulmhof Station and then taken directly to the mansion, where they were told to strip and get into the gas vans, supposedly to take showers. Once they were locked in the vans, they were gassed by carbon monoxide entering the rear compartment through a concealed pipe. Other Jews were forced to empty the vans and bury the bodies. Even Eichmann was repelled by this murder factory when he witnessed what happened to the hapless Jews.

> I followed the van and then came the most horrifying sight I've ever seen in my life. The van stopped alongside a wide pit, the doors were opened and the bodies thrown out. The limbs were still supple as if the victims were still alive. They were thrown into the pit. I saw a civilian pulling out teeth with a pair of pliers and then I left quickly. I rushed to my car and departed and said no more. I was through. I had had it. A white-coated doctor said I ought to look through the peephole and see what went on inside the van. I refused. I couldn't. I couldn't speak. I had to get away. Frightful, I tell you. An inferno.

While the Kulmhof operation sickened Eichmann, it didn't deter him from his responsibility of liquidating the Jews. It only encouraged him to find a new and better way. Consequently he wholeheartedly backed Christian Wirth's experimentation in Poland. Wirth selected an area along the Lublin-Lwow railway for this initial death camp installation. It was near the Polish village of Belzec where, in May 1940, the Nazis had established a labor camp to which 7,000 Jews from Lublin, Warsaw, and Radom had been deported. Wirth decided that he wanted nothing to do with the gas vans or mobile death units. He wanted a stationary unit. In the center of the camp he had three "shower rooms" constructed, each 16 feet by 16 feet by 6 feet. To camouflage these death chambers, he planted geraniums around them and kept the grass neatly cut so that his victims thought they were being ushered into modern shower rooms where they could wash their bodies of the grime and dirt accumulated from the long trip to the camp in cattle trains.

Instead of the warm water and soap they expected, however, they received the exhaust gases from diesel engines. And to make the entire procedure as efficient as possible, Wirth had wide doors on both the front wall and back wall. This made it much easier to take the corpses out of the rooms after the gassing.

Belzec death camp opened on March 17, 1942, and, in the minds of Wirth, Himmler, Eichmann, and other Nazis bent on eliminating the Jews, it was a great success. For the following nine months it was the main death camp. Jews were brought to Belzec from all the villages and hamlets of Eastern Galicia and even some from as far away as Rumania, Czechoslovakia, and Germany. Wirth was so pleased with the killing center that he added three additional gas chambers for a total of six. This permitted the SS men to deal with 15,000 Jews a day! The SS officers and men stationed at Belzec were proud of their new camp, so proud that a sign was erected over the entrance that stated: "Entrance to the Jewish State." Hanging from the large doors through which the Jews entered the gas chamber was a banner made from a synagogue curtain which stated in Hebrew: "This is the gate of the Lord into which the righteous shall enter."

Obersturmführer-SS Kurt Gerstein, who was in the prussic acid business and was considered a poison gas expert, was sent to Belzec in August of 1942 to check on Wirth's installation. When the war ended, Gerstein gave a report to his American captors about Belzec shortly before he committed suicide. His report is a vivid eyewitness account of the procedure used at the killing center.

> For a number of men there still flickers a lingering hope, sufficient to make them march with resistance to the death chambers. The majority know with certainty what is to be their fate. The horrible, all-pervading stench reveals the truth. Then they climb some small steps and behold the reality. Silent mothers hold their babies to their breasts, naked; there are many children of all ages. They hesitate, but nevertheless proceed toward the death chambers, most of them without a word, pushed by those behind, chased by the whips of the SS men.
>
> A woman of about forty curses the chief of the murderers, crying that the blood of her children will be on his head. Wirth, an SS officer, himself strikes her across the face with five lashes of the whip and she disappears into the gas chamber. The SS men push people into the chambers as Wirth orders them to fill it up well. The naked people stand on each other's feet. About seven to eight hundred people in an area about a hundred square meters. The doors close. Outside other transports, loaded with Jews, wait their turn. But the diesel engine is not working. Fifty minutes pass, seventy minutes. The people in the death chamber remain standing. They have no choice. Many are weeping. After two hours and forty-nine minutes the diesel engine finally starts. Many have

already died in the crowded chamber. Twenty-five minutes pass. Many are still alive. After thirty-two minutes all are dead.

Jewish workers open the doors on the rear wall. The dead, having nowhere to fall, stand like pillars of salt. Even in death families may be seen standing pressed together, clutching hands. It is only with difficulty that the bodies are separated in order to clear the place for the next group. The blue corpses, covered with sweat and urine, are thrown out. So are the bodies of babies and children. A couple of workers are busy with the mouths of the dead, opening them with iron pegs, searching for gold teeth. Others search the private parts of the bodies for gold and diamonds hidden by the victims. Wirth points to a container and exclaims: "Lift it up and see how much gold is in it."

By the spring of 1943 almost all the Jews of the eastern Galicia area had died in the gas chambers of Belzec, and Wirth had similar installations scattered throughout Poland: Sobibor, near the Ukrainian border, which could "process" 20,000 persons a day; Treblinka, 75 miles northwest of Warsaw, which had 30 gas chambers and handled at least 25,000 persons a day; and he even added several gas chambers to the concentration camp at Lublin, known later as Maidanek, to handle the overflow. Wirth, dubbed the "Death Camp King," was the star of the murder operation but his elevation to the throne aroused the jealousy of others determined to topple him from his glorified position. One who succeeded in dethroning Wirth was Rudolph Höss.

Höss was born in Baden-Baden in 1900 to a shopkeeper who hoped his son would become a Catholic priest. Höss embraced violence instead of love. Although he was not quite fifteen years old when World War I started, he managed to join the German army and see action at the front where he was wounded several times. He was awarded the Iron Cross, First and Second Classes. When he was discharged from the army after the war he was one of the first veterans to join the *Freikorps*, the paramilitary unit that virtually replaced the disbanded armed forces of the defeated country. Instead of entering a Catholic seminary, he entered a prison when he was arrested along with Martin Bormann, later Hitler's private secretary, and accused of murder. Both men were found guilty of killing Walther Kadow, a teacher who was suspected of informing on *Freikorps* members to the occupying French. After five years he was released from jail and promptly became a member of the SS, working his way up the ranks until he was a Hauptsturmführer-SS by 1940.

In the summer of 1941, Himmler summoned him to SS headquarters and told him: "The Führer has ordered the Final Solution of the Jewish question and we have to carry out the task. For reasons of transportation and isolation, I have picked Auschwitz for this. You now have the hard job of carrying this out."

Auschwitz was a small town situated between the Vistula and its tributary, the Sola, about 150 miles southwest of Warsaw. When Höss took command of the camp, it was one of many such detention or work camps and was of no special interest to either the Nazis or the outside world. That soon changed, however. Höss enlisted the aid of German firms and experts to construct the gas chambers, explaining that he wanted units capable of disposing of 2,000 people at one time. While these firms were considering their bids for the construction, Höss visited one of Wirth's death camps, Treblinka. He was disgusted with what he saw. The gas chambers were too small and the carbon monoxide piped into them came from old captured transport-vehicle and tank engines that often failed to run. Then the bodies had to be buried. The whole procedure for which Wirth had been praised so highly was completely unacceptable to the ambitious Höss. One "improvement" he was determined to have at Auschwitz were ovens to burn the bodies instead of having to bury the corpses.

He had six extermination chambers constructed—two large ones that could accommodate 2,000 in each and four smaller ones capable of holding 1,500 each—by German Armaments Incorporated. The firm adhered closely to Höss's demand that the "Corpse Cellars" have gas-proof doors and observation windows of double eight-millimeter glass. The ovens were designed by the German firm of Topf and Company of Erfurt. There were five furnaces, each with three doors, that utilized body fat as fuel. One tall chimney provided the necessary draught for all five of the furnaces. The furnaces, however, could only handle 2,000 bodies while the combined gas chambers could liquidate 10,000 persons. As Höss complained to a psychologist at Nuremberg: "The killing itself took the least time. You could dispose of 2,000 head in a half hour but it was the burning that took all the time. The killing was easy; you didn't even need guards to drive them into the chambers; they just went in expecting to take showers and instead of water we turned on poison gas."

One of the reasons the killing was accomplished so quickly was because Höss didn't use carbon monoxide as Wirth did in his death camps. He used a new agent. After visiting Treblinka and deciding that carbon monoxide was not lethal enough and much too slow, he began investigating the other poisons he might be able to use. He discovered that Deutsche Gesellschaft für Schädlingsbekampfung (German Corporation for Pest Control) had a deadly chemical called Zyklon B, the generic name of which was prussic acid. It was an insecticide and had a special odor to warn human beings of its presence. Other than the odor, however, Höss considered it an ideal killing agent and tried it in one of his gas chambers. He was amazed—and happy—to discover that all the victims were dead within ten minutes. He immediately ordered Zyklon B to be delivered to Auschwitz in unlimited quantities and the firm, controlled by the industrial conglomerate I. G. Farben, was quick to comply. Then Höss added that he didn't want the warning odor agent incorporated into the Zyklon B shipped to his camp, and company officials hesitated. Even without official notice of the reason, they were well aware of why Höss wanted the odor eliminated, but their hesitation didn't stem from moral grounds. Their patent on the Zyklon B had expired earlier and only their warning indicator in the agent was patented. Without it, competitors would move in and share the market. Himmler, however, made certain that they complied promptly with Höss's request. It meant Höss would become the most successful mass murderer in modern history and I. G. Farben's dividends for the remaining years of the war would be double those of 1940 and 1941.

Mass transports began arriving at the camp once the new facilities were completed and the supply of Zyklon B was adequate: 400,000 persons from Hungary; 250,000 from Poland and Upper Silesia; 100,000 from Germany; 90,000 from the Netherlands; 90,000 from Slovakia; 65,000 from Greece;

and 11,000 from France. Höss became so busy that he set up another camp at nearby Birkenau although he had to improvise. Here he used two old farm buildings made airtight as makeshift gas chambers, and it was necessary to bury these victims. He tried to speed up the process at this auxiliary death camp by putting the corpses into a pit lined with rags soaked in paraffin and setting them afire. Much to his disgust, it still took six to seven hours to cremate 100 bodies in such a pit.

In Auschwitz, however, the operation normally moved very smoothly. When they stepped from the train the prisoners were assembled on a special ramp where their baggage was taken from them and they were assigned their destination. Those fit for work were taken to living quarters in the camp, those destined for extermination were taken to a large underground dressing room adjoining one of the gas chambers. The room had several benches and hooks for clothing, making plausible the SS guards' explanation that they were going to be given showers and deloused. The prisoners were even instructed to remember where they hung their clothes, indicating to them that they would soon return to the dressing room. They were then directed into the gas chamber which was equipped with fake shower heads, further duping them into the belief that all was well. As soon as the guards escorting them into the chamber departed and the doors were closed, however, the Zyklon B pellets were dropped into the room and the victims died within minutes. At times there were problems but not often. In his statement to Allied interrogators, Höss told about one incident:

> I remember one incident especially well. One transport from Belsen had arrived and two-thirds of it, mostly men, were in the gas chamber and one-third still in the dressing room. When three or four armed SS Unterführers entered the dressing room to make the prisoners hurry undressing, mutiny broke out. The light cables were torn down, the SS men overpowered and disarmed, and one of them stabbed. As the room was in incomplete darkness wild shots were exchanged between the sentry at the exit and the prisoners inside. When I arrived I ordered the doors to be shut and I had the process of the gassing of the first party finished and then went into the room with the guard, carrying small torches, and we forced the prisoners into one corner from where they were

taken out singly into another room in the crematorium and shot, by my order, with small caliber weapons.

I. G. Farben was not content with the profit being made from its Zyklon B. Officials decided to build a plant near the Auschwitz death camp to manufacture synthetic buna rubber needed by the German armed forces. The terrain was unsuitable but the possibility of obtaining slave labor from Höss's camp overrode any disadvantages. Farben director Carl Krauch contacted Himmler and asked if the labor requirements of such a new plant could be met by camp inmates. There was no problem. Farben could have all the inmates it needed. Höss was soon providing 1,000 Jews a day to work on the construction of the factory. Relations were so good between the SS and the Farben officials that they had a joint Christmas party in 1941 "which was festive and ended up in heavy drinking." At this very time, the inmates of Auschwitz had no suitable clothing for the winter weather, not enough food to maintain their strength, and no hope. They had to walk the seven kilometers to the construction site through the snow each day and return in the evening after a hard day's work. Many had to be carried back to the camp by their friends. Those who could not move were shot on the spot.

One Farben civilian employee at the new plant stated in a letter to an acquaintance in Frankfurt that the inmates of Auschwitz were important to the company. "That the Jewish race is playing a special part here, you can well imagine. The diet and treatment of this sort of people is in accordance with our aim. Evidently an increase in weight is hardly ever recorded for them. That bullets start flying at the slightest attempt of a 'change of air' is also certain as well as the fact that many have already disappeared as a result of 'sunstroke.' "

The "sunstroke" referred to in the letter from the Farben employee was certainly not caused by the sun. It was the result of the treatment at the camp. In the testimony of one SS man who was stationed at Auschwitz, this fact is made clear:

The mere view of the tightly drawn, high, double-barbed wire fences with the signs reading "Attention! Danger!", the towers manned by sentries with machine guns and carbines, and the bleak living blocks put every newcomer into a hopeless state of mind as he realized that from there he would never return to freedom. And there were indeed few who did not come to a tormented end there. Many committed suicide after a few days. When out on a working party they would run through the chain of sentries in order to be shot or they "went into the wire," as it was termed in camp language. A high voltage shock, a round from a machine gun, and death spared them the tortures to come. Whenever shots were heard during the night, everyone knew that once again despair had driven yet another human being into the wire and that he now lay there, dressed only in rags, a lifeless bundle within the so-called neutral zone. This was a strip of gravel two meters wide which ran along the inner wire obstacle and anyone entering this strip was fired upon.

Others were found hanged by their belts at their bedsides in the morning. In such cases the prisoner responsible for order in the block would report the number of suicides to the camp commandant. The "Identification Service" would then hurry to the scene and photograph the corpse from all angles and statements would be taken from the other occupants of the room to ascertain whether the wretched suicide had not perhaps been murdered by other camp inmates. The farcical hypocrisy displayed on these occasions was unsurpassed, as if the SS authorities of a camp in which thousands of people were systematically murdered daily were the least bit interested in the fate of one unfortunate man.

Besides gassing and shooting prisoners, Höss, who had now replaced Wirth as the "Death Camp King," often resorted to injections of phenol. It is estimated that at least 25,000 inmates of Auschwitz were murdered in this manner. Often when a man was questioned about some camp incident, rather than return him to his block and schedule him for death by gassing at a later date, he was given the lethal injection on the spot. Guards would grab his hands, he would be blindfolded, and a doctor would inject the phenol with a long needle into the inmate's chest. Death was not instantaneous. The victim was usually stretched out on the floor, and left to die.

Höss, like Ohlendorf, was a prime example of how a man's mind could be programmed by the Nazis to understand only the slogan of the SS: "Believe! Obey! Fight!" In his own opinion he was a perfectly normal man with one characteristic that he wished he didn't have—he considered himself more sensitive than most people! He tried to explain this incredible statement to interrogators by saying: "I must confess that the gassing process had a calming effect on me. I always had a horror of the shootings, thinking of the number of people, the women and the children. I was relieved that they were spared those bloodbaths."

A psychologist at Nuremberg, Captain G. M. Gilbert, inquired of Höss whether he had a normal social life. Höss admitted that he had never had close friends even as a child and that he hadn't changed as he matured. He felt more comfortable when he was alone. Asked if he loved and had compassion for his wife, he said he loved her but a real spiritual union was lacking. He also revealed that sex was never an important factor in his life, that he could take it or leave it. After his wife discovered what he was doing at Auschwitz, he said, they rarely had intercourse. Both lost desire. His rationalizing of his actions was much the same as Ohlendorf's.

"We were all so trained to obey orders without even thinking that the thought never occurred to anybody to disobey. Someone else would have done it anyway. You can be sure it wasn't always a pleasure to see those mountains of corpses and smell the continual burning but Himmler ordered it and had explained its necessity. I never really gave much thought to whether it was wrong. It just seemed a necessity," Höss explained.

At Auschwitz he was overseer of the execution of more than 2.5 million inmates and starved to death another half million. He accomplished his task so well that a 1944 SS citation commended him as a true pioneer in this area because of his new ideas and educational methods. Captured by the Russians, Höss was sentenced to death at Warsaw and, ironically, was executed at Auschwitz in 1947.

The I. G. Farben corporation fared much better, both on the slave labor charges and the financial profit from Zyklon B. Carl Krauch, the director who guided the building of the buna plant at Auschwitz with inmate labor, was found guilty at Nuremberg in 1948 of slavery and mass murder but was sentenced to a mere six years in prison. I. G. Farben was ordered dismantled but it was a futile order that was not carried out by the Allies. Today the three companies that resulted from the so-called dismantling procedure—Bayer-Leverkusen, Farbwerke Höchst, and BASF (Badischeanilin und Sodafabrik)—are each larger than their parent company I. G. Farben. The company that had equated slave labor with a consumable raw material survived. International business interests tied to the German chemical company were much stronger than the moral outrage over the millions that died at Auschwitz because of Zyklon B and slave labor.

7

The Bari Incident

Himmler was never satisfied with the operation of the death camps despite the success of Zyklon B. He was constantly searching for more economical methods to exterminate large segments of an unwanted population and, ironically, an Allied catastrophe in 1943 gave him an opportunity to test a war gas. The Luftwaffe bombing of Allied merchant ships in the harbor at Bari, Italy, on December 3, 1943, was one of the German Air Force's most successful missions of the entire war. Twenty-five ships were sunk, instantly killing 2,000 persons. It was the worst Allied naval disaster except for Pearl Harbor; and it seriously delayed Allied efforts to overrun Italy. But the real horror of the event and one of the best-kept secrets of World War II was the unleashing of 100 tons of poison gas!

On July 10 the Allied forces invaded Sicily and started a drive toward the Axis-held Continent. Hitler and his staff prepared for the step-by-step path obviously planned by the Allies: Sicily, Italy, southern France, and ultimately Germany. Determined to stop the Allied forces, the Führer resorted to every weapon and called upon every man available, but serious problems faced him. His Luftwaffe was engaged night and day by the USAF and the RAF; the fall of Italian dictator Benito Mussolini fifteen days after the Allied invasion of Sicily cost Hitler between 30 and 40 Italian divisions that he had depended upon to defend Italy; and the 16 remaining German divisions stationed in Italy were spread so thin that unless the exact invasion area and time of invasion were accurately forecast, there was little hope of repulsing an Allied landing. Hitler had one weapon that he had not yet used in the war—poison gas. Near the end of July reports reached London and Washington that the Führer was moving to Italy some of the quarter of a million tons of toxic munitions he had stored east of the Rhine. These included Tabun, a colorless, odorless gas that attacked the human nervous system through the lungs or eyes, causing death within one to five minutes.

In August 1943, President Roosevelt, alerted by the reports about the possible use of chemical agents by the Germans, issued a statement outlining Allied policy on the use of poison gas.

> From time to time since the present war began there have been reports that one or more of the Axis powers were seriously contemplating the use of poisonous or noxious gases or other inhumane devices of warfare. I have been loath to believe that any nation, even our present enemies, could or would be willing to loose upon mankind such terrible and inhumane weapons.
>
> However, evidence that the Axis powers are making significant preparations indicative of such an intention is being reported with increasing frequency from a variety of sources. Use of such weapons has been outlawed by the general opinion of civilized mankind. This country has not used them, and I hope that we never will be compelled to use them. I state categorically that we shall under no circumstances resort to the use of such weapons unless they are first used by our enemies.
>
> As President of the United States and Commander-in-Chief of the American armed forces, I want to make clear beyond all doubt to any of our enemies contemplating a resort to such desperate and barbarous methods that acts of this nature committed against any one of the United Nations will be regarded as having been committed against the United States and will be treated accordingly. We promise to any perpetrators of such crime full and swift retaliation in kind and I feel obliged now to warn the Axis armies and the Axis peoples in Europe and in Asia that the terrible consequence of any use of these inhumane methods on their part will be brought down swiftly and surely upon their own heads. Any use of poison gas by an Axis power, therefore, will immediately

be followed by the fullest retaliation upon munition centers, seaports, and other military objectives throughout the whole extent of the territory of such Axis country.

This stiff warning from Washington didn't stop the rumors that Hitler was still stockpiling chemical weapons in Italy. After careful consideration the White House granted permission to the army to ship a supply of chemical bombs containing liquid mustard to the battle zone. By the time this decision was made, the ships loaded, and the convoy assembled for the long voyage, southern Italy was in Allied hands and a depot had been established at the city of Bari on the heel of the peninsula. The American merchant ship *John Harvey* under the command of Captain Elwin F. Knowles was selected to carry the shipment. The 701st Chemical Maintenance Company headed by First Lieutenant Howard D. Beckstrom, a unit trained to handle large-scale shipments of toxics, was ordered to Baltimore to board the *John Harvey*. The assignment was to nursemaid the 2,000 M47A1 hundred-pound mustard bombs to Italy.

The bombs needed care. Only slightly more than four feet long and eight inches in diameter, each bomb held from 60 to 70 pounds of liquid mustard, enough to contaminate an area from 15 to 40 yards in diameter, depending upon environmental conditions at the time of explosion. Beckstrom and his men had to check continually for any evidence of contamination due to leaks in the bomb casing caused by corrosion or vibration. They also had to keep a check on the pressure inside the casing to make certain they were not building up to a dangerous level that might cause detonation. When Knowles was briefed by Beckstrom on the dangers inherent to such load, he just shook his head and muttered, "We'll just put the cargo in the hold and pray. We don't have any other choice."

The crossing from Baltimore to Oran, Algeria, where the *John Harvey* lowered anchor on November 18, was uneventful. Two days later Knowles left Oran with a convoy headed for Augusta, Sicily. Again there were no problems and the *John Harvey* reached Augusta on November 25 without incident. There had been several submarine wolf pack alerts and a formation of German bombers had been spotted just south of Sicily, but there had been no actual attacks on the bomb-loaded ship. On November 26, after Beckstrom had inspected the mustard bombs carefully and found nothing wrong, the *John Harvey* moved slowly out of Augusta and set course for Italy. The convoy passed through the Strait of Otranto that separates Italy from Albania and went up the Adriatic Sea to Bari. The fifteen merchant ships entered the breakwater of Bari harbor, passing through the submarine nets strung between the Molo Nuovo and Molo San Cataldo, only to discover that the harbor was jammed with ships waiting to be unloaded. When he received orders to moor at pier 29 outside the inner breakwater of the port, Knowles was apprehensive. It was one thing for a ship loaded with conventional cargo to tie up at a dock for several days in plain view of any German planes in the area but his was not such a cargo. He wanted to tell the British port director about the mustard bombs on the *John Harvey* in hopes the Britisher would give the ship preference in the unloading sequence, but since he was not supposed to reveal the contents of his ship he was stymied. Secrecy about the transporting of poison gas to the war zone was paramount. So for five days Knowles sweat out the situation. On the sixth day, as the sun was setting, he saw a German reconnaissance plane high in the sky over Bari harbor. Without a doubt the Luftwaffe pilot could see the large number of merchant ships jamming the harbor.

Oberleutenant Werner Hahn, the pilot of the Me-210, had no trouble detecting the Allied ships far below him nor in recognizing that they made an excellent target for the German bombers. He immediately streaked back to his base in northern Italy to inform his commander. Hahn knew that Field Marshal Wolfram von Richthofen, commander of Luftflotte Two, was eagerly awaiting his report, and that all available Luftwaffe bombers were fueled and loaded with bombs at the scattered airfields in northern Italy, ready to take off for Bari the moment the word was given. Richthofen had been watching the harbor for several days well aware that the merchant ships were piling up, well aware, too, that Field Marshal Albert Kesselring, commander in chief of the German troops in Italy, had ordered him to find a way to slow down the British and American forces in Italy. The question was where to hit the Allies to hurt them the most, to halt the flow of supplies and men. Richthofen thought the answer was Bari.

Fifteen minutes after Hahn's report reached his office, Richthofen had convinced Kesselring to send all the available bombers in Italy to bomb the ships in Bari. The 105 Ju-88s, including several carrying flares to bathe Bari harbor in brilliant light, headed east until they were over the Adriatic and then turned south toward Bari. At 7:25 P.M. the lead plane turned west directly toward Bari harbor and dropped to an altitude of only 45 meters.

The unloading at the docks in Bari was going smoothly despite the fact that darkness had fallen over the harbor. So confident was the British port director that the Luftwaffe posed no threat that far south that he had ordered all lights in the harbor turned on to aid with the work. Consequently neither the merchant seamen, the Allied soldiers in the area, nor the Italian dockhands heard or saw the Luftwaffe bombers until the Ju-88s made their first low-level pass across the harbor. Several of the merchant ships received direct hits on this initial bombing run. One of the badly damaged ships was the *John Harvey*. Shrapnel from a near hit had started a fire in the hold of the ship laden with the mustard gas bombs but no one in the harbor paid particular attention to this one ship. Other vessels on each side of the *John Harvey* were also aflame and three had received direct hits and were already sinking. By the time the German bombers circled around for a second run over the harbor the *John Harvey* was a mass of flames and beyond saving. Before the crew members could evacuate the ship there was a tremendous explosion. From the spot where the *John Harvey* had been seconds before rose a vast fountain of flame with multicolored jets streaming in all directions. It shot more than a thousand feet into the air. There was nothing left of the ship nor of Beckstrom and his chemical warfare men nor of Captain Knowles. The only men who could have warned the others at Bari that December night that a large amount of deadly mustard had been released over the harbor were dead.

It was a dawn to chill the soul of those still alive in Bari when light spread across the sky on December 3. Fires were burning in the harbor and a huge pall of smoke hovered over the port and the city. Flames still flickered in various sections of Bari, too, especially in the badly damaged old section. Communications were nonexistent. First aid stations and hospitals were packed with burn and shock victims and the wounded. But there was one mysterious aspect about those being treated. Many of the patients were complaining about burns and blisters although they denied being close to any flames. Others had severe burning sensations in their eyes and couldn't see clearly. At first the doctors and nurses believed that the victims were so shocked by their experiences that they were in error about not being trapped by the flames. All patients were treated for normal burns and given ointment to soothe their burning eyes.

The first indication the medical personnel at Bari had that they faced an unusual problem was in the resuscitation wards of the hospitals, where the men brought in supposedly suffering from shock, immersions, and exposure were bedded. The normal treatment for their irritated eyes did no good. Weeping became very marked and was associated with spasms of the eyelids and a morbid fear of light. Within 24 hours the eyes were swollen and the patients complained they were blind. Another factor puzzling the doctors was the pulse and blood pressure readings of the men supposedly in shock. The pulse beat was barely evident and blood pressure was down in the range of 40 to 60 millimeters of mercury, and yet the patients did not appear to be in clinical shock. Then, without warning and for no apparent medical reason, the patients began dying. Men who had been complaining of burning eyes but nothing else suddenly passed away. Supposedly minor shock victims died without warning despite the excellent treatment they were receiving.

On December 5, three days after the disastrous raid by the Luftwaffe on the ships in Bari harbor, the following report was sent to the commanding officer of the British Ninety-eighth General Hospital:

> Subject: N.Y.D. Dermatitis Cases received from local air raid on night
> 2nd-3rd December 1943.
> To: Officer Commanding, Ninety-eighth General Hospital
> Sir:

I respectfully submit the following report written at your request and at short notice. It should be regarded as an interim report.

1. About 430 casualties were received from the incident.

2. No official notification was received till the following morning that N.Y.D. [not yet diagnosed] (D) cases might be amongst the casualties.

3. As a result I was considerably puzzled by the extremely shocked conditions of the patients with negligible surgical injuries.

4. Many of these patients were treated as "immersion" cases and were wrapped in blankets to warm them up. This naturally aggravated the subsequent development of the dermatitis.

5. The complaint, rarely seriously made of "smarting eyes" was considered due to oil fuel and not regarded as of any importance.

6. I have in the Surgical Division 140 cases of this condition.The remainder are in the Medical Division.

7. There have been ten deaths in my Division due to this condition. I expect this number will probably be more than doubled.

8. Seventy percent of the cases are severe. I expect there will be a high incidence of severe sepsis. This will raise nursing problems in a Forward Field Hospital.

9. Expert advice on this condition is requested.

A.L. d'Abreu
O.i/c Surgical Division

An emergency call was made from Italy to Allied Force Headquarters in Algiers as soon as the medical personnel admitted their patients were dying for an undetermined reason. Lieutenant Colonel Stewart Francis Alexander, the twenty-nine-year-old doctor serving as consultant in chemical warfare medicine, was immediately ordered to Bari to investigate the medical mystery. Since no one at the Allied Force Headquarters was aware that the *John Harvey* had been carrying mustard bombs, Alexander had no clues to the unexplained deaths—only the suspicion that a toxic agent might be involved.

Alexander and the Allied medical personnel at Bari were still confused on December 5, but Oberstgruppenführer-SS Karl Wolff, the German military governor of northern Italy, knew exactly what was causing the deaths. Six hours after the Luftwaffe raid on the ships in Bari harbor, three SS men who had infiltrated the Allied troops at Bari and were living in the city had obtained a piece of bomb casing. An Italian frogman still loyal to the Germans had recovered the piece from the bottom of the harbor. Within a few minutes the SS men, led by Dieter Gollob, had identified it.

"It was easy," Gollob said later. "The marking M47A1 was on the metal casing and a call to our headquarters in the north soon verified that it was a hundred-pound bomb that was often used by the Americans for carrying liquid mustard."

The condition of the victims made Gollob certain that one of the sunken ships had been carrying mustard bombs. When the casing had been split open by the fires and explosions, the mustard had mixed with the oil in the harbor from the damaged ships. Seamen who had to abandon their vessels and swim for their lives were saturated with the oil-mustard mixture and unless they immediately took a shower or bath after reaching shore, the mustard was absorbed into their systems. Even more deadly was the mustard that turned to gas because of the extreme heat and which had drifted over the city. The citizens of Bari were completely unaware of the deadly poison hidden in the "clouds" sweeping over both the old and new sections of the town, and took no precautions. Nor did they have the first aid or hospital facilities available to the military and merchant seamen. The inhabitants, having survived from the beginning of the war until late 1943 without serious damage to their city, weren't prepared for the catastrophe. When many of them began dying after breathing the mustard vapors that floated overhead, there was near panic.

Gollob's report was relayed immediately by Wolff to Himmler in Berlin. It was obvious to the veteran SS officer that the Bari incident offered Himmler a wonderful opportunity for a propaganda coup against the Allies. World opinion undoubtedly had held Hitler back from using poison gas and Roosevelt's pronouncement in August that any nation that would use such a weapon would be classed inhumane and uncivilized both emphasized the importance of the disaster at Bari. But Wolff, a member of the Nazi party since 1931 who had joined Himmler's entourage in 1933, completely underestimated the inhumane character of his superior. Or perhaps he was unaware that in 1939 Himmler had the doctors on his staff conduct experiments involving liquid mustard. It was applied to the skin of selected prisoners in the concentration camps and their symptoms were observed and photographed up to the time of death. These initial tests were so successful in Himmler's view that he ordered further experiments on a larger scale. According to one witness, the prisoners subjected to the liquid mustard suffered such appalling pain one could hardly bear to be near them. In 1942, however, Himmler became so engrossed in the gas chambers and crematoria that he failed to follow up on the liquid mustard experiments. When he received word from Wolff that the entire population of Bari had been subjected to the poison, he was delighted.

Wolff had planned for the Reichsführer-SS to publicize the fact that the Allies had unleashed the liquid mustard on Bari, playing down the fact that the Luftwaffe bombers had been the immediate cause of the disaster. Once the incident was publicized in the newspapers and broadcast on the radio, Wolff knew that the confusion and frustration of the Allied medical personnel in the Bari area would end and they would know how to treat the victims. Despite his long SS career, Wolff was much more humane than Himmler. This was later proven in early March 1945, when he arranged a meeting with American authorities in an effort to stop the fighting in Italy. Himmler, however, decided that the Bari disaster gave him the opportunity to get revenge on the Italians whom he considered traitors because their government had deserted Hitler. He also wanted to determine the effect of mustard on such a large number of persons, in keeping with his quest to find new ways of exterminating the Jews. Himmler kept the secret of the mysterious deaths from the Allies until they were able to determine the cause on their own.

It was a diabolical scheme of which Wolff did not approve. There was nothing he could do about Himmler's decision, however, without endangering his own life.

Meanwhile Alexander, the doctor from Allied Force Headquarters in Algiers, was trying desperately to stop the deaths. His concern is obvious in the final report he submitted: "The type of death merits special attention as it was described as most impressive by those who witness them. Individuals would be remarkably clear mentally and suddenly stop breathing. At first it was thought they died because of blast injuries but clinically this was disproven." It wasn't until the ninth day after the Luftwaffe raid on the harbor that Alexander learned that a bomb casing discovered by an English diver had contained mustard. Three days before that, however, he had concluded that the victims were suffering from some type of chemical burn and he had changed his treatment. As soon as he was told that the chemical was definitely mustard, he was able to prescribe even better procedures and dramatically reduce the number of daily deaths. As his report stated later: "Eighty-eight percent of the deaths occurred within the first two weeks and only 10 deaths occurred subsequent to the 14th day." The delay in starting the proper treatment, a delay that could have been avoided if Wolff had been permitted to implement his plan of publicizing the disaster and its cause, greatly increased the number of fatalities. Of the victims treated at the military first aid stations and hospitals in the Bari area, 13.6 percent died from exposure to the mustard. How many of the civilians who were not admitted to the military medical units died will never be known. Himmler undoubtedly obtained his revenge and he also learned the effect of such a large-scale application of mustard. He discovered that while the victims suffered terribly before they died (despite the fact that their final moments were often surprisingly rational) the mustard took much too long compared to Zyklon B. The involvement of the SS in the Bari disaster was kept top secret, but this was not nearly as surprising as the action of the Allied officials.

Alexander routinely routed a copy of his final report to the British chemical warfare headquarters at Porton and expected no reply. Consequently he was shocked when he was informed that Prime Minister Winston Churchill had read the report and did not believe there were any mustard casualties at Bari. Despite the absolute proof that the victims had died of exposure to the mustard, all British reports were ordered to read that the cause of death was "N.Y.D.—not yet diagnosed." Nor were the reports ever changed.

Himmler and other SS officials didn't live long enough to learn that the tragic poison gas incident at Bari did have its redeeming features. Alexander's final medical report on the disaster suggested that the effects of mustard poisoning noted in the Bari casualties might have significant effect in treating cancers of the bloodstream and lymph glands, specifically leukemia and Hodgkin's disease. The head of the Memorial Hospital in New York, Dr. Cornelius P.("Dusty") Rhoads, read the Alexander report and concurred. His enthusiasm was contagious, and he soon had the support of such men as Frank Howard, vice president of Standard Oil, and Alfred Sloan and Charles Kettering, two of the founders of General Motors. Sloan donated an initial four million dollars to start the construction of the Sloan-Kettering Institute, the first institute devoted entirely to cancer research.

It was at the Sloan-Kettering Institute that the nitrogen mustard compounds were developed, based primarily on the information contained in Alexander's report. Later other drugs were developed, all of which are used in cancer treatments today.

The Reichsführer-SS who had been directly responsible for so many deaths during the Third Reich was ironically also indirectly responsible for saving many lives during the postwar years.

8

The Hangman's Last Ride

Himmler's brilliant subordinate, Reinhard Heydrich, was also the greatest threat to the Reichsführer's eminence. Himmler needed Heydrich's creative talent but it also made him jealous. Hitler was exceptionally proud of the tall, lean Heydrich. After the Gleiwitz raid in Poland that started World War II, the Führer was effusive in his praise of Heydrich's leadership and courage, much to the chagrin of Himmler. Heydrich's subsequent role with the *Einsatzgruppen*, his trickery that resulted in the Soviet army purge, and his blackmail files earned him the rank of Obergruppenführer-SS by 1941. He had already earned the enmity of Canaris and the Abwehr, who considered him an arrogant meddler in their affairs. He also shared a mutual love-hate relationship with Himmler. Heydrich took the hatred in stride, however, knowing that he had the full support of Hitler.

At the Wannsee Conference on January 20, 1942, when the plans were made for *Die Endlösung* (the Final Solution), Heydrich was chosen to head the program, despite the fact that both Hitler and Himmler were aware that Heydrich was suspected of having Jewish blood. Both, however, regarded him as much too valuable to the extermination program to ruin his career because of this suspicion. In fact, Hitler was convinced that Heydrich's possible non-Aryan origin would drive him harder—and he was right. Heydrich, who had been appointed Deputy Reich Protector for Bohemia and Moravia on September 27, 1941, carried out the program in Czechoslovakia with such brutality that he earned the title of "a young evil god of death."

As the terror increased, so did the resistance of the Czechs. Fires, slowdowns in the factories, and sabotage were rampant throughout the country. At the Skoda munitions works in Pilsen, a craneman called "Old Vacek" dumped a ladle of molten lead on a group of visiting German army officers, burning fourteen to death. When the Gestapo agents climbed the ladder after him, Vacek dove head first out of the cab 60 feet to the floor, killing himself. The following day another explosion ripped through the same factory, killing several Germans and destroying the power plant. Heydrich immediately proclaimed a state of emergency in six key districts, arrested Premier Alois Elias on charges of treason, executed six workers and sentenced 24 more to prison, and condemned two Czech generals to the firing squad.

One Czech who was prominent in the resistance was a young captain on the general staff of the Czech army, Jaroslav Sustr. While part of the staff went to London and set up headquarters there after the Germans moved into Czechoslovakia, he stayed behind to sabotage the Nazi war effort. He got a job as an inspector of northeastern Bohemian operations for an oil company, and for a time was successful in impeding the Germans by putting powdered sugar in the gasoline and sand in the grease. Eventually he was caught and jailed. He escaped by bribing the guards and made his way back to his home in Pardubice. When the Gestapo started to close in on him, he traveled by back roads to Prague and hid in a monastery dressed in a monk's habit, loaned him by a friendly Benedictine priest. When the opportunity arose, he crossed into Yugoslavia and became a valued member of General Draza Mihailovich's resistance force.

By 1941, Sustr was in England working with President Edouard Benes in the London headquarters of the Czech government in exile. Tiring of administrative work, he volunteered to train paratroopers for sabotage and intelligence work behind German lines. Several times he jumped with the two or three paratroopers assigned to a mission, helped them establish a secret base in the country, and then returned to England without incident. After each such trip, however, he reported to London that conditions in his homeland were getting worse, that Czech citizens were getting desperate. It was then that the plot was hatched to assassinate Heydrich, and Sustr was given the responsibility of selecting and training the men to do the job. He immediately traveled to a camp in Scotland where Czech soldiers were training, and after watching the men for several days, picked two. The first was a locksmith from Slovakia named Josef Gabchik who had been in combat in France earlier in the war. The second was Jan Kubis, an experienced underground fighter, who had escaped from the Gestapo after being tortured. His buttocks were branded with seven swastikas. Sustr told the men of the plan, emphasizing the dangers involved, and was delighted when the pair agreed to handle the mission.

The training was long and difficult. They were taught to parachute, to handle Sten guns and hand grenades, and they spent hours studying photographs of Heydrich and the layout of Prague's Hradcany Castle where Heydrich had established his headquarters, as well as of his residence 15 miles outside Prague in the village of Panenske Brezany. Both places were guarded night and day by SS men. Heydrich's house had a ten-foot wall around it while the castle was protected by a stone wall and moat. Sustr, knowing the area well, suggested they try to assassinate Heydrich while he was traveling between his headquarters and his home. Gabchik and Kubis both agreed with Sustr although they, too, had read an intelligence report which explained that Heydrich's limousine drove at speeds of 100 mph or more during the trips.

The two Czechs bid farewell to Sustr early in the evening of December 28, 1941, boarded a C-47 in England, and headed out over the Channel on their fateful mission.

Meanwhile, Heydrich continued his reign of terror in Czechoslovakia, but followed Hitler's advice of offering the Czechs both the carrot and the stick. He began playing off the workers and peasants against the bourgeois intellectuals. He increased the food rations for factory workers, provided new clothes for them, and even set up rest homes where the loyal laborer could take a periodic short vacation. He also revised the Czech social security system to benefit workers in sabotage-free plants. Hitler was so proud of Heydrich's accomplishments that he began calling him "the man with iron nerves." The Führer intimated to his historical officer,

Dr. Wilhelm Scheidt, that he was grooming Heydrich to be his successor, and that his appointment as Deputy Reich Protector for Bohemia and Moravia was a first step in this direction. When this word got back to Himmler in Berlin, the Reichsführer-SS was in a bad mood for days.

This chance remark by Hitler to Scheidt may have had a vital effect on history. Gabchik and Kubis landed safely near Prague from the C-47 the night of December 28, 1941, and made their way to the city without any problems. Once they contacted the waiting underground members and were provided with the necessary forged papers and a hideout, they were ready to carry out their mission. But for the next four months they were stymied. After reconnoitering both the castle and Heydrich's residence, it became clear to the pair that Sustr was right—that their target could not be attacked in either place: too many SS guards, too many walls and moats. In early May, however, Kubis received a note through the underground that supposedly came from London. Only one word was on the paper: Holesovice. Since he had never before received such a strange message from the Czech government in exile in London, Kubis used the verification procedure given to him before his departure from England. London stated they had sent no such message. Yet the resistance radio operator, whose loyalty to the underground fighters was checked and rechecked, swore that he had picked up the one-word message on the London frequency. Kubis decided that it was a German trap.

For several days he and Gabchik waited expectantly for the SS or Gestapo to come to their hideout, but nothing unusual happened. Nor was there any explanation of where or from whom the strange message had come. After a week of tense apprehension, Kubis decided to act. He recognized Holesovice as the name of a suburb of Prague. He had visited it many times since his arrival because it was on the route Heydrich traveled between Hradcany Castle and his residence. Nothing in the suburb had attracted his eye but since the strange message intrigued him, he made yet another trip to the area. Walking around the suburb slowly, he watched to see if he were being followed, but saw no such evidence. He was ignored. Just as he was about to leave the suburb, however, a Mercedes driven by an SS officer sped down the street from the direction of Prague. As the automobile neared him, the driver suddenly applied the brakes and slowed to a mere 10 mph to make a hairpin turn. At that moment Kubis found the spot to attack Heydrich. He had never noticed the sharp turn before, nor how slowly a driver would have to manipulate the turn.

The note? In 1945, during the Nuremberg investigation of Gottlob Berger, an SS general, Hauptsturmführer—SS Siegfried Hamler told court reporter S/Sgt. William A. Wegle that he had sent the note to the Czech underground on orders of Himmler himself. He stated that while Himmler was not aware of Kubis and Gabchik, the Reichsführer-SS did know that the Czech underground had long planned to assassinate Heydrich. When Scheidt told him that Hitler had inferred he was grooming Heydrich as his successor, Himmler decided Heydrich had to go. While Himmler was careful not to become directly involved in the operation, his order to Hamler was his way of aiding the assassins. Kubis had been under SS surveillance from the moment he left his hideout that day to go to Holesovice, and it was Hamler who slowly drove the car around the hairpin to demonstrate to the Czech resistance fighter that it was an ideal spot for the attack. If Hamler were telling the truth at the Nuremberg interrogation, it was only one more example in a long list of betrayals of one Nazi official by another for personal reasons.

Kubis alerted his companion Gabchik of his find and, after contacting London for approval, set the date for the assassination attempt. May 27 was chosen. Kubis decided they needed help, so he enlisted the aid of two Czech underground members, and early on the morning of the 27th the four men set out for Holesovice on their bicycles. Whether they were kept under surveillance by SS men acting under secret orders from Himmler, no one knows, but they reached the Prague suburb without incident. Kubis stationed the two underground members along the road leading to the hairpin turn from the direction of the village of Panenske Brezany where Heydrich had his residence. The first Czech would use a mirror to notify the second that Heydrich's Mercedes was approaching. That man would immediately flash the warning to Gabchik, who would be waiting at the sharp turn with his Sten gun. Further along the turn, Kubis would be ready with his hand grenades in case Gabchik failed to kill Heydrich. By 7:30 A.M. the four men were in position and ready.

Heydrich, always conscious that he was the most hated man in Czechoslovakia, never made the morning trip from his home to the castle headquarters at the same time. Some mornings he was very early, others very late. He was confident that this precaution, plus the speed of his car and his well-armed bodyguard, would make a successful attempt on his life impossible. On May 27 he departed his chateau later than usual. It was a warm day and the sun was already shining brightly, so he ordered his driver, Oberscharführer-SS Klein, to keep the top down on the Mercedes. As usual Klein drove fast, very fast, although the streets in the village were narrow and had several turns. Once out of the village and on the highway to Prague, he increased the speed of the Mercedes until he was going nearly 100 mph. As he neared Holesovice, however, Klein took his foot off the accelerator and let the car's momentum carry them near the hairpin turn. Neither he nor Heydrich paid any attention to the man standing on the sidewalk 200 feet from the sharp turn, so they missed seeing him flash a mirror signal to another man much closer to the turn. Just as Klein braked hard to slow the Mercedes for the hairpin turn, the second underground member alerted Gabchik as planned.

As soon as Gabchik received the signal and was certain that Heydrich's car was nearing the hairpin turn, he opened his worn briefcase and took out the Sten gun. He had time for a quick glance at Kubis a few feet further down the road and saw that the latter had taken his hand grenades from the briefcase he was carrying. When he turned his eyes back toward the road the dark green Mercedes with Heydrich and the driver both in the front seat nosed around the turn. Without hesitation, Gabchik stepped to the edge of the sidewalk, raised the Sten gun to his shoulder, took aim and pulled the trigger. At that distance he couldn't miss with the machine gun—except that the gun didn't fire! Gabchik pulled the trigger again and again as he kept Heydrich in the sight but the gun was useless. He heard the brakes squeal as Klein brought the Mercedes to an even slower speed, saw Heydrich pull a revolver from his uniform.

Kubis couldn't believe that Gabchik wasn't shooting. He

watched in horror as Heydrich's car moved past Gabchik and came closer and closer to where he was standing. Heydrich was now waving his revolver, well aware that an attempt was being made on his life by Gabchik, but as yet he hadn't noticed Kubis. Kubis took advantage of Heydrich's mistake, pulled the pin from the grenade in his hand, waited two seconds as Sustr had taught him back in England and Scotland, then lobbed the grenade toward the car. For a second or two he thought the grenade was a dud. Nothing happened. When it did explode, however, the Mercedes was lifted off the road momentarily, then disappeared in a cloud of smoke. Kubis was knocked backward by the explosion and by the time he regained his balance the smoke was clearing. Instead of seeing the two Nazis lying dead in the car, Kubis saw both the driver and Heydrich leaping out of the Mercedes and yelling at him.

A bullet hitting the ground a foot away from where he was standing aroused Kubis. He ran for his bicycle and leaped on. Only the fact that two streetcars arrived on the scene and stopped, saved him. He rode between the cars and that protected him from Heydrich and Klein for a few seconds. Pedaling as fast as he could, with Klein in pursuit, Kubis reached the house of an underground member he knew well; there he was hidden temporarily. Klein, losing sight of him, returned to the damaged Mercedes to report to Heydrich.

Heydrich's actions during the minutes after the assassination attempt at the hairpin turn were amazing. By the way he leaped from the damaged car, fired several shots at Kubis and then turned his attention towards Gabchik, it appeared that he was uninjured in the blast. He was, however, a dying man. His body had been pierced in numerous places by steel, other parts of the car, and even fragments of the seatcovers. Despite these wounds, which proved fatal within nine days, Heydrich chased after Gabchik, who was unable to get to his bicycle because of the excited crowd. Gabchik took cover behind a telephone pole and began firing his revolver at Heydrich. He missed with the first two shots and Heydrich had time to duck behind another pole about 25 feet behind Gabchik. Periodically they each fired a shot without results. Finally Gabchik saw Heydrich pull the trigger and shake his head in anger when the gun didn't fire. Realizing the SS officer's gun was empty, Gabchik left the protective cover of the telephone pole and began running down the street. He had only gone a few steps, however, when a bullet passed close to his head. He looked back and saw that Klein, the chauffeur, had joined in the chase. Once again Gabchik dove behind a telephone pole.

The duel between Gabchik and Klein didn't last long. Klein made the mistake of stepping into the open to get a clear shot at Gabchik and the Czech resistance fighter shot him in the hip. Klein went down screaming in pain and Gabchik hurried away. He saw a streetcar moving away from the nearest corner, noticed that the conductor had obligingly left the door open, ran and jumped inside. At Wenceslaus Square in Prague, Gabchik stepped off the car and walked to the next stop, where he took a second streetcar to the home of his girlfriend, Liboslava Fafka. He arrived just in time to hear the radio announcement of the assassination attempt:

> This morning on the twenty-seventh of May at ten-thirty o'clock an attempt on the life of Acting Reichsprotector Heydrich was made in Prague. A reward of ten million crowns is offered for the capture of the culprits. Whoever hides the criminals or gives them any help, or has any knowledge of their identity or description of their appearance and does not inform the authorities will be shot with his whole family. This is by order of the Oberlandrat in Prague. Other announcements will be made in due course.

The entire city was in an uproar by the time Kubis and Gabchik found temporary shelter after the assassination attempt. Heydrich was loaded into a bakery truck and taken to the Bulov Hospital along with Klein, who was bleeding profusely from his hip wound. As soon as Heydrich's headquarters at Hradcany Castle were alerted, the hospital was surrounded by SS troops and Heydrich's room was guarded closely to prevent another attempt on his life. Berlin was notified of the incident and the best surgeons in Germany were immediately ordered to Prague to treat the critically wounded Heydrich. The most important news for Czech citizens was that Karl Frank, the Nazi secretary of state for the protectorate, had taken over Heydrich's official position. Hitler told him to use any means he wanted to find the men who tried to assassinate Heydrich and to obtain the Führer's revenge from the entire Czechoslovakian nation. Yet even the most pessimistic Czech citizen didn't anticipate the horror the country was facing.

When it became evident that it was too dangerous for Kubis and Gabchik to stay in the hiding places they had found immediately after the attack, they were moved by the underground to the Czech Orthodox Church of Saints Cyril and Methodius, where Vladimir Petrek, the chaplain, hid them in a crypt under the floor. It was a depressing, cold, and damp place with little light and stale air, but in the situation both men were delighted to use it. Frank stepped up his punishment of the country as Heydrich's condition worsened. More than 10,000 Czechs were arrested and executions took place every night in Prague. Sustr, with the government in exile in London, predicted that the worst was yet to come, and warned the Czech resistance fighters. Kubis and Gabchik were told of the warning but there was nothing they could do. They felt guilty that because of their actions so many innocent citizens were suffering and dying, but the London government in exile considered the attack a great victory.

The price for the victory went up considerably when Heydrich died of his wounds on June 4. A state funeral was held in Berlin on June 9 in the Chancellery. Hitler and 600 of Germany's leading officials and industrialists attended to pay homage to Heydrich. In addition there was evidence that the Czech puppet government, headed by President Emil Hácha and his staff, was supporting the Nazi attitude that a great crime had been committed when Heydrich was killed. Fifty thousand Czech workers marched in protest in Prague on the day of the funeral, angry about the assassination. Even Himmler praised Heydrich at the service, affable now that Heydrich was no longer a threat to him personally. If Hitler suspected Himmler of any involvement in the assassination, there was no public mention of it by the Führer. After Heydrich was buried at the Invalidenfriedhof cemetery, Hitler gave Hácha one more warning that he would not permit such actions by the Czechs to go unpunished.

The next day the Czechs discovered what Hitler meant. Early in the morning SS troops surrounded the small mining village of Lidice near Prague and slowly moved into the center of the puzzled population. The men and boys were ordered to march to a farming area where, without explanation or mercy, they were lined up against the walls of nearby barns and shot. Back at Lidice the grieving women and young girls were forced into trucks and taken to concentration camps. Frank then ordered the city completely razed. It was the worst such revenge massacre that the Nazis perpetrated, so horrible that only the SS could carry it out.

Frank also discovered through German agents that Sustr had trained the assassins in England and Scotland. He immediately rounded up Sustr's mother, wife, father, and brother and had them executed by the SS.

But Kubis and Gabchik were still undetected. After the Lidice massacre they offered to go sit in a Prague park with a sign around their necks stating that they had killed Heydrich, and take the poison from the capsules they carried with them. Chaplain Petrek talked them out of it, explaining that it would be a victory for the Nazis and wouldn't stop the reprisals. So they remained in the crypt. But time was running out for them and many others in the Czech resistance. Czech parachutist Karel Cruda, who had trained in England with Kubis and Gabchik and knew of their mission, had been dropped into the country on another mission which later was aborted. He was staying with his mother on her farm near Prague, but after Heydrich died and the village of Lidice was obliterated, he lost his nerve. He didn't want his mother and sister to die nor did he want to die himself, so he took up Frank's offer that anyone revealing information about the identities of the assassins by June 18 would be protected and so would his family. In addition the informant would receive 20 million crowns.

Cruda took the train to Prague on June 14 and went directly to the Gestapo headquarters in the city. While he was revealing the names of Kubis and Gabchik and listing the names and addresses of various underground fighters, London was making last-minute plans to get the parachutists out of Czechoslovakia. Sustr radioed Prague that the men should be moved to the small city of Kladno northwest of Prague, where a British plane would land in a meadow on the outskirts of the city and pick them up. It was heartening news for Kubis and Gabchik. But as they prepared for the move, the SS troops closed in on their hideout in the church. Cruda's information had doomed them.

Unbeknownst to the two Czech resistance fighters, the SS had already visited the homes of the underground members with whom the pair had first taken cover. The occupants of the homes were either killed, committed suicide, or were taken to Gestapo headquarters to be questioned. Step by step the SS moved closer to the crypt at the church on Resslova Street where Chaplain Petrek had hidden them.

On the night of June 17 Kubis had guard duty on the balcony of the church with another parachutist hiding with them. Gabchik and three other parachutists stayed in the crypt under the floor to sleep. The men were in high spirits, knowing that they would be moving from Prague to Kladno the next day. At 5:30 P.M., however, the church was surrounded by SS troops. According to eyewitness accounts, Kubis and his companion spotted the SS troops from their position on the church balcony and, knowing they couldn't get back into the crypt fast enough, opened fire on the Germans. The battle lasted two hours. The SS made attack after attack on the balcony, but because of their position the Czechs managed to keep the Germans at bay. It wasn't until daylight that the SS finally was victorious. A grenade tossed accurately onto the balcony critically wounded Kubis. His companion, also wounded, took poison. The angry SS troops rushed Kubis to the hospital in hopes of saving his life so they could savor their revenge, but he died thirty minutes later in the operating room.

Cruda identified the corpse of Kubis as one of the assassins but denied that Kubis' dead companion was the other. Karl Frank, who had arrived at the hospital on Charles Square to see the dead assassins, immediately ordered the SS commander back to the church to hunt Gabchik. Although Chaplain Petrek refused to speak despite every effort by the SS to make him do so, the Germans soon discovered the entrance to the crypt. When they lifted the door, however, they were greeted by a blast from Gabchik's machine gun. The door was quickly replaced. Since it was certain death for any SS man brave enough or foolhardy enough to open the door again, Frank and his staff looked around for another way into the crypt. When they located the ventilation slot to the crypt, which opened onto the street, they tossed tear gas grenades through it. Gabchik and his companions threw them back out. When a floodlight was brought to the ventilation opening in an effort to blind those inside the crypt, Gabchik immediately shot it out with his Sten gun. Frustrated, the SS brought a smoke-making machine to the church and stuffed the nozzle of the hose leading from the machine through the ventilation slot. Gabchik pushed it back out. When Frank ordered firemen to use water, a hose was inserted through the slot and 600 gallons of water a minute began pouring into the crypt. Gabchik calmly cut the nozzle off the water hose and pushed the jagged end of the hose back through the opening, where the water and smoke both hampered the attacking SS troops.

For six hours, the four men in the crypt held off the SS troops, but, outnumbered and short on ammunition, they finally were defeated. SS explosives experts blasted open the main entrance to the crypt, which had been walled over years before. Gabchik and his three companions thwarted several frontal assaults attempted by the SS down the wide steps uncovered by the blast, but when their ammunition ran low and the SS began throwing hand grenades into the crypt, they made their final decision. Each of the resistance fighters killed himself with the final bullet remaining in his revolver.

With Gabchik and Kubis dead, the Czechs hoped the bloody aftermath of the Heydrich assassination was over. It wasn't. Men, women, and children suspected of any type of underground activity were shot. Chaplain Petrek, his sexton, bishop, and church elders were executed. Within two months after the assassination an additional 1,600 persons died at the hands of the SS. It was an unmatched bloody episode carried out by the most brutal aggregation in history—a carnage that helped convince the Nuremberg War Crimes Tribunal that the SS was a criminal organization and that all of its members were war criminals. Cruda was tried before a Prague court in 1946, found guilty and hanged, as was Karl Frank. In general, however, most of the SS men involved in the massacre escaped postwar punishment.

There is only farmland where the village of Lidice once stood. Nearby is the new village of Lidice, where a small museum is a reminder of the SS massacre. In Prague, at the Resslova Street church, whose walls are bullet-scarred, the

9

The Hitler-Göring Art War

When Major-General Jacques Philippe LeClerc's French 2nd Armored Division entered Berchtesgaden on May 4, 1945, his soldiers discovered Hermann Göring's private train standing in a siding of the railroad station. Inside the train was the Reichmarshal's personal art collection, which he had removed from his Karinhall estate outside Berlin, intending to hide the treasures in nearby bunkers. The Frenchmen, however, took one look at the paintings, shrugged their shoulders, and turned away. They were more interested in the stock of champagne and whiskey located in a car at the front of the train.

The next day the American 101st Airborne Division arrived in Berchtesgaden, and while the paratroopers were just as interested in the drinking stock as the Frenchmen, the military government officer accompanying them, Major Harry Anderson, quickly recognized the value of the train's cargo. He ordered the men of the 101st to move the paintings and other art treasures from the train to a Luftwaffe officers' recreation building at Unterstein, a suburb of Berchtesgaden, where it could more easily be guarded. After making certain that everything had been unloaded from the train, Anderson had the paintings appraised. Even he was surprised to learn that he had in his possession more than 500 million dollars worth of art. But his collection was not yet complete.

A German citizen of Berchtesgaden tipped off Anderson that Frau Emmy Göring, the Luftwaffe commander's second wife, was residing at Zell-am-See, Austria, and had more of the Göring art collection in her possession. Anderson and his staff made a hurried trip to Zell-am-See and discovered Frau Göring did indeed have a large number of art treasures, including thirty canvases from the famous Renders collection of Brussels. As the major was leaving the Göring apartment (Frau Göring was staying in a castle owned by a South American friend), Frau Göring's nurse handed him a package.

"The Reichsmarshal gave me this the last time I saw him and told me to guard it with my life," she explained. "He said if I should ever be in need I could sell it and make a fortune."

The major took the package and when he returned to Unterstein he opened it. To his surprise it was a painting by the Dutch master Jan Vermeer entitled "Christ and the Adulteress," a priceless treasure. This particular painting of the Göring collection was later discovered to have an amazing history; but in 1945, when Anderson obtained it from the nurse, the question in his mind was where and how the painting had come into Göring's possession. It was a mystery that was slowly unraveled during the postwar years, one that revealed a little-known art war between Hitler and Göring that involved the SS.

Hitler had a lifelong interest in painting. His fondest hope as a youth was to attend the Academy of Fine Arts in Vienna. In October 1907, at the age of seventeen, Hitler traveled to Vienna and presented himself at the academy headquarters on the Schillerplatz. He took a two-day examination that covered a wide range of subjects and required test drawings. Hitler, as confident of his ability then as in later years, felt certain he had passed and prepared to enter the academy as a full-time student. Consequently it was a shock to him when he discovered that he failed the examination. He blamed his failure on discrimination, although he never explained the charge any further. Shortly after he returned from Vienna to his home in Linz, his mother died and left him a small amount of money. Hitler promptly moved to Vienna and the following October applied to take the examination again at the academy. He felt certain he would pass this second time, that the judges would realize they had made a mistake. He was wrong. He wasn't even permitted to take the test.

> The following gentlemen performed their test drawings with insufficient success or were not admitted to the test: No. 24 Adolf Hitler, Braunau am Inn, 20 April 1889, German, Catholic, Father senior official. Four classes in Realschule. Not admitted to the test.

With his dream of attending the Academy of Fine Arts shattered, Hitler's only painting activity after that was accomplished when he was starving. He had spent his small inheritance and had no job. In order to earn enough money to buy food, he painted postcard-sized watercolors and for a while did quite well. Later he branched out into window posters. When World War I began, however, Hitler's paintbrush was traded for a gun; after the war his main interest was politics. Yet he never lost his interest in art and once he became chancellor and his armies began rolling across Europe, he discovered he had an opportunity to not only accumulate a great fortune in art treaures for himself but to obtain the revenge he wanted so badly because of his snubbing by the judges at the Academy of Fine Arts.

Some of Hitler's happiest hours were spent during his triumphant return to his hometown of Linz after the Austrian Anschluss of 1938. He arrived on March 12, staying at the Weinzinger Hotel, where he consulted with the director of the Linz museum. Hitler told the stunned director that he intended to transform Linz into the artistic capital of Europe. He vowed that he would construct a Führermuseum that would house the largest art collection in the world. Armor, rare books, manuscripts, sculptures, tapestries, stamps, coins, furniture, and other objets d'art would be exhibited in other buildings. Hitler emphasized that he personally intended to supervise the development. The director didn't have the courage to ask Hitler where he intended to obtain the art treasures he planned to exhibit in Linz.

Hitler knew the answer but didn't want it known publicly. He intended to loot museums and private collections all over Europe as the German army conquered country after country. After careful consideration, he decided that his political and military problems would not leave him sufficient time to select those items he wanted for Linz after his conquest of Europe was complete. He gave orders to amass as large a collection as possible and the final selection would be later. To this end, Martin Bormann sent a letter to Hans Heinrich Lammers, state secretary of the Reich Chancellery, on June 26, 1939, stating:

> On behalf of the Führer I wish to inform you that he has asked the director of the Dresden Art Gallery, Dr. Hans Posse, to build up the new Linz Art Museum. The Führer wishes that Dr. Posse for the time being receive one thousand reichsmarks for travel and other expenses. For his work with the new Linz Art Museum Dr. Posse shall receive one thousand reichsmarks per month expenses beginning July 1, 1939.

Dr. Lammers was an Obergruppenführer-SS and made certain Posse had all the money required to travel throughout Europe hunting art treasures for Hitler.

Hitler also organized a special commission to handle the problems of the proposed Linz collection. It was named Sonderauftrag Linz on all official papers, but its existence was kept secret from the public. Hitler insisted that the headquarters of the commission be in Munich, since he wanted the art treasures looted from across Europe stored in the air raid shelters under the city's Nazi headquarters. Hitler was in supreme command of Sonderauftrag Linz, but because of pressing responsibilities in Berlin and on the battlefronts, he designated Martin Bormann second in command. Bormann, at this early stage of the war, was not well known even within the Nazi party, but already Hitler had bestowed upon his secretary a great deal of power. Bormann, sitting in the innermost sanctum of Hitler's headquarters, kept the SS and Himmler at a distance. He didn't want Himmler to obtain so much power that the Reichsführer-SS would interfere with his own influence with Hitler. Nor did he agree with many of Himmler's ideas about developing the perfect Germany and establishing an SS state, considering such plans as claptrap that weakened Hitler's aim of conquering Europe. Yet, when it came to the actual looting of the European museums of their art treasures and forcing private collectors to give up their personal holdings, Bormann relied upon SS personnel. He knew that Himmler had the most ruthless and most disciplined organization in the Reich.

Bormann insisted that Posse hire Friedrich Wolffhardt, an active Nazi party member, to aid in the looting. Wolffhardt was a Hauptsturmführer-SS and an ideal man for the job. He was tall, blond, and polite but his outward appearance and attitude covered an inner brutality. For the Hitler collection, he plundered museums as pirates plunder merchant ships at sea. Wolffhardt thought it was a waste of time to try to negotiate with museum officials on a legal basis, to offer them a small price just to keep within the law. When he saw something he wanted for the Hitler collection, he took it, especially rare books and manuscripts, which fascinated him.

Wolffhardt was tireless in his efforts and traveled back and forth across Europe, taking possession in one way or another. He was always proposing clever plans to obtain the treasures.

> Eventually Buemming informed me confidentially of the Gutmann library in Vienna. The Jew Gutmann is in America. His daughter (Baroness Ferstel) has contrived to obtain the precious Dürer collection through various intrigues but there still exists a Rembrandt collection.
>
> Buemming suggests that the library with its valuable French 17th and 18th century books be sold at auction in Lucern through Hoepli-Milan in order to provide the Reich with foreign currency. The total value of the library is likely to amount to 500,000 Swiss francs.

Wolffhardt's scheme in this instance was to confiscate the Gutmann library and sell it to obtain foreign currency to purchase additions for the Hitler collection in neutral countries, where many private collections had been deposited at the time of the Nazi takeover in 1933. Thus, money obtained by looting private collections still in Germany was used to purchase even more select private collections previously sent out of the country to avoid Nazi confiscation. It was a very successful and profitable scheme.

There was considerable satisfaction at Hitler's headquarters about Wolffhardt's achievements. In November 1943, he sent Bormann a letter detailing some of his past and on-going activities in behalf of the Hitler collection.

> Considering we have 20,000 items, apart from those on the way and still more expected, the employment of ten trained librarians and five to ten bookbinders would not be too much for taking care of this literature. Additional materials and facilities would be indispensable. The war in its present form makes me waive any request for an enlargement of the project. We are doing here what we can and this is no more than our duty.

He was doing quite a lot. At the time he wrote the letter Wolffhardt was "negotiating" for a collection valued at 80,000 reichsmarks as well as another valuable library in Holland, and he was proud to announce that he had obtained nearly 800 rare books as a "gift." Three months later the 20,000 items had multiplied to 45,000 and a quarter of a million more were "under consideration." His one complaint was that the SS security forces interfered with his collecting in many instances because they burned libraries in occupied countries before he could loot them. Until the end of the war he was trying to halt this practice but with little success.

Wolffhardt, while angry with the SS security services, did have aid from other SS sources, however, as did Posse, in building up the Hitler collection. When Posse discovered the famous Pieter Breughel painting "The Hay Harvest" in Radnitz Castle in Czechoslovakia among the Lobkowitz collection, he immediately earmarked it for Hitler's project. Afraid that it might go to the Kaiser Friedrich Museum in Berlin instead, he didn't hesitate to enlist Bormann's aid.

> I have only just learned through a memorandum from the Director of the Kaiser Friedrich Museum in Berlin that the famous Lobkowitz collection in the Protectorate will be seized by the Reich. In addition to armor and "objets d'art," the collection includes highly valuable German, Italian, Spanish, French, and Dutch paintings, among which is "The Hay Harvest" by Pieter Breughel the Elder for which the Kaiser Friedrich Museum has been negotiating for some time prior to the confiscation proceedings.
>
> It would be advisable to suggest to the Reichsprotector von Neurath that an inspection of the Radnitz items be arranged so that claims may be filed in time by the German museums and, above all, by the Führermuseum.

Posse's suggestion assured him of obtaining the coveted painting for his Hitler collection. Constantin Freiherr von Neurath, whom Hitler had appointed Reichsprotector of Bohemia and Moravia on March 18, 1939, was a loyal follower of the Führer. The day after Hitler came to power in 1933, von Neurath joined the Nazi party and the SS with the rank of Gruppenführer-SS and became Hitler's adviser on foreign affairs. Although too conservative for Hitler in many matters, when the Führer's interests were made clear to him, von Neurath usually came to his support. So it was with the Lobkowitz collection. Posse had his choice, and among the items he chose was, of course, "The Hay Harvest."

The controversy over the Lobkowitz collection emphasized Posse's problems in trying to build the Hitler collection for postwar Linz. Although he was the most powerful man in Germany, and feared by millions, Hitler's orders regarding the art treasures of Europe were not always obeyed. Bureaucratic red tape, subterfuge, intrigue, and procrastination often interfered with the Führer's wishes. Other Nazi leaders were interested in building their own art collections or making their lives financially secure by looting private collections in occupied countries and selling the paintings. Others, such as Hermann Göring, appreciated great works of art and wanted the ego-satisfaction, pleasure, and prestige of owning and being able to display works of the masters.

Hitler's strongest competitor in the art war was Göring. He knew and loved art. He was considered an expert on Renaissance painters and the Dutch school. Like Hitler, Göring intended to have a postwar showplace, the Hermann Göring Museum. He even made definite plans to open his new museum on his sixtieth birthday, which would be in 1953. This would be two years after the scheduled opening of Hitler's Führermuseum in Linz. Meanwhile he housed his paintings in his four homes—Karinhall, Castle Mauterndorf, Castle Veldenstein, and his palace in the Leipziger Platz—as well as his hunting lodge. When it came to financing his art search throughout Europe, Göring didn't lack funds. He had an income of more than a million reichsmarks a year from his salaries of Luftwaffe chief, Minister of Prussia, comptroller of the German economy, and from his stock holdings and book royalties. Soon after the Nazis took power, he established an art fund to which his friends in the industrial world were expected to contribute if they wanted their share of the rearmament jackpot. Nor was Göring afraid to compete with Hitler although the Führer rarely realized it. The art treasures of Paris were a good example.

When Paris was occupied by the German troops Hitler expected his Linz collection to grow spectacularly. He was careful, however, in his approach to the French cultural authorities. Unlike the looting of Poland's museums, churches, and public buildings under the direction of Standartenführer-SS Kajetan Muehlmann, when the resentment of the Polish citizens was ignored, Hitler planned to purchase the art treasures of France for less than magnificent sums, but thereby partially assuage the French people. He had unlimited funds from the Reich treasury to do so. As his first step in obtaining the vast quantity of paintings and other treasures available in Paris, Hitler denied access to these objects of art until a complete inventory could be made by his own personal representatives. Sixteen days after the German troops occupied Paris, Field Marshal Keitel ordered General von Bockelberg, governor of Paris, to safeguard the art treasures until Hitler's representatives were ready to make their selection.

> The Führer, on receiving the report of the Reich Minister of Foreign Affairs, has issued an order to safeguard for the time being objects of art belonging to the French state and also such works of art and antiquity which constitute private property. Especially the Jewish property is to be taken into custody by the occupational powers against removal or concealment after having been labelled with the names of their present owners. There is no question of expropriation but certainly of a transfer into our custody to serve as a pawn in the peace negotiations.

This order supposedly gave Hitler and his representatives sole possession of the Paris art treasures until the best of the lot had been culled out for the Linz postwar collection. But Göring outwitted both Keitel and Hitler and he did it through an organization Hitler had personally set up to insure the Führermuseum got the best of everything. This was the Einsatzstab Rosenberg, under the command of Alfred Rosenberg, the notorious Nazi ideologist. This task force was organized in January 1940 for the specific purpose of inventorying and confiscating art treasures in occupied countries. Hitler selected the right man for the assignment since Rosenberg was rabidly anti-Semitic and many of the greatest art collections were owned by Jews. Hitler had given him a free hand to loot Jewish collections and he did so with a will. It resulted in the biggest art seizure in history. Between October 1940 and July 1944, Rosenberg's official report stated, he had confiscated nearly 22,000 art objects which had been carried to Germany in 137 freight cars as well as hundreds of trucks. Among these art objects were 5,281 paintings, including works by such masters as Rubens, Rembrandt, Gainsborough, and Goya; hundreds of icons; 6,000 handmade objects; and 2,500 pieces of seventeenth and eighteenth century furniture. He valued the French acquisitions at one billion dollars.

Rosenberg operated out of the Musée du Jeu de Paume near the Place de la Concorde in Paris. All confiscated items, and there were thousands, were brought to the Jeu de Paume and put on exhibition for Posse and *Sonderauftrag Linz* representatives. According to a decree issued on November 5, 1940, after the selections were made for the Hitler collection, Göring had second choice, Einsatzstab Rosenberg third choice for distributions among other Nazi leaders and, fourth, the German museums were welcome to what was left. That was the way it was supposed to work and Rosenberg, with the help of the SS and Gestapo, was expected to oversee the entire program.

Göring, over whose signature the November 5, 1940, order of preference was issued, never abided by the order. Instead he went to work on the Rosenberg organization and on Rosenberg himself. He sent a letter to Rosenberg stating his personal opinion about how the Einstzstab should view the overall art treasure situation, emphasizing, of course, his own interests.

> I have promised to support energetically the work of your staff and to place at its disposal that which it could not hitherto obtain, namely transportation and guard personnel, and the Luftwaffe is assigned to give the utmost assistance. I already possess today

> through purchase and barter perhaps the most important private collection in Germany, if not Europe. However, I still need a few pieces from the Jewish cultural goods, a very small percentage of the hundreds and thousands of paintings.

Rosenberg, a loner who didn't make many friends, was vulnerable to flattery, and Göring made certain he received a great deal. He wrote Rosenberg letters praising his work and made certain that Rosenberg knew that copies of the letters were also forwarded to the Führer himself. Göring, however, didn't place all his bets on Rosenberg alone. He bribed many of the Einsatzstab employees, overwhelmed others with gifts and personal attention, and even suggested to a few how they could increase their own fortunes by selling a painting or two on their own. Before long Göring was summoned to the Jeu de Paume first whenever a French collection was seized and before the art treasures were inventoried. He would make his selections and have them sent to Karinhall before Posse or other representatives of the Hitler collection were aware there was a new stock of paintings to view. Of course, he was prudent enough to make sure Hitler obtained enough fine paintings so that his suspicions were not aroused.

Göring and Rosenberg worked together very well and Hitler was completely outwitted in the contest for French art treasures. The Führer had quantity but Göring had the quality. Bormann was the first to get wise to the special arrangement between Göring and Rosenberg and after the Luftwaffe failed during the Battle of Britain he decided that Göring, its chief, was vulnerable. He convinced Hitler to break up the Einsatzstab Rosenberg despite Göring's vehement protests. Bormann sent a blunt note of dismissal to Rosenberg.

> The Führer wishes that the art objects seized by your staff be transferred as soon as possible to the Führer's experts for further handling. Expert for the remaining collections which the Führer wishes to build in Linz at the present time is Dr. von Hummel.

Hitler changed his tactics. Instead of relying on Rosenberg to notify Posse when art treasures had been confiscated and were ready for viewing, he once again relied on the SS as he had in Poland. Muehlmann, who had looted the Polish museums under the guidance of the governor-general, Hans Frank, went into action again in Holland on the trail of the famous Fritz Mannheimer collection. Mannheimer was a wealthy Jewish banker who moved to Amsterdam from Stuttgart when it became obvious to him that Hitler would come to power. Over the years he bought paintings as investments and for the pleasure they gave him, and by the advent of World War II, his collection was one of the most valuable in Europe. When Nazi influence forced his Dutch bank into bankruptcy, Mannheimer died suddenly of a heart attack. Hitler wasted not a moment, but told his SS art thief to get the Mannheimer collection for the Linz museum. This time Göring recognized the danger of trying to oppose the SS, so he remained in Berlin. Using typical SS tactics, Muehlmann offered the creditors holding the Mannheimer collection a small amount of money for the collection, informing them that if they didn't accept the offer he would confiscate the entire collection as enemy property. The creditors tried to get other buyers interested but none wanted to compete with the SS, so the entire collection went to Hitler for a tiny fraction of its actual value.

In Italy the SS looted art treasures in behalf of both Göring and Hitler. When several valuable collections were en route from Naples to the Vatican because of Allied air raids, the SS confiscated many of the paintings and forwarded them to Göring in Berlin. When the German 362nd Infantry Division overran northern Italy, the SS following in their tracks obtained more than three hundred paintings from Florentine galleries for Hitler's personal museum.

As the war turned against the Germans and the Allies closed in from all sides, both Hitler's and Göring's art treasures became vulnerable to air raids and advancing troops. Hitler's overflowing art collection was stored in the Führerbau at Munich, Schloss Thürntal outside Kremsmünster, a monastery along the Czech border, and Schloss Neuschwanstein, the castle built by Bavaria's mad King Ludwig. But as the Allied air raids became more numerous, Hitler ordered all four depositories evacuated. He wanted the art treasures hidden underground. One such sanctuary was the Merkers salt mine west of Weimar. Other salt mines used for storage were those at Alt Aussee southwest of Salzburg. Thousands of items were moved to these mines but Hitler, concerned that some of his art treasures might be lost or stolen during the transfer, ordered Himmler to take an inventory. Bormann issued the order on January 26, 1945:

> Based on the Führer's orders, the existence of all confiscated works of art, especially paintings, objects of artistic interest and weapons of artistic importance, in Greater Germany and the Occupied Territories is to be reported to the Führer's advisers in such matters who, on consideration of the individual cases, will send a report to the Führer through me so that the Führer can himself decide what use he will make of the acquired articles. This ruling must be strictly upheld by all branches of the SS.

There were thousands of paintings stored in the main salt mine at Alt Aussee, of which nearly 7,000 were earmarked for the postwar Linz museum by Hitler. In addition to the paintings, many of which were by old masters, there were valuable drawings, prints, sculptures, coins, armor, books, and even theater archives. But Hitler hadn't concentrated on the collection for Linz alone. He was also looking out for himself. In the mine were 200 paintings and seven rugs to be used in a castle he liked at Posen as well as 500 paintings, innumerable pieces of sculpture, and a complete library for his beloved Berghof near Berchtesgaden.

Göring, too, had connived to store some of his art treasures at Alt Aussee as well as the bunker at Berchtesgaden as the war neared an end. He was still in the midst of transferring his collection to the bunker and cave when the area was overrun by Allied troops who found many of his valuable paintings in the train on the siding at Berchtesgaden. Later other Allied soldiers located the hidden bunker and retrieved the remainder of his collection.

It became the task of the Monuments, Fine Arts, and Archives Section (M.F.A.& A.) of the Allied Expeditionary Force Supreme Headquarters to track down the looted art treasures. Captain Robert Posey of the unit learned from a young German art student that the most likely place for the stolen art to be hidden were the salt mines in Austria. The student also warned him that the SS was guarding the mines. Wisely, Posey stayed behind the fast-advancing U.S. Third

Army that was heading for Alt Aussee. When they reached that city, they came face to face with the SS troops assigned the responsibility of guarding the Hitler collection, but the feared elite of the Nazi forces decided that paintings weren't cause enough to die. They surrendered.

Troops of the 80th Infantry Division of the U.S. Third Army gained control of the salt mine at Alt Aussee within a matter of hours, and close behind came Posey. Using acetylene lamps, the captain and Private Lincoln Kirstein explored the dark labyrinth. At first they found nothing. Then, nearly a half mile into the mine, they came to an iron door blocked by rubble. Once they had forced a path through the rubble, they opened the large door. When their eyes became accustomed to the darkness, they were stunned to see art treasures in every nook and cranny of the large room. That was only the first chamber. There were many others in the mine, each filled with valuable works of art. By October 1945 more than 100,000 pieces of art were removed from the salt mine, their value astronomical. Later Posey and his men found other important works of art in Munich, Berlin, and in the countryside where both Hitler and Göring had tried to hide their collections.

After the war the long, tedious, and difficult task of trying to find the rightful owners of the looted art began, a search that continues today.

The SS had helped both Göring and Hitler seize the greatest art of Europe but Himmler's black-uniformed troops were subject to an irony. For years they guarded Göring's Vermeer, "Christ and the Adulteress," with their lives, thinking it priceless. In 1947, however, it was discovered that the painting was a fake, that it had been painted by a man named Hans von Meegeren, not the master Jan Vermeer. By this time Göring didn't care. He had ended his life by taking poison on October 15, 1946, two hours before he was to be hanged.

10

Holocaust Millionaires

The SS, while looting the art of Europe for both Hitler and Göring, didn't overlook its own financial interests. The aesthetic beauty of the valuable paintings, sculptures, and other art treasures meant little to them, but the millions in hard cash those objects could fetch for those from Himmler down to the lowest-ranking SS member could buy more prosaic material luxuries or provide a financial nest egg for the future. They satisfied this craving for wealth in a number of innovative ways.

In one stroke of inhumane genius, the SS devised methods of obtaining large sums of money by preying on their already brutally treated concentration and death camp prisoners. The actual schemes employed varied from camp to camp. Food was of primary importance to the prisoners. There was never enough and what little was provided was of inferior quality. Yet the SS officers and noncommissioned officers in charge of prisoner-food distribution even skimmed the best off the top of this meager supply and sold it on the black market outside the camps. Toward the end of the war, the German people were on reduced rations in many sections of the country, and this stolen food brought large sums into the illegal coffers of the SS. Obviously, the short-changed prisoners, scheduled for a slow starvation diet at best, suffered from this SS thievery, and large numbers died of malnutrition. When a medical survey indicated that more than 70 percent of the concentration camps' deaths stemmed from that cause, Himmler decided that all prisoners destined for heavy manual slave labor in German industry should be given a supplementary ration. Without the prisoner labor, the SS would not collect the money the German industrialists paid for these services. The additional ration included good-quality sausage, a delicacy coveted by hungry German civilians. This new order was a boon to the SS administrators. They immediately intercepted the sausage shipments to the camps and sold the meat at high prices to those Germans who had the money to purchase it. The prisoner laborers never saw the sausage. When the industrialists complained that the slave labor was too weak to maintain proper productivity, an investigation was begun. The report, issued on March 17, 1945, stated:

> The field office of the Todt Organization reports that post mortems of prisoners in an outside labor detail from Buchenwald reveal a state of chronic starvation. They are unable to account for this since the prisoners received supplementary rations for heavy manual workers. Their letter hints at the possibility of irregularities in the issuing of the rations.

Since the Third Reich lasted less than two more months, it was much too late to do anything about the "possibility of irregularities."

Prisoners were allowed to have money sent to them every month so that they could purchase additional food from the canteen in order to survive. Relatives and friends, often at great personal sacrifice, did their best to provide as many reichsmarks as possible, believing they were saving the lives of the prisoner. In many instances, however, they were donating more money to the private fund of the SS. Items in the canteen were ridiculously overpriced. Salad, for example, was priced ten times its cost to make; sugar and later saccharine, when sugar was unavailable, was upped in price twenty-five times its cost; and German tea, which was much preferred by the prisoners to the coffee substitute, was auctioned off to the prisoner with the most money at prices ranging to 100 times the actual cost. At Buchenwald alone more than 2 million reichsmarks were obtained by SS personnel for their private fund by this scheme.

The "voluntary contribution" contrivance lined the pockets of the SS, too. Any excuse for such a contribution from the prisoners was acceptable to the SS and when none was readily available the guards, administrators, or camp commandant devised one.

"We even were asked to contribute for a new uniform for the Führer after the July assassination attempt," says Karl Becker, a prisoner at Dachau. "We would much rather have contributed for flowers for his funeral."

Knowing that only a few of the prisoners had any money, the SS guards would "suggest" that each barracks contribute a certain sum to the collection. The prisoners were told bluntly that if their barracks fell short of its expected donation there would be extra duty, night roll calls, and restricted rations. Consequently, those prisoners who did not have any money to give insisted that those who did contribute generously so that their barracks would receive high marks. This caused ill-feelings among prisoners, much to the delight of the SS personnel.

"Our barracks was expected to give seventy-five reichsmarks for Hitler's new uniform," Becker explained. "Instead we gave one hundred in the futile hope of getting better treatment."

Of course, the "voluntary contributions" never left the camp SS office. It was spent on such items as cars, motorboats, homes, wine, and other items harder and harder to get in the war-pressed Third Reich.

After 1941 the prisoners were permitted to receive packages as well as sums of money. Himmler surmised, correctly, that foreign prisoners would receive food packages from their home countries where farm products were much more plentiful than in Germany. The SS was ordered to examine every incoming package and appropriate whatever was wanted. As usual, the prisoners suffered while the SS made a fortune selling the hard-to-get products on the black market.

Each prisoner was expected to make a profit for the SS. Very careful records were kept at most of the concentration and death camps of the expenses and profit associated with each individual, just as a manufacturer keeps records on the efficiency of machinery in his factory. Gold teeth, for example, were a lucrative item. Even while the prisoner was still healthy enough to perform slave labor for which the SS was paid by the industrialists, his gold dental work was coveted by his guards and camp administrators. If he was unfortunate enough to become ill and had to report to the infirmary, his sickness was automatically diagnosed as incurable. A nurse would visit him, give him a lethal injection, and the SS physician would extract the gold teeth. If the possessor of the gold teeth didn't become ill enough to report to the infirmary, his death sentence was delayed until malnutrition made him too weak to work. He was then taken to the gas chamber, gassed, and his gold teeth were extracted. There was no escape.

SS records captured after the war indicated that Oswald Pohl, the concentration and death camp administrator, demanded "profit" from each prisoner and distributed a suggested efficiency chart to each of his colleagues showing how such a profit could be made.

Daily farming-out wage, 6 to 8 marks, average			6.00
Minus:	1. Food	0.60	
	2. Clothing Depreciation	0.10	
		0.70	5.30

Multiplied by 270 (average life span of nine months) 1,431 marks

Efficient utilization of the prisoner's body at the end of nine months increases this profit by the return of:

1. Dental gold
2. Personally owned clothing [part of which was used in other camps, reducing expenses for new clothing while part was utilized in respinning for army uniforms]
3. Valuables left by the deceased
4. Money left by the deceased

From these returns must be deducted the average cremation cost of two marks per body but the direct and indirect profit per body averaged at least 200 marks

In many cases it can run to many thousands of marks.

The total profit per prisoner, at an average turnover rate of nine months, therefore can run to at least 1,630 marks

It is possible at times to obtain additional revenue from the utilization of bones and ashes.

Were the camps really profitable? After the war when Fritz Stangl, commander of the Treblinka extermination camp, was located in Brazil and an effort was made to extradite him to Germany to stand trial, his SS dossier was made public. This dossier stated that in one year's time Stangl had delivered to Berlin 2.8 million U.S. dollars, 11 million Soviet rubles, 250 kilograms of gold wedding rings, 350,000 pounds sterling and 20 freight cars of women's hair, among other items. Multiply these amounts by the number of camps and it is obvious that the SS raked in a grisly fortune from the camps.

What happened to the money, gold, and other items once they reached Berlin? This question has been only partially answered and after more than a quarter of a century the search still continues for much of this SS booty. It is known that Bormann discovered in late 1943 that there was a secret SS fund hoarded in the Reichsbank in Berlin, a fund derived from the profit on the Jews killed in the camps. Shipments from the camps were deposited in the bank under the fictitious name of Max Heillger, but the money was controlled by Dr. Walther Funk, president of the Reichsbank. Bormann recognized an opportunity to accumulate a fortune for himself from the fund and promptly began doing so. Knowing that there was a possibility that Germany might lose the war, he began shipping money from the fund out of the country. Funk, thinking Bormann was acting on behalf of Hitler, didn't object when Bormann had his own personal secretary, Dr. Helmut von Hummel, withdraw money from the bank for "party expenses." The withdrawals became larger as time passed. None of the money, however, was used for party expenses. Instead, Bormann, with the help of Otto Skorzeny, shipped the money in armored trucks to ports in southern Spain where German U-boats took it to Argentina. Juan Perón, Argentina's strongman, was a Hitler sympathizer despite the official neutrality of his country, and Perón made certain that Bormann's treasure was kept in a safe place. During the postwar years much of this money was used by Skorzeny, who survived the fall of the Third Reich, to aid SS personnel who escaped to South America.

Not all the SS treasure got out of Germany, however. Much of it was hidden in Bavaria—and may still be hidden there since millions have never been found. A collection of gold coins belonging to Bormann was discovered after the war near the Schloss Fuschl outside Salzburg, but a large number of gold bars made by Degussa, a German company, from the gold teeth of camp victims have never been located. As the war neared its end and more and more SS officials began taking their personal treasures to Bavaria, the local citizens became suspicious of the truck convoys. Skorzeny, however, found a solution. He suggested that several small SS hospitals be built in the area so that he could use ambulances plainly marked with the international Red Cross symbol to transport the shipments of gold, jewelry, and money.

Once this plan was put into effect, Skorzeny was deluged with requests from SS and other Nazi officials to hide their fortunes in the mountains around Berchtesgaden. Eichmann, the top administrator of the genocide operation, arranged to have 22 iron boxes of documents and gold moved to the Obersalzberg area. Ernst Kaltenbrunner, the successor to Heydrich as chief of the SD, asked Skorzeny to help him get a few personal belongings to Bavaria. These included: 50 kilograms of gold bars; 50 cases of gold coins and gold articles, each case weighing 100 pounds; 2 million American dollars; 2 million Swiss francs; 5 cases filled with diamonds and precious stones; and a stamp collection worth 5 million reichsmarks. Even Funk asked Skorzeny to help by concealing the state treasury on the Obersalzberg. Skorzeny denied to Allied interrogators that he had done so but there are lingering doubts about the truth of his statement since a large portion of the Nazi treasury has never been located.

One man who did not ask Skorzeny or anyone else to help him conceal a personal fortune as the war neared its end was Himmler. There has been a great deal of controversy over this since the war. Some historians and Nazi survivors believe that the Reichsführer-SS had already stashed away a personal fortune in Switzerland. If that was true, the fortune was never found. It is a fact, however, that during the later stages of the war Himmler, through Walter Schellenberg, was in touch with Jean-Marie Musi, the son of the former president of Switzerland, with a plan to send 5,000 older German Jews to Switzerland. Himmler originally agreed to the plan in May of 1944 but later decided that the Jews could go to Switzerland only if a certain sum was paid. The payment demanded was so large that the Swiss could not raise it and the plan was dropped.

Gottlob Berger, of the SS Central Security Office, stated during his testimony at Nuremberg that he negotiated with Hungarian officials in September 1944 on behalf of Himmler for a payment of 2 million penges in return for the release of Hungarian Jews from the death camps. Berger claimed that the money was for Himmler's personal use, not for the SS in general. In addition, during the months before the beginning of the first deportations from the Warsaw ghetto, more than $4,000,000 worth of goods were seized from the Jews imprisoned behind those walls, goods which were sold for the profit of Himmler's SS fund.

So it was entirely possible that Himmler had a fortune hidden away for his personal use after the war. His lifestyle, however, indicates that the ex-chicken farmer may have spent much of any such money as quickly as he stole it. Himmler spent not in luxurious living nor on a collection of art treasures as did Göring; nor on beautiful women and magnificent homes as did Joseph Goebbels, Hitler's minister of propaganda; nor on sophisticated living as did Albert Speer, Hitler's minister of munitions and armaments. Himmler's money was spent on more bizarre pet projects. The 13 million reichsmarks he lavished on his beloved Wewelsburg Castle near Paderborn is a typical example.

Himmler was convinced that he could communicate with great men of the past and didn't hesitate to tell associates about the regular meetings he held with King Heinrich I, King Arthur, and others. It was, in fact, his "close contact" with King Arthur that led to the reconstruction of the fantastic Wewelsburg Castle. The castle in Westphalia had once been owned by Wewel von Buren, a knight who spent his time robbing other wealthy landowners. After the death of von Buren it went through many reconstruction modifications and uses, ending up as a triangular mass of stone that from the outside appeared impenetrable. Himmler was fascinated by the structure as well as the legend that a Westphalian castle would be the one edifice that would survive an attack from the east. He decided he had to have it for the SS at any expense.

Himmler encountered no problems in obtaining the castle since the maintenance costs were bankrupting the local government which had seen to its upkeep. In July 1934 it was turned over to him for an annual fee of a single reichsmark. He immediately informed the Reich Minister of Economics that he needed a financial grant to meet the building costs that would be encountered in modifying the castle to his standards and ordered SS architect Hermann Bartels to draw up a new design along the lines suggested by Himmler. Within a year the work was completed, most of it accomplished by slave labor from the concentration camps. Each room in the reconstructed castle was furnished differently. The solid oak furniture, tapestries, heavy brocade curtains, carved doors, thick carpets, and wrought-iron accessories were of the best quality and very expensive. When Berlin frowned at Himmler's repeated requests for money to finance the reconstruction and furnishing of his castle, Himmler shrugged off the criticism and turned to his SS Economic and Administrative Department which owned several prospering firms.

Publicly the SS owned no companies but secretly it completely controlled four large businesses. The German Excavation and Quarrying Company that was composed of 15 stone, brick, and other building materials divisions was exceptionally profitable, as was the German Equipment Company that specialized in tools for industries from breadmaking to iron foundries. This company profited too, from the locations of many of its plants. Its factories were set up near the concentration camps; they used slave labor and also sold supplies to the camps. The third company covertly controlled by the SS was started at the personal insistence of Himmler himself who believed religiously in the medicinal qualities of herbs. It was the German Experimental Establishment for Foodstuffs and Nutrition, a firm that planted herb gardens around all the concentration camps. As one camp survivor stated later: "Himmler's herbs didn't save one prisoner but probably hastened the death of thousands." The fourth of the quartet of SS companies was the Society for Exploitation of Textile and Leather Work. Its factory was constructed at the concentration camp for females at Ravensbrück. The slave laborers from the camp produced uniforms for the Waffen-SS, to the profit of their masters.

With these resources, Himmler had no problem getting the money he needed for his castle. He simply dipped into the profits of these companies. His own private apartment was constructed in the southern wing of the castle and was a shrine to the memory of King Heinrich I. Himmler had a library of 14,000 books, a huge collection of weapons, and a large hall where the SS leaders met. He never permitted more than twelve guests to sit at the huge table in the hall, basing this restriction on the practice of King Arthur's Knights of the Round Table. Himmler's table wasn't round but he still abided by the advice he supposedly received during his séances.

The rooms of the reconstructed Wewelsburg Castle fascinated visiting SS leaders. There was a Frederich Barbarossa room that was always kept locked and was reserved for the Führer. Hitler never visited the castle, however, much to the disappointment of Himmler, but the Reichsführer-SS covered up this embarrassment by starting the rumor that Hitler was going to be buried there. After Hitler's disappearance at the end of the war, one of the first areas searched for his body was this room in the Wewelsburg Castle. As everywhere else they searched, the Allied investigators came away empty-handed. There were also rooms named for Otto the Great, Philip of Swabia, Henry the Lion, Conrad IV, and Friederich Hohenstauffen, to name a few. Each room was furnished with genuine period pieces and often personal items such as garments, armor, or shields that belonged to the hero for whom the room was named. A fortune in SS funds was spent by Himmler's aides as they scoured museums and private collections all over Europe for the items.

But what happened to the money that remained when the Third Reich collapsed? If no special SS funds were found in Switzerland, where Himmler had allegedly established secret bank accounts, where is the money today? One method used by Himmler to conceal those SS funds was discovered by Allied investigators after the war. Low-ranking SS officers were approached by their superiors on orders from the Reichsführer-SS and asked for the identification number of their personal bank accounts. These were usually insignificant accounts used by the SS officer or his wife to handle personal bills and other expenses. These officers were then asked to sign two blank sheets of paper; and, having been drilled in the strict discipline of the organization, they did not hesitate. With the end of the war all German banks came under the control of the Allies. During the ensuing investigation many of the SS officers were shocked to learn from Allied officials that instead of having a few thousand reichsmarks in their account they had several million! These hidden funds were extremely difficult to trace because of the traditional secrecy of banks so it has never been learned just how vast a fortune the Nazis stored away for the hoped-for Fourth Reich. Nor has the rumored Nazi treasure hidden in the Aussee region in Austria yet been found. We will say more about that later.

11

The SS Sex Association

On June 10, 1942, the day after the state funeral was held for the assassinated Heydrich, the SS troops moved into the small mining village of Lidice near Prague and rounded up the citizens, as we have seen. The men and older boys were marched to a farming area, lined up against the wall of a barn, and shot. The women and young girls were loaded into trucks and taken to concentration camps. Yet, before any of the young boys or girls were despatched to the grave or the camps, each was examined very carefully by the SS. They were made to undress, their heads, chests, and hips were measured, they were weighed and photographed from all angles. Why?

A telegram found in the SS files after the war gives the explanation. It was sent on June 12 by Horst Böhme, the security chief in Prague.

> By order of the supreme command the community of Lidice in the Protectorate of Bohemia and Moravia has been razed to the ground in connection with the attempt on the life of Gruppenführer Heydrich. The whole male population has been shot. The women have been sent to a concentration camp for life. The children were examined for the capacity for Germanization. The non-Germanizable will be sent to you and you will send them on to local Polish camps. There are ninety children, unaccompanied by members of their families. They will be sent to Lodz in a special coach attached to the regular passenger train to Lodz. The train will arrive on Saturday 13 June 1942 at 2:30 hours. I therefore

request you to ensure that the children are met at the station and immediately sent to a suitable camp. Special care is not required.

Thirteen of the children from Lidice were selected by the SS for the *Lebensborn* (Fountain of Life) program and were sent to the home established for this purpose at Pushkau. Later the thirteen were adopted by German families to be raised as a superbreed for the Third Reich. In addition to the thirteen children selected, six pregnant women of Lidice were given the best of care until their children were born, and then, after three weeks with their mothers, the babies were examined for their qualifications for Germanization. All six babies were selected but, unfortunately, five of them later died due to the stress their mothers experienced during the Lidice massacre when their husbands were murdered.

"How can we be so cruel as to take a child from its mother?" Himmler asked piously, then answered: "How much more cruel to leave a potential genius with our natural enemies."

The *Lebensborn* program, the breeding establishment formed by Himmler in 1936 to increase the birthrate of the "superrace," was another manifestation of the emotional bankruptcy of the SS. The basic idea of the program was to select ideal German women and encourage them to have intercourse with SS men, who were considered the racial and political elite of the Reich. The pregnant women were housed in maternity centers established throughout the country by Himmler; there they received excellent medical care until their children were born. After birth the mothers received extra benefits from the government and the babies were watched over very carefully since they were to be the model future citizens of the Thousand Year Third Reich. It wasn't until nearly three decades after the end of World War II that the secret documents of the *Lebensborn* program revealed its much wider scope. Especially revolting was the kidnapping of hundreds of thousands of foreign children for the purpose of adding to Germany's breeding stock, children who were never returned to their parents. Many of the "Germanized orphans" are still unaware of their origin.

Himmler, in his fanatical desire to build a superrace for Nazi Germany, attempted to control every aspect of the SS man's life, including his sex life. He let it be known that he expected the SS man to marry, preferably between the ages of twenty-four and thirty, and have a family. The SS member and his fiancée had to undergo a complete physical examination by an SS physician and receive the approval of Himmler or one of his designated subordinates before they could marry. Once the go-ahead was given, the couple were married in a civil ceremony since SS regulations prohibited a church service. After the civil ceremony, the local SS commander conducted a unique service during which the marriage vows were repeated before him, the couple exchanged rings and were handed bread and salt by the SS leader. Himmler did everything possible to divorce the SS from the church and to promote the local SS commander as the "priest" for the area. He also emphasized to each SS member that he expected him and his new wife to raise a large family.

Himmler was not successful in either program. More than half the SS members attended church or retained their church membership regardless of their activities in the field. And most SS wives refused to raise large families. A survey taken in 1939 revealed that most SS families had only one child, not atypical among parents who were relatively young, and among those only just coming out of a period of severe economic depression. It was this slow breeding by his SS men, however, that forced Himmler to establish the *Lebensborn* program under the auspices of the SS Race and Resettlement Bureau. He hoped to develop a child-reservoir to increase the population and at the same time provide superrace-quality babies for the Third Reich. Himmler was convinced that his SS men were virile and sexually aggressive, that the small families were the fault of their wives. He decided that if he provided the women security during their pregnancy and afterward, the SS members would gladly handle the rest of the procreative activity.

Where did the women come from for the program? Himmler gave preference to the wives and girlfriends of the SS members. After them any pregnant German woman who met his strict racial requirements was accepted. To handle what Himmler expected to be an overflow crowd, maternity homes were established in twelve locations. Heim Pommern in Pölzin and Klosterheide in Brandenburg were the first two homes. Later, the estate that would become a Heim Wienerwald was seized from its Jewish owners by the Gestapo and became a part of the *Lebensborn* program. Others followed: Hochland in Bavaria; Friesland near Bremen; Wernigerode in the Harz Mountains; and Neulengbach in the Wienerwald. But his SS men seemed reluctant to jump between the covers with the willing women and the *Lebensborn* homes remained half-empty. Not that Himmler didn't keep trying to encourage them. On October 28, 1939, he issued a blunt order for the SS members to procreate.

> Beyond the bounds of civil laws and constraints which at other times be needful, it may prove to be a noble duty—even outside marriage—for German women and girls of good blood to become, not irresponsibly but in a spirit of profound moral solemnity, the mothers of children fathered by departing soldiers of whom fate alone knows whether they will return home or die for Germany.

He emphasized that the SS would guarantee guardianship and education of the children until they came of age and give them financial support. When his order aroused protests he tried to clear up any misunderstandings. He explained piously that he did not want SS members trying to bed down the wives of soldiers who were on active duty. He also emphasized that even the Führer sanctioned these illegitimate children, so the SS members could feel confident that they were doing their nation a great patriotic duty. Himmler's efforts brought only mediocre results.

Underage girls were considered fair game for the *Lebensborn* program by Himmler. While he told the SS members that they must not forcibly take the advantage of young German girls, it was another matter if the girls recognized their sensible duty to the Führer and agreed to procreate. One of the first questions asked of a young German girl when she enrolled in an *Arbeitsmädchen* (Labor Maids) unit was whether she would have a baby for the Führer. If agreeable, she was transferred to a camp where she was visited by SS men. She would stay there for a year, have the child, receive 1,000 reichsmarks and be discharged. The *Bund Deutscher Mädel* (League of German Girls) was also fair game for the

SS. This was the feminine branch of the German youth movement and had two general age groups: the *Jungmädel* (Young Girls) from ten to fourteen years of age, and older girls from fifteen to twenty-one. They were repeatedly told that they should dedicate themselves to comradeship, service, and physical fitness for motherhood. To Himmler all three of these aims added up to one objective: babies for the Third Reich. As he told them, "You can't all get a husband but you can all be mothers." Many did become mothers despite the objections of their parents. If the parents did have the temerity to object or threaten to punish the girl, they were promptly visited by the SS. Many such parents ended up in a concentration camp.

Himmler was a firm believer in soldiers enjoying themselves when on leave. He included his SS members in the soldier category although many of them never got any closer to the combat front than a death camp. Martin Bormann concurred and with Hitler's permission issued Circular 83/44, which stated, in part: "The creation of a good social environment for the soldier on leave from the front is essential for reasons of population policy." Party headquarters in each region was expected to arrange social functions, bringing together the German soldiers and willing girls of the *Arbeitsmädchen* and *Bund Deutscher Mädel*. The girls on these occasions did not wear their uniforms but attractive dresses provided them by the Nazi party. Each social function allotted a certain amount of leisure time during which Himmler hoped the soldiers and the girls would further the cause of *Lebensborn*.

Himmler and Bormann understood the various problems that often made a man look for a different woman; both of those men had mistresses themselves. Bormann's reason for taking a mistress was simple. He looked upon women as sex objects. The fact that his wife Gerda had ten children and submitted to him whenever and wherever he desired had nothing to do with increasing the German population for the glory of the Führer. Bormann often suggested that his large family should be a model for all Germans, but in truth it was merely the result of a selfish, crude sex drive that he had no wish to control. His affair with Manja Behrens, an actress with the Dresden State Theater and in movies produced by the Tobis Film Production Company, was a scandalous affair that violated all marriage vows. Nor did he try to keep the affair secret. In fact he flaunted it in the face of his wife, writing her detailed letters about his trysts with Manja. "She attracted me immensely," Bormann wrote his wife. "I fell madly in love with her. I arranged it so that I met her again many times and then I took her in spite of all her refusals. Oh, my sweet, you can't imagine how happy I am with the two of you! Really, Heaven has been kind to me. All the happiness you have given me through yourself and all the children, and now I have M. besides. I shall have to be doubly and trebly careful now and see that I keep well and fit."

Gerda Bormann accepted her husband's philandering and at times even encouraged it. She really had no choice. She had the insight to understand that in the end he would rely upon her, not the actress nor any of his other women-of-the-moment. But his actions induced her to suggest that after the war perhaps it would be best for a man who was physically capable to have his two wives lawfully. Bormann was skeptical at first but the more he thought about the idea the more he agreed. Finally he decided he would discuss it with that other Third Reich population enthusiast, Heinrich Himmler.

Himmler's personal approach to sex was entirely different from Bormann's although the net effect was similar. In fact, Himmler's bottom line added up to two illegitimate children while Bormann, despite his various women and his bragging about his sexual prowess, had none. Himmler tried to be very discreet about his love affair and did everything possible to keep it secret, as though he were ashamed. This was not only opposite of Bormann's boasting, but also of the publicly announced *Lebensborn* program of the SS. As a youth Himmler was always prim and correct in his relationship with girls. He insisted to his friends that a girl should be protected because she was so much weaker than a man and be loved for her childlike purity. In 1928 he married Margarete Concerzowo, a nurse seven years older than he. She operated a nursing home in Berlin and was a strong believer in using herbs to cure her patients. This attracted Himmler since he, too, was a supporter of herb treatment and later made such products the mainstay of one of his SS-controlled commercial enterprises. After their marriage, Marga Himmler sold the nursing home and bought a small farm ten miles from Munich where she and Himmler raised chickens and produce for the marketplace. Both seemed happy with their humdrum existence.

The situation changed when Himmler was appointed head of the newly formed SS in January 1929. The small farm and the chicken-raising business didn't project the right image for the chief of the SS so they sold the farm and moved to a home on the Tegernsee. Later he established an official residence in Berlin in the fashionable Dahlem section and a headquarters on Prinz Albrechtstrasse. Marga, however, gradually became lost in the web of Nazi intrigue. She stayed at the Tegernsee with their children—an adopted boy named Gerhard and a daughter of the marriage named Gudrun. Not that Marga Himmler really cared about her husband's prolonged absences. Their marriage had turned platonic long before Himmler reached the top hierarchy of the Nazi party. She was much more interested in her herbs than her husband. All she required was sufficient support money and her two children.

Himmler, on the other hand, was still interested in herbs but he also had an intense interest in his personal secretary, Hedwig Potthast—so interested that they produced two children: Helge, a son, and Nanette Dorothea, a daughter. There was no question but that Himmler was deeply in love with Hedwig; he didn't live with her merely for sex, but because he wanted her companionship and warmth. It never fails to startle us that this man who could love one woman deeply could order numberless other women and children to the gas chamber. Even Walter Schellenberg, his high-ranking subordinate, found Himmler difficult to understand.

> Himmler's first marriage had been unhappy but for his daughter's sake he had not sought divorce. He now lived with a woman who was not his wife and they had two very nice children to whom he was completely devoted. He did what he could for these children within the limits of his own income but although, after Hitler, Himmler had more real power than anyone else in the Third Reich, and through the control of many economic organizations could have had millions at his disposal, he found it difficult to provide for their needs.

The strait-laced Himmler finally went to Bormann and asked for 80,000 reichsmarks to build a house for his mistress in the Schneewinkel-Lehen, near Berchtsgaden. He received it at a very high rate of interest. This gave Bormann an opportunity to raise with Himmler the possibility of legalizing having more than one wife. One reason he felt confident in broaching the subject was that he had discovered that Hitler was concerned about the loss of German men in the fighting and was wondering how to make up this loss after the war. Bormann drafted a memorandum after a conversation with Hitler on the subject, a document entitled "Safeguarding the Future of the German People." In the paper he pointed out that the numerical strength of "racial Germans" would be disastrously depleted after the war and while there was no doubt Germany would win the military war, there was an excellent chance it would lose it "racially" unless drastic readjustments were made. The drastic readjustments?

> As the Führer stressed, after this war we will have 3 to 4 million women who either no longer have husbands or will not get any. The drop in the birth rate resulting from that would be impossible for our people to accept; how many divisions—the Führer emphasized—would we be short in twenty to forty-five years and beyond that!
>
> Now it is a fact that women who find themselves without a man after this war cannot have children by the Holy Spirit but only by men who have survived. [But] from the standpoint of the good of the people, increased population by only a portion of these men is desirable. Good men with strong character, physically and psychically healthy, are the ones who should reproduce extra generously.

Both Himmler and Bormann saw bigamy in a favorable light. Himmler's viewpoint differed only in that he concentrated as much on the personal lives of the man and woman as he did on the national requirements of population increase. According to Himmler:

> The fact that a man has to spend his entire existence with one wife drives him first of all to deceive her and then makes him a hypocrite as he tries to cover it up. The result is indifference

> between the partners. They avoid each other's embraces and the final consequence is that they don't produce children. This is the reason why millions of children are never born, children whom the state urgently requires. On the other hand the husband never dares to have children by the woman with whom he is carrying on an affair, much though he would like to, because middle-class morality forbids it. Again it's the state which loses, for it gets no children from the second woman either. The law is in direct contradiction to our crying need—children and still more children. We must show courage and act decisively in this matter even if it means arousing still greater opposition from the church—a little more or less is of no consequence.

Himmler assured Bormann that he supported Hitler's plan to change all existing marriage laws after the war. He emphasized that in his plan to augment the Führer's overall proposal, he wanted the SS and the heroes of the war to have special privileges, that they should be permitted to immediately take a second wife as a mark of distinction. Holders of the German Cross in Gold, the Knight's Cross and the Iron Cross, First Class, should be granted this favor. Since these men had already proven themselves in combat, they would, Himmler believed, produce superior children for the Reich. Had this plan worked successfully, monogamy might have been completely abolished in the future.

The Reichsführer-SS didn't overlook the fact that supporting two wives and their children would be costly. He suggested that each war hero be given a farm in the east and the guarantee of a well-paying government job. He should also be exempt from paying income tax. Himmler's plan projected a merry, enjoyable future for the man. But what about the women involved? he was asked. Wouldn't they compete for the husband's favor and argue with each other? According to Himmler, the first wife should receive special privileges and the title of Domina. But he added that he didn't particularly care whether the wives were happy or not as long as they produced the needed children. "Who will ask in 300 or 400 years time if a certain Fräulein Müller or Schultz was unhappy?"

Although Himmler and Bormann saw more or less eye to eye on bigamy, the Reichsführer-SS jealously guarded his elite empire and prerogatives against encroachments by Bormann in the latter's capacity as Hitler's personal secretary. When Leonardo Conti, the Reich Director of Health, decided that every Third Reich district should have an advisory center for infertile couples, he asked Bormann for the necessary permission. Bormann readily granted it to aid population growth, an innovation that did not have to await the end of the war. The centers advised early marriage but discovered after a nationwide survey that far too many women remained unmarried. Conti decided that the Nazi party and medical bodies should arrange to bring suitable mates together through planned introductions. The suitability was to be physical as well as mental, and this required the doctors to examine each young woman. If these two approaches, children by a lover or by a tested stranger didn't appeal to the women, Conti had a third idea: artificial insemination. He even suggested a semen bank provided by superior males, to be used by women rated highly by the medical staff of the Reich Ministry of Health.

Himmler was outraged. He felt that Conti and Bormann were treading on SS territory. In no uncertain terms he told Bormann to order the medical experts to confine their efforts to curing sterility and that the SS would take care of the population-growth efforts. That was the end of Conti's advisory centers.

As was his custom, however, Himmler tried out some of Conti's ideas himself. He was always willing to adapt someone else's suggestions as long as he was in control and received the credit. The human semen bank idea fascinated Himmler and he experimented with human semen as a substitute for plasma in blood transfusions. He obtained the semen from the brothel in Stuttgart. Everyone involved in the experiment was pledged to secrecy, especially when the experiment failed completely.

When it came to abortion, Himmler was very strict. Before the Nazis took power, there were approximately 700,000 abortions a year in Germany. Himmler was determined that the state should not lose that many babies and set out to do something about it. He insisted that women having an abortion should be sentenced to prison for life and the abortionist sentenced to death. When he discovered the Reich Ministry of Justice was not following his suggestions, he complained to Hitler and, while the Führer did not insist on such harsh punishment, he did order the courts to stop being so lenient. This strict attitude toward abortion applied only to German women. Hitler's feelings were clear when, on July 22, 1942, he talked about the restrictions on abortions in Germany:

> If any such idiot tried to put into practice such an order in the occupied Eastern territories, I would personally shoot him. In view of the large families of the native population, it could only suit us if girls and women there had as many abortions as possible. Active trade in contraceptives ought to be actually encouraged in the Eastern territories, as we could not possibly have the slightest interest in increasing the non-German population.

The Polish Red Cross estimated after the war that as many as 40,000 babies born in concentration camps were killed by the SS, while enforced abortions more than equaled this number.

What were the results of Himmler's varied programs to increase the German population? In most cases they were a failure. The *Lebensborn* program didn't attract many SS members despite Himmler's urging. One survey showed that of the 12,000 children born to SS leaders, only 135 were born out of wedlock. The same men who acted so ruthlessly in the field or at the death camps were conventional when it came to sex and marriage. The illegitimate birth rate as a whole remained at the same level or dropped. Himmler's strict marriage laws, however, had to be relaxed as the war continued. In 1943, when he had to decide between the severe rules he had established earlier or increasing the number of marriages of SS members, he chose the latter. He decided that quantity was more important than quality. Abortions among Germans remained high despite Himmler's efforts to present a different propaganda picture by falsifying the yearly reports.

The most tragic results were those of the "Germanization" program. Those children who were not selected for adoption during the final weeding out were often sent to concentration camps where many eventually died. Those who were adopted by German foster parents discovered that their ordeal did not end with the collapse of the Nazi empire. Some didn't know they were adopted. Many of the German foster parents didn't want to give up the children. Even the Allies were reluctant to become involved in the delicate problem. Of all the Polish children kidnapped under the ''Germanization'' program and adopted by German parents, only 15 percent were repatriated. More than three decades after the end of the war, the heart-rending search continues.

12

Mysterious SS Playboy

One of the most perplexing mysteries of the Third Reich concerns the fate of Hermann Fegelein, Hitler's brother-in-law. During the postwar years, when many secret documents have come to light from European and American archives and Allied intelligence reports have become available, the role of Fegelein has become a subject of investigation. It appears that he was much more than just the notorious ''SS playboy'' who chased women more than he did enemies of the Reich. Whether he was a loyal Hitler supporter who died in Berlin at the Führer's side, was executed by Hitler because the Führer suspected him of plotting with Himmler to betray Germany to the Allies, or was actually a Russian spy in Hitler's headquarters who escaped to the Soviet zone during the final days of the war, there is no question that Fegelein duped a great many people.

It certainly wasn't a superior education that enabled Fegelein to outwit so many others. He was born in Ansbach, Middle Franconia (a region of Bavaria), on October 30, 1906, and had very little taste for even elementary schooling. He did like horses, however, and although nearly illiterate, he was hired as a groom. Eventually he became a jockey, but was barely surviving on his meager income when he had the good fortune to meet Christian Weber. Weber was one of the original members of the Nazi party, a horse fancier, and a typical Munich street fighter. After listening to Hitler speak at some of the early party rallies, Weber became a devoted follower. It wasn't unusual for him to help keep order at a rally with his fists or with a long whip. Since he was a huge man, nearly as wide as he was tall, and with a Kaiser mustache that made him look even fiercer, not many of Hitler's opponents were willing to meet him eyeball-to-eyeball. Weber, once the fighting was over for the evening, preferred the company of pretty young women and liked to down large quantities of beer. In this he was matched by the young jockey Fegelein. Fegelein, a handsome, flamboyant youth, had no problem attracting young women but he often lacked money to buy the beer he also loved. On the other hand, Weber had the money for the drinks but his personal appearance kept many of the young girls at a distance. Weber, always an opportunist, decided it would be to his social benefit to join forces with the young jockey so he hired him to handle his horses.

It was a fateful union for both. Not only did Fegelein provide Weber with the feminine companionship he desired, but he was also excellent with the horses. Horses were the one interest of his life to which he was constantly loyal. As he accompanied Weber to many of the Nazi party meetings, mainly to help the older man meet some young women after the meeting was over, Fegelein became acquainted with Hitler but developed no interest in politics. He was impressed, as most seventeen-year-old boys would have been, when Weber helped save Hitler's life during the Munich Beer Hall Putsch, but it was Weber's physical courage that delighted him, not the fact that he had been involved in a political revolution. When Weber was sentenced to five years in prison for his part in the battle, Fegelein took care of the older man's horses and his women.

Hitler never forgot the loyalty and courage of Christian Weber and once he came to power he made certain that Weber received his share of the money available to the Nazi party. Through various business contracts, many of them of questionable legality, Weber soon became a very wealthy man. Fegelein became his protégé. He encouraged Fegelein to join the Nazi party and, through Weber's influence and Fegelein's ability to handle horses, the ex-jockey became the commander of the first SS cavalry unit. Fegelein was overjoyed. He wore the flashy uniform of the unit with great pride, knowing that it accented his tall, slim body, just as he knew that his riding ability made him a standout performer at all the SS horse shows. Even Hitler, who had no real love for horses, was fascinated by Fegelein's daring feats in the saddle.

Fegelein moved up the promotion ladder rapidly and by 1942 he was the SS inspector for all cavalry units with the rank of brigadier general (Oberführer-SS). Some of his hopes were dashed when he was ordered to the Russian front in 1943. The bitter cold and rough living conditions were considerably more depressing than the comfortable life to which he had been accustomed as an SS inspector, but ultimately this move was of great help to his career. On October 30, 1943, he was wounded in action and was evacuated from the front lines after being awarded the Knight's Cross with Oak Leaves. Back in Germany and recovered from his wounds, Fegelein, with the help of Weber and other Nazi officials with whom he had become friendly, managed to obtain an appointment as Heinrich Himmler's liaison officer with Hitler. It was a position that obviously suited Fegelein. He was with the top Nazi hierarchy, able to dress in his immaculate uniform and mingle with the rich and the powerful, and, as always, have his choice of the beautiful women who frequented Hitler's headquarters.

As much as he enjoyed the company of beautiful women, in and out of bed, Fegelein didn't spend all his time cultivating their friendship. He had learned his lesson well from his association with Christian Weber: A patron could do wonders for his career. From his position at Hitler's headquarters, he soon discovered that the two men who could do him the most good were his immediate superior Reichsführer-SS Heinrich Himmler and Hitler's secretary and confidant, Martin Bormann. Fegelein understood something that many of Hitler's associates overlooked—that Bormann was fast becoming the most powerful man in the Reich next to Hitler himself. Bormann, from his unique post as guardian of the door to Hitler's office, largely controlled who saw the Führer. Even those who were granted an audience with Hitler had to explain their subject to him first. If Bormann felt the matter wasn't important enough or that it interfered with some other matter he was personally championing, he turned the visitor away.

Over a period of time, Bormann became master of Hitler's headquarters, and was both feared and hated.

Fegelein, rather than oppose Bormann, joined him. Before long, Bormann, Fegelein, and Wilhelm Burgdorff, Hitler's military adjutant, became close friends and drinking companions. "General Burgdorff and Fegelein came and stayed an hour," Bormann wrote to his wife on August 22, 1944, "and at 1:30 A.M. I was with the Führer for half an hour." Later, he wrote: "Fegelein and Burgdorff invade my room most nights and there is shoptalk and discussion of current problems over a bottle of wine." Gradually Fegelein's influence in the discussions became more and more pronounced and he and Bormann worked together closely—so closely that Himmler began to worry about whether Fegelein was looking out for the interests of the SS at Hitler's headquarters, as was his responsibility, or for his own personal career.

Himmler had more to worry about in this respect when he discovered that Fegelein planned to marry Gretl Braun, the sister of Eva Braun, Hitler's longtime mistress. Gretl spent a great deal of time at the Berghof with Eva, and Hitler liked her much better than Eva's other sister Ilse. Ilse opposed many of the Nazi principles and actions and was outspoken in her criticism when she visited Eva at the Berghof or in Berlin. She probably would have been imprisoned for speaking as she did to the Führer, were it not that Eva eventually learned to keep her sister out of Hitler's sight. Gretl, however, had no interest in politics. Her interest was in men, and at the Berghof she had a field day with the young, handsome, and virile officers and guards. She was fun loving and was one person who could tease Hitler about his eating habits, dress, and personal superstitions, and she could make him smile. Hitler was determined to find a husband for Gretl for two reasons. First, he wanted her to find a well-placed officer who could support her and provide the luxuries she coveted. Now those were often provided out of party funds or Hitler's personal funds. Second, if Gretl were married, it would make Eva socially acceptable in public as the sister of the wife of one of his staff officers. As his mistress Hitler kept Eva behind the scenes except in the privacy of the Berghof or her villa in Munich.

As a matchmaker the Führer had his problems, however.

He set his sights on Walter Hewel, Foreign Minister Ribbentrop's liaison man at headquarters, but Hewel wasn't interested in Gretl. When Hitler continued to pressure him, Hewel promptly married Elisabeth Blanda, a wealthy playgirl who frequented the parties held by the top-ranking Nazis. SS Colonel Fritz Darges was another good prospect. Darges, a military adjutant at Hitler's headquarters, spent a lot of his free time with Gretl, so much so that Hitler and Eva thought it only a matter of time until the pair announced their plans to marry. When Gretl became pregnant, however, Darges took off for the eastern front. He apparently deemed it better to face the Russians than the remainder of his life with Gretl Braun. Another man who had been enjoying the favors of Gretl was Fegelein, just as he had also been squiring Elisabeth Blanda around the Berghof and the nightclubs of Berlin before she married Hewel. Now it was his turn to come under pressure from Hitler to marry the pregnant Gretl. Fegelein looked at the situation in a completely different light than Darges. He saw many advantages in legally marrying the sister of Hitler's mistress, not the least of which was his hope that he and the Führer would become much closer, bettering his own position within the Nazi hierarchy. That was considerably better than being shipped off to combat.

Gretl and Fegelein had an elaborate wedding at the Eagle's Nest, the mountaintop retreat Bormann had built for Hitler above the Berghof on the Obersalzberg. It was an all-day, all-night affair, one of the most expensive parties ever held there. Hitler, who seldom visited this retreat sitting high on Kelstein peak, despite Bormann's having spent millions of reichsmarks constructing it for his use, attended the wedding and gave Gretl an expensive tiara but stayed only a few minutes. The day after the wedding, Bormann threw a large party for the couple in his home on the Obersalzberg, violating his own directive of a few weeks earlier, which stated: "The longer the war lasts, the more important it is that leading party members set an example for other comrades of fighting spirit, of trust in victory, and of modesty in their personal conduct." The entire wedding party was drunk for two days.

Fegelein was barely settled in his marriage and was still trying to figure out how he could get Gretl away from his side long enough so that he could see a few of his former girlfriends, when the attempt was made on Hitler's life on July 20, 1944. The attempt was made at a war conference held at Hitler's headquarters in East Prussia when Colonel Claus Schenk Graf von Stauffenberg, a wounded war hero who had become disillusioned with Hitler and the Nazi party, planted an explosive device in a briefcase next to the conference table. Four men present were killed and several wounded but Hitler was only slightly injured. The SS was immediately set on the trail of the conspirators, and Fegelein played an important role in the search. Field Marshal Günther Hans von Kluge was one of the many officers who knew the attempt was to be made but who did not actively participate in it. When von Kluge disappeared, Fegelein was charged with the responsibility of finding him. Hitler was fond of von Kluge and had great confidence in his military planning, so much so that when Field Marshal Gerd von Rundstedt failed to halt the Allied advance in Normandy after the June 6, 1944, invasion, the Führer had replaced him with von Kluge. On August 15, however, Hitler received word that von Kluge had disappeared somewhere on the western front. Hitler was puzzled and rebuffed Fegelein when the latter suggested that von Kluge had probably been involved in the assassination attempt. However, later that day German intelligence agents monitored a British radio signal inquiring about the whereabouts of von Kluge. In a complete turnabout, Hitler became convinced that not only had von Kluge been involved in the July plot but that he was at that very moment meeting with the Allies to negotiate a surrender of the entire western front. He appointed Field Marshal Walther Model to replace von Kluge and ordered von Kluge back to Germany.

Von Kluge was found—dead. Model's report stated that he had died of a cerebral hemorrhage brought on by the stress of trying to halt the Allied advance. Hitler wasn't convinced, thinking that Model was trying to save the reputation of a fellow German officer. He ordered a secret autopsy by SS doctors and kept the death of von Kluge a secret from the German public. On August 28 Fegelein sent Bormann a report that disclosed that von Kluge had poisoned himself with cyanide. Fegelein also presented evidence that von Kluge had been trying to contact the enemy but a fighter-bomber had destroyed his command car and he had to abandon the plan.

Von Kluge was given a modest burial, without the customary honors bestowed upon such a high-ranking officer, and the cause of his death was kept secret. Many of his compatriots who were in on the secret refused to believe that he had voluntarily committed suicide. They were convinced that Fegelein forced him to take the poison just as Field Marshal Erwin Rommel was forced to do when his indirect involvement with the conspirators was learned by Hitler. Fegelein never denied the rumor.

The von Kluge affair and Fegelein's part in solving the case brought him closer to Hitler than before. When the final German gamble of the war, the Ardennes offensive, was being planned, Hitler, reading reports on the German generals that had been written from information gathered by the Gestapo, decided that the generals could no longer be trusted. He designated the Sixth SS Panzer Army to lead the offensive. The Gestapo reports were fed to him by Fegelein with Bormann's approval. When Hitler became disillusioned with Göring's leadership of the Luftwaffe and appointed General Ritter von Greim his deputy, it was Fegelein and Bormann who supported Greim. During the last days of the war Greim succeeded Goring.

According to a report declassified by U.S. Army intelligence a quarter of a century after the war, Fegelein was alleged to have saved Hitler's life from a would-be poisoner. The report is based on information received from Hans Fegelein, the general's father, on September 21, 1945, by Walter Hirschfeld, a counterintelligence agent. Hans Fegelein stated:

> Did you happen to hear about the Morell affair? Morell [Hitler's personal physician] and Himmler plotted in the last days to kill the Führer by means of a poison injection. It was Himmler's plan. The Führer was at that time very excited, you see, because those saboteurs did not bring the new atomic bomb into play although it would have meant a change in the course of the war. The Führer believed up until the last moment that these people would finally carry out his order; when nothing happened, he became so nervous that people thought he was no longer normal.

> My son Hermann discovered this plan of Himmler and Morell—there may also have been more involved—and he immediately reported it to the Führer. According to my son's orders, Morell

> should have been arrested but he managed to obtain the plane which was standing ready for the use of Hitler, Eva Braun, and my son, and he escaped in that. I have heard that the SS later arrested him.
>
> As far as that atomic bomb is concerned, the Americans need not be so proud of that. I know for certain that this invention was turned over to the Russians.
>
> That is a German invention, anyhow. The engineers who were in the Führer's headquarters at the last, and the Führer himself, were awaiting daily the use of the atomic bomb in combat. But those saboteurs never put it to use. I would only like to know why it was not used against the Russians. When the Russians first entered Germany there was still time and there were certainly plenty of opportunities. The Führer realized fully that the atomic bomb could decide the outcome of the war and for that reason he believed in a German victory up until the last minute.

Hirschfeld was an undercover agent for G-2 who posed as a Nazi who had escaped arrest. He turned over 15,000 reichsmarks to Hans Fegelein to win his confidence. The money was later recovered. Hans Fegelein's version of the Morell affair differs from that accepted by Allied investigators in several respects. Himmler was not considered one of the plotters, nor was it thought that General Fegelein was the one who discovered the poison in Dr. Theodor Morell's pills. It was generally thought that Dr. Erwin Giesing, an eye, ear, and nose specialist who had been called in to check Hitler, discovered that the antigas pills Morell had been giving the Führer for months contained small amounts of strychnine and atropine which, over this long period of time, were cumulatively poisoning him. (However, it was always perplexing to historians why Giesing, instead of being rewarded by Hitler for his discovery, was paid his fee and sent away while Morell remained the Führer's doctor several more months.) From the testimony of Hans Fegelein, it appears that General Fegelein conducted an investigation of Morell which resulted in discovery of the plot by the doctor and Morell during the latter days of the war. Morell did fly out of Berlin in late April 1945 while by this time Himmler was estranged from Hitler and out of the Führer's reach.

Hans Fegelein's comments on the atomic bomb were obviously based on wishful thinking and not fact. Skorzeny, Hitler's commando chief, and his saboteurs never used the atomic bomb for the simple reason that the German scientists never produced one. They tried, but time ran out on the Third Reich before they succeeded.

The Hermann Fegelein mystery deepens in the last few months of the war. He and Bormann became daily confidants of Hitler as the Allies closed in on Berlin from the west and the Russians from the east. They spoon-fed the Führer what they wanted him to hear and had considerable influence on his decisions during this period. At the same time they both were looking out for their own futures and, being realists, understood in early 1945 that there was a strong possibility that Germany would be defeated. In fact, Fegelein was aware of Himmler's attempt to negotiate a surrender with the Allies but didn't relay the word to the Führer. Fegelein was aware that Hitler no longer trusted the Reichsführer-SS, in any case. He did, however, tell Hitler on the night of April 17 that secret talks between SS General Karl Wolff and Allen Dulles, station chief of the Office of Strategic Services, were in progress in Switzerland concerning the surrender of German troops in Italy. Fegelein emphasized that Wolff was attempting to get the Americans to renege on the promise they had made to the Soviets to exact an unconditional surrender from Germany. Wolff was attempting to get America to help Germany repel the Soviet troops once the German and American armies had stopped fighting each other. Hitler favored the talks as long as there was a chance of splitting the Allies. Fegelein was told to inform the SS general to continue his negotiations.

The fact that Wolff was in contact with an Allied agent didn't concern Hitler nearly as much as the fact that there was a leak in his headquarters. Both the British and the Russians were receiving secret information about Hitler's war conferences, often only hours after the conference ended. As the end neared there was a steady flow of information from the Berlin bunker relayed via Switzerland to England and the Soviet Union. In one instance Hitler had drawn up a promotion list in one of his conferences but, after the others attending the conference left the room, he decided to delay the promotions for several days. Within 48 hours the British radio was broadcasting the names Hitler had listed on the promotion sheet. He knew then that the leak was coming from one of his intimate associates. Long after the war, Reinhard Gehlen, Hitler's chief espionage agent on the eastern front and later head of all intelligence activities for West Germany, stated that he and Admiral Wilhelm Canaris, chief of the Abwehr, suspected Bormann. They suspected that he was using a secret radio transmitter to send messages to Russia. Gehlen even testified that the missing Bormann, who has never officially been located by the Allies, was seen in the 1950s in East Berlin attending a theater. Others believe, however, that the Russian agent in Hitler's headquarters was Hermann Fegelein. He has never been found, either.

Both Bormann and Fegelein were in the bunker with Hitler during the final days of the Third Reich. Earlier, Hitler had decided that he would make his last stand on the Obersalzberg, the Alpine Redoubt that concerned General Eisenhower and the Western Allies. American and British intelligence agents suspected that Hitler intended to gather thousands of his SS officers and men in the Bavarian mountains to fight a guerrilla war after Berlin fell. The Allies knew that it would take months to dig out such a mountain force but they needn't have worried: Hitler changed his mind. He vowed that he would stay in Berlin, win or lose. Many of those who had been with him through his years of glory wanted no part of the bunker and had no intention of dying with their Führer. But Bormann and Fegelein stayed, as did Eva Braun. Fegelein sent his wife Gretl to the Obersalzberg, promising to join her later, but she never saw her husband again. There are conflicting reports from those who were in Berlin at the time as to just what happened to Fegelein.

It is known that Fegelein was in and out of the bunker periodically until April 28, but after that date eyewitness accounts of his whereabouts and actions vary considerably. On that date Hitler was stunned to hear on the Allied radio that Himmler, Fegelein's superior officer, had contacted the U.S. and England and promised Germany's unconditional surrender. After he had the report verified, the Führer went into a rage, promising everyone within earshot that he would have Himmler executed as a traitor. After castigating Himmler and his actions, he suddenly recalled that he hadn't seen Fegelein, Himmler's liaison officer with whom he had been conferring daily until a few days earlier. Hitler immediately became suspicious and demanded that Fegelein be summoned to his office to throw some light on Himmler's contact with the enemy. But no one could find Fegelein in the bunker.

Fegelein was not in the bunker. He had slipped out on April 25, supposedly for a trip to Hohenlychen to confer with Himmler. However, the Russian artillery and Allied planes blocked his path and he returned to Berlin. He didn't go back to the bunker, though. He went to his apartment on the Kurfürstendamm, changed into civilian clothes, and drove to Number 10-11 Bleibtreustrasse, which was located about four miles from the bunker. Fegelein had never permitted his marriage to interfere with his woman-chasing, and for several months he had kept the apartment on Bleibtreustrasse for a tall blond mistress. He was in bed there with his mistress when he received a telephone call from the bunker. Otto Günsche, Hitler's personal adjutant and a drinking companion of Fegelein's, knew about the aprartment and the mistress. When Hitler began searching for Fegelein, Günsche called to tip him off. Fegelein told his friend that he would be back at the bunker within two hours. As soon as Günsche hung up, Fegelein called Eva Braun, his sister-in-law, and told her she was a fool to stay in the bunker, that if she would join him they could go to the Obersalzberg together.

What happened next has never been ascertained except that Fegelein soon disappeared. Hanna Reitsch, in the bunker at the time, believed that Eva Braun told Fegelein that she would never leave the Führer's side but that he should join his pregnant wife Gretl at the Berghof. Reitsch didn't believe Eva Braun told Hitler about the telephone call from Fegelein. General Johann Rattenhuber insists that Fegelein was forcibly brought back to the bunker by an SS detachment, but Colonel Peter Hoegl, who was in charge of the detachment, says that Fegelein volunteered to return when they confronted him at the Bleibtreustrasse apartment. He had a valise with him that contained jewels, more than 100,000 reichsmarks, 3,000 Swiss francs, road maps, and passports. A passport which included a photograph of his blond mistress was British. This evidence, in addition to Himmler's surrender overtures to the

Allies, was too much for the Führer, according to Colonel Nikolaus von Below, the Luftwaffe adjutant at Hitler's headquarters, and he ordered Fegelein executed as a traitor. Bormann wrote in his diary: "Treason and treachery by Himmler—unconditional surrender—announced abroad. Fegelein disgraced—the coward tried to clear out of Berlin in civilian clothes!" Hans Baur said Eva Braun begged Hitler to save Fegelein's life for her sister Gretl's sake but the Führer refused. Fegelein was shot two hours before Hitler and Eva Braun were married.

Or was he? Did he and Bormann escape from the bunker together and go to Russia if, as some suspect, both were Russian agents during the war? Or did Hitler, Eva Braun, Fegelein, and Bormann all escape from Berlin hidden in the last plane to leave the capital? Considerable controversy surrounds the disappearance of all four. There was an American investigation, a British investigation, and a Russian investigation, none of which agreed. In addition there is the confusing and changing testimony of the bunker eyewitnesses, who alter their stories to fit the occasion. The American undercover agent Walter Hirschfeld, posing as an SS officer who had had a prominent part in the German counterfeiting scheme "Operation Bernhardt," visited Fegelein's father many times in September 1945. He told the elder Fegelein that he had sketches showing the place of concealment of the plates used for the counterfeiting and where the jewelry and precious metals, bought with the counterfeit funds in neutral countries, were hidden. During a talk with Hans Fegelein on September 20, the old man said: "I think I can say with certainty that the Führer is alive. I have received word through a special courier. My son hinted that the Führer lives. I telephoned my son only two days before the capitulation."

Hirschfeld then asked: "Do you really believe that the Führer is still alive?"

"Yes, I am positive of it, for my son Hermann sent me a courier *after* the capitulation."

"When you got the message were Hitler, Hermann, and Eva still in Germany?" Hirschfeld asked.

"Yes, at that time they were still in Germany. The courier told me that Hermann had told him to tell me that 'the Führer and I are safe and well. Don't worry about me; you will get further word from me even if it is not for some time.' "

Hirschfeld tried to shake the old man's story. "But that sounds so unreal. Even many SS officers state that the Führer is dead and his body was burned."

"Don't let yourself be taken in by propaganda. They are all trusted and true SS men who have orders to make these statements."

Merely wishful thinking by an old man who loved his son? When Hirschfeld expressed doubt that Hitler, Fegelein, or Eva Braun was still alive, the elder Fegelein raised himself up from the bed in which he was resting because of a sore leg and said, with tears in his eyes: "Herr Hirschfeld, you can believe me. I've told you no lies and no fancy stories. I know for certain that the Führer and my son are still living. Otherwise my life would be finished. I have no reason to mislead you and have no intention of lying to you."

Hermann Fegelein has not been seen since April 1945. Yet, at the conclusion of Hirschfeld's report, the undercover agent states: "I think I can safely say that Hans Fegelein's statements about Hitler, Hermann Fegelein, and Eva Braun, that is, that they are alive and that he learned this through a courier, have a basis in fact."

The mystery of the SS playboy has not been solved yet.

The black-uniformed SS were the pride of the Third Reich, the image Hitler wanted to project to the world.

Sentenced to death for the shooting of American prisoners at Malmédy, Peiper was released from prison in 1956 when influential SS veterans threatened to abandon the Western cause and support the Russians.

SS-Obersturmbannführer Jochen Peiper was a dedicated Nazi whose wartime atrocities were finally avenged when he was killed at his home in France in 1976. (*Reprinted from Charles Whiting's* Death of a Division, *courtesy of Stein and Day/Publishers*)

Bodies of death camp victims awaiting cremation

Mass grave at Bergen-Belsen

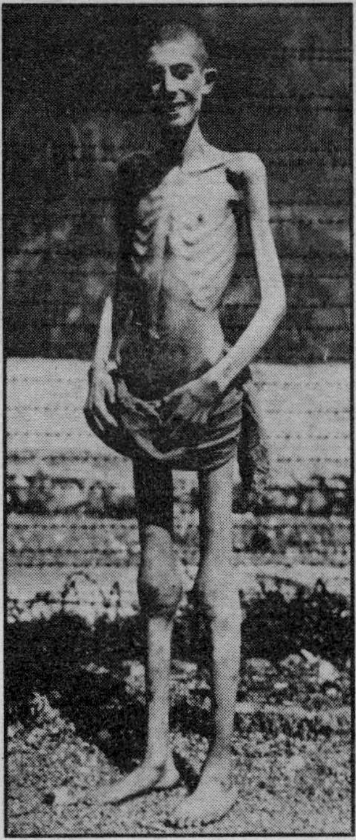

A survivor of Ebensee

Ernst Kaltenbrunner, chief of the Security Service of the SS. He was hanged on October 16, 1946, after being found guilty at the Nuremberg trials.

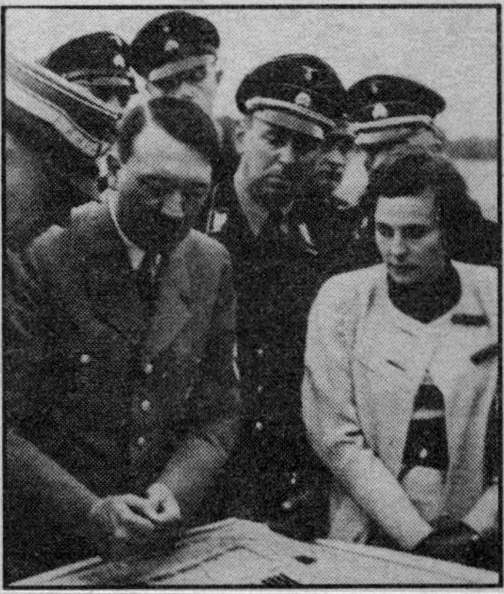

Leni Riefenstahl, Hitler, and SS officers discuss plans for the famous film *Triumph of the Will.* Riefenstahl directed the film.

Himmler, an ex-chicken farmer, never wavered in his ambition to make his SS the master of Germany.

Josef (Sepp) Dietrich, first commander of Hitler's SS bodyguard, was one of the most brutal of all SS officers.

Ernst Röhm, notoriously homosexual chief of the SA. When Röhm became too powerful, Hitler had him murdered and then elevated the SS above the SA.

Heydrich (foreground) with Himmler and his adjutant Karl Wolff in October 1935.

U.S. soldiers discover an open grave containing murdered children near an SS camp.

Karl Koch commanded the concentration camps at Buchenwald and Bachsenhausen. His wife Ilse earned the title "Bitch of Buchenwald." Her hobby was collecting lamp shades, bookcovers, and gloves made from the skin of murdered concentration camp inmates.

Theodor Eicke, inspector of concentration camps and SS guard formations.

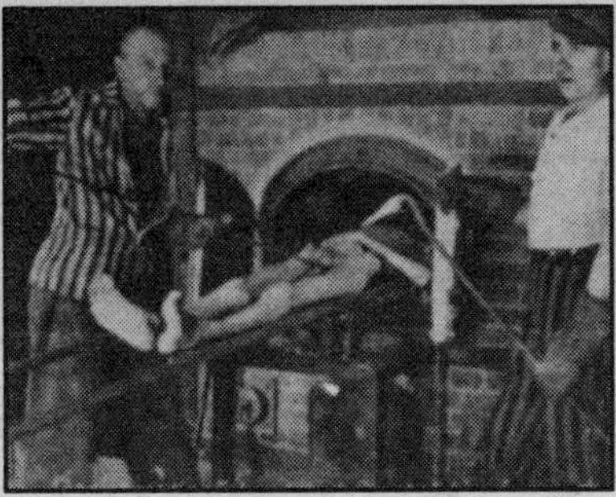

Crematorium at Dachau

SS General Jürgen Stroop, who destroyed the Warsaw ghetto. Its residents were sent to the death camps.

Inmates demonstrate how SS guards tortured them.

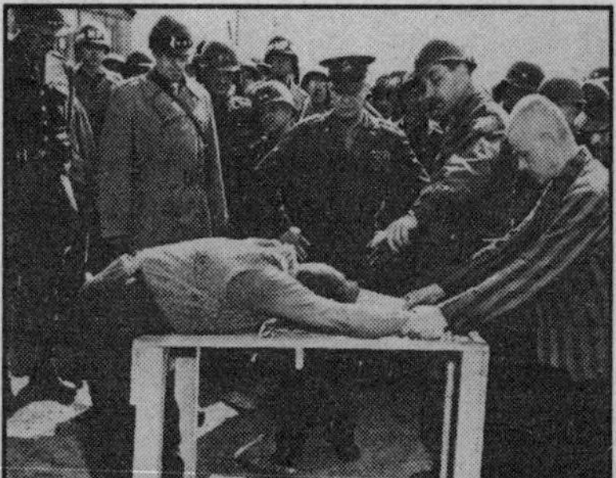

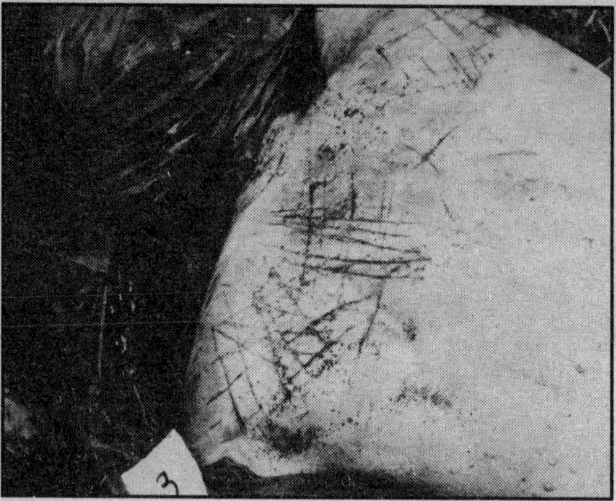

The back of a dead inmate who had been tortured.

An American officer interrogates an SS guard.

SS-Obersturmbannführer Karl Wolff, the German military governor of Northern Italy, wanted to publicize an allegation that the Allies had unleashed mustard gas on Bari.

Dr. Stewart Alexander finally discovered the cause of the mysterious deaths at Bari.

Reinhard Heydrich, head of the Reich Security Service, chosen by Hitler to administer the "Final Solution." As governor of Czechoslovakia, he was assassinated near Prague in spring 1942.

Memorial marking a mass grave at Lidice, Czechoslovakia, the village wiped out by SS troops in retaliation for the assassination of Heydrich.

Hitler was constantly searching for art treasures for the museum he planned for his hometown, Linz. The SS was often used to gather the booty.

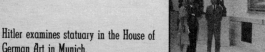

Hitler examines statuary in the House of German Art in Munich.

Oswald Pohl (right) at Nuremberg in 1947. Pohl made certain that all valuables taken from Jewish prisoners went into the SS coffers.

Box of gold wedding rings taken from gassed victims by the SS. Such valuables went to secret SS accounts in the Reichsbank.

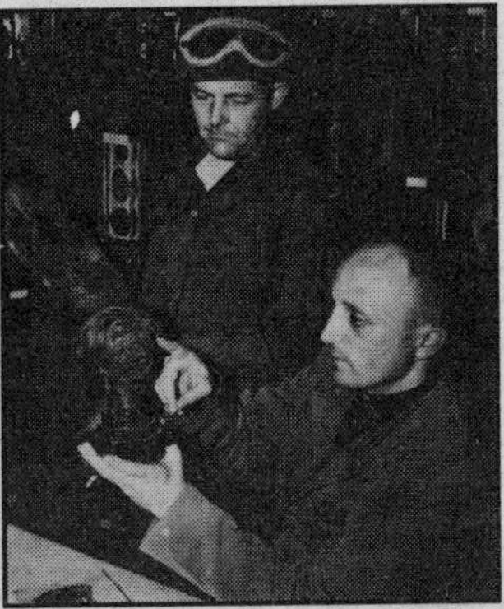

Not content with the worldly goods of their victims, the SS sometimes made souvenirs of their victims' bodies. Here is the shrunken head of a Polish prisoner and a lampshade made of human skin.

Bormann (at left) partying with other members of Hitler's inner circle. He conspired with SS-Chief Himmler to propose the postwar legalization of bigamy so as to propagate more Germans for the colonization of Europe.

By early 1945 the German situation was already desperate. These Waffen-SS troops were no longer hand-picked elite, but ordinary young conscripts.

Hermann Fegelein, Himmler's SS liaison officer at Hitler's headquarters. His disappearance at the end of the war remains a mystery. Some have suggested that he was a Soviet agent.

Hitler and his mistress Eva Braun have been rumored still alive and in hiding ever since the end of the war. The Führer had said, "The conflict (between the Russians and the Western Allies) must come... When it comes, I must be alive to lead the German people, to help them arise from defeat, to lead them to final victory. Germany can hope for the future only if the whole world thinks I am dead."

Hans Baur, Hitler's personal pilot, had been in the bunker. He offered to fly the Führer to safety.

Allen Dulles (right) was one of those who recommended that the U.S. employ the Gehlen organization. (*U.S. Army*)

SS horse farm at Fischorn near where a large part of the secret SS treasure was located after the war. Much of it is still missing.

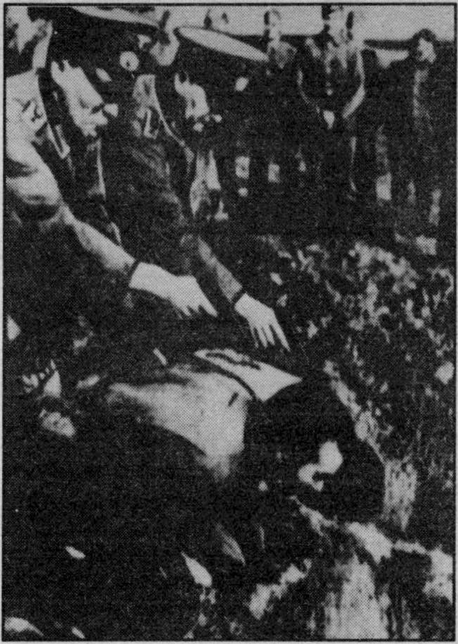

SS officers murdering Russians beside an open grave.

Arthur G. Trudeau, U.S. Army G-2 officer who warned Washington that SS officers working for U.S. Intelligence after the war were unreliable. He was right.

Unlike most of his comrades, this SS guard met justice. He is being dragged from a moat by two American soldiers and a Dachau concentration camp inmate while other prisoners look on.

German civilians forced to bury victims after a concentration camp is liberated. The U.S. Army concluded that millions of Germans participated directly or indirectly in the Nazi crimes, yet full acknowledgment is still rare among the perpetrators.

13

The Führer's Shadow

The disappearance of Hermann Fegelein after the fall of the Third Reich has not caused as much controversy as the disappearance of his inner circle companion Martin Bormann. Over the years since the end of World War II, Bormann has been reported seen in more than half a dozen countries, has been accused of having been a long-time Soviet agent presently residing in East Berlin, and bodies identified as his have been numerous. Yet there is no official verification of his death nor that he still lives. Both he and Fegelein simply vanished, leaving behind a multitude of theories as to what actually happened.

Even in life Bormann was a mystery man. He appeared, to outsiders, a mere officeholder in the Nazi organization who had no leadership qualities and who had a repelling rather than compelling personality. Even his physical appearance was unattractive. Short, overweight, rough, and with a broad face that seldom smiled, he always looked rumpled and unpleasant. His language was coarse, blunt, and tactless, yet he considered himself handsome and a lady-killer. In his position as Hitler's private secretary, many of the Nazi officials and military officers who were not a part of Hitler's inner circle and who visited the Führer's headquarters infrequently, believed Bormann to be merely Hitler's "go-fer." They mistakenly thought he had no power, no influence, and that all he did was get Hitler his sweets when he was hungry, take care of domestic matters on the Obersalzberg, and pay Hitler's private bills. Many of these same Nazi officials and generals died early deaths because they grossly underestimated that inconsequential-appearing secretary.

Bormann's ruthlessness became evident early. He was a member of the *Rossbach Freikorps*, a post-World War I paramilitary unit dedicated to the elimination of those whom they considered traitors to the Fatherland. During his turn of duty with this unit, he participated in the murder of his former elementary schoolteacher, Walther Kadow. His partner in that crime was Rudolf Höss, who later became infamous for his brutality at the Auschwitz death camp. Both went to jail for that murder. It was the last time Bormann resorted to physical violence, however. He had learned his lesson. Instead of continuing along the lines of Höss who became more physically brutal as the years passed and as the Nazi party got stronger, Bormann switched tactics. He decided he could gain more power and influence by developing administrative skills and worming his way into positions of authority. There he could use those skills to improve his personal status. He held various posts on his way up the Nazi ladder: district leader, regional press officer, a staff member of the SA, and Gau secretary.

During this period he developed a technique that he was to use again and again in the succeeding years. Bormann quickly learned that the man who controls an organization's money has a great deal of leverage. He organized a fund to aid party members injured in the fights that usually erupted when Hitler gave a speech prior to coming to power in 1933. Of course, he named himself administrator of this fund. No one but Bormann knew how much was in the fund and no one but Bormann took money from it. This put him in a unique position of power in those early days of the party. Yet he stayed completely in the background, subservient to Hitler. He always conferred with his Führer before allocating from the special fund, letting Hitler believe that as head of the party he, not Bormann, controlled the money. Hitler, busy with other matters, usually told Bormann to do as he thought best but was grateful that he had been consulted. At that time some other party members were trying to usurp the leadership of the organization, and Bormann's appearance of loyalty confirmed to Hitler that here was a man who could be trusted.

Hitler didn't forget. Seven months after Hitler came to power in 1933, he promoted Bormann to Reichsleiter (Reich Leader) and installed him as chief of staff to his deputy, Rudolf Hess. Bormann's gain was Hess's loss. Bormann immediately began undermining Hess in his subtle, unrelenting manner, never missing a chance to ingratiate himself with Hitler. Alfred Rosenberg indicated how Bormann did so:

> Whenever I visited Hess, [Bormann] was often present; later on, almost always. When I had dinner with the Führer, Bormann and Goebbels were usually there. Hess had obviously got on the Führer's nerves, and so Bormann took care of the queries and orders. Here is where he began to make himself indispensable. If, during our dinner conversations, some incident was mentioned, Bormann would pull out his notebook and make an entry. Or else, if the Führer expressed displeasure over some remark, some measure, some film, Bormann would make a note. If something seemed unclear, Bormann would get up and leave the room, but return almost immediately—after having given orders to his office staff to investigate forthwith and to telephone, wire, or teletype.

In addition Bormann encouraged Dr. Henry Picker, a lawyer at Hitler's headquarters, to secretly record the Führer's private conversations. He refused to accept any responsibility for the transcripts in case Hitler objected, but often would request copies from Picker so he could extract information he thought important. The Picker transcripts survived the war and helped give insight into not only Hitler's character but Bormann's as well.

Hess was oblivious of Bormann's tactics, not realizing until it was too late that his chief of staff was draining from him his power and influence with both Hitler and the party. When Bormann suggested to Hess that the jurisdiction over certain areas by Nazi leaders should be changed, Hess hesitated at first because such a reorganization would reduce the power of many of the old-line party stalwarts. However, when Bormann showed him that the new jurisdictional areas would give Hess more concentrated power within the party, Hess went along with the plan. Hans Frank testified at the Nuremberg war crimes trials that Bormann's reorganization program was aimed at eliminating most other important party offices except his own. He still had Hess to contend with, but not for long.

Shortly before noon on May 11, 1941, Hitler was informed that Rudolf Hess had left Germany in a Messerschmitt 110 headed for England. In a letter he left behind for Hitler, Hess stated that he hoped through friends in England to end the war with the British. It was a propaganda disaster for the Third Reich and Hitler was furious. Indicative of his trust and reliance in Bormann, however, Bormann was the first man with whom he consulted after learning of Hess's flight. Albert Speer and other high-ranking Nazis who were at the Berghof that day to meet with Hitler had to sit idly by while Bormann and the Führer discussed the turn of events. Bormann suggested that Hess should be declared insane in the press releases concerning the affair. This was an error because the British, upon questioning Hess, discovered that he was quite sane, albeit excited. Bormann then put out a second press release stating that Hess suffered from mental confusion brought on by mesmerists and astrologers whom he had been consulting and that a thorough investigation was being made in Germany to find the individuals responsible.

Neither press release was taken seriously by the Allies but there was considerable confusion about the purpose behind the Hess flight, not only in the Western world but in Germany, too. Albert Speer, Reich Youth Leader Baldur von Schirach, and other Nazis who were aware of Bormann's duties at Hitler's headquarters were convinced that Hess felt that he was being replaced by Bormann as the Führer's confidant, that he was losing his influence with Hitler. If he could arrange peace terms between Germany and England his prestige, he felt, would once again soar with Hitler. Others believe Bormann even knew ahead of time about his superior's plans to fly to England and encouraged him, considering it an excellent opportunity to get rid of Hess and move one more step up the Nazi ladder himself. One fact is certain: as soon as Bormann learned that Hess had flown to England he immediately denounced him as a traitor and insisted that everyone connected with Hess—except himself, of course—should be considered a suspect conspirator and investigated, even Ilse Hess, his wife. Hitler agreed and turned the matter over to Bormann.

On May 13 Bormann was promoted. The title Hess had held was changed when the position was given to Bormann but the power of the office remained virtually intact. The official announcement stated:

> The Führer has issued the following decree: The former office of Deputy to the Führer henceforth is to be known as the Party Chancellery. It is to be under my personal orders. Its chief executive is, as before, Reichsleiter Martin Bormann.—Adolf Hitler.

From that date until April 1945, Bormann consolidated his power and influence until by the time of his mysterious disappearance he was the most feared of Hitler's inner circle. Day by day he found ways to expand his area of responsibility and each time he did, other Nazi leaders suffered a setback. He became a maker and breaker of careers. Eventually he became the sole hub of communication between the party and Hitler. Every piece of correspondence, every telephone call, every telegram intended for Hitler, had to go first to Bormann. Robert Ley, head of the German Labor Front, tried to circumvent Bormann and was reprimanded not only by Bormann but also by Hitler himself. Hans Frank stepped out of bounds by spending party money on paintings, jewelry, furs, and similar items without first contacting Bormann, and he received the same headquarters treatment as Ley. Word soon got around that Himmler's Gestapo was watching over those Nazi leaders whom Bormann mistrusted and they conformed to his directives.

Bormann had the reputation of being blindly devoted to Hitler, and Hitler, of course, loved it. But investigations since the fall of the Third Reich and the discovery of previously unknown documents throw considerable doubt on Bormann's loyalty to the Führer or, at very least, upon the reasons for his loyalty. The records clearly show that over the years Bormann's main concern was Bormann and that he exploited Hitler's trust for his own ends. Now, one must wonder if he did not seek gain in the service of the Soviet Union, too. When Reinhard Gehlen, Hitler's respected espionage chief on the eastern front, testified in 1971 that Bormann had been rescued from Berlin by the Soviets in 1945 and that informants had told him they had seen Bormann entering an East Berlin theater in the 1950s, certain actions of Bormann between 1941 and 1945 took on another perspective. For instance, why do the Russians refuse to release Rudolf Hess from Spandau prison more than three and a half decades after the end of World War II? Hess was in England before Hitler ordered the invasion of the Soviet Union so it is obvious he played no role in that action. Why then are the Soviets so bitter? Is it because Bormann relayed to them the real reason Hess went to England, that Hess was trying to get the English to join with the Germans in the war against the Russians?

Even more intriguing is the Bormann treasure and what happened to it after World War II. He had access to party funds but was very careful about their use except for the benefit of the Führer himself. Hitler's Berghof, the famed Eagle's Nest, and the many other buildings on the Obersalzberg south of Munich were built with millions of reichsmarks provided by Bormann because he knew Hitler loved the area. With others, however, Bormann was usually very tight-fisted, and exacted an exorbitant rate of interest for money borrowed. Nor did he take any of the party funds for his own nest egg that he was determined to accumulate before the war would end. He was too clever for that.

Early in the conflict Bormann was so busy with Nazi party affairs and consolidating his own power that other than his beautiful home on the Obersalzberg he really had very little personal fortune. Gradually, however, he came to realize that Germany might well lose the war. Concluding that if he were going to lose his exalted position by Hitler's side in case of defeat, he didn't want to be poor, too, Bormann devised a plan that amassed millions for him in reichsmarks and foreign currency. On August 10, 1944, he arranged to have most of the prominent German industrialists meet in the Hotel Rotes Haus in Strasbourg. While he did not appear at the meeting in person, he let it be known to the industrialists that he was not averse to the transfer abroad of money, machine tools, specialty steel, and secret blueprints for use after the war ended. This could not be done openly, so Bormann called upon Hjalmar Schacht, the German financial wizard, to camouflage the assets so that the new firms to be established abroad would appear to have no connection with their Nazi sponsors. To help with the physical transfer of the money and materials, he enlisted the aid of Otto Skorzeny, Hitler's commando chief.

It was a dangerous plan because, at the same time that Bormann and his industrialist friends were building up a huge equity in foreign countries for postwar use, Hitler was demanding that every German contribute as much of his or her wealth as possible to support the war effort. Those caught doing otherwise were executed without trial. The Führer never suspected that his most "loyal" inner circle member was a ringleader of those who were building private fortunes outside Germany. Dummy factories, existing only on paper, or firms using Argentine, Spanish, or Swiss "fronts," were quickly established. Bormann discovered that the officials of these "neutral" countries were very agreeable to the transfer of the Nazi hoard to their jurisdiction—for a price. He was more than willing to pay the price since it wasn't coming out of his pocket but from the Nazi industrialists.

Skorzeny and the SS provided the protection Bormann needed. When Bormann needed armored trucks and a guard detachment to move consignments across Germany and France to submarine bases in southern Spain, he notified Skorzeny who provided whatever was needed. It is interesting to note that Bormann stayed clear of any arrangement with Himmler at this time. Bormann considered the Reichsführer-SS weak. He dismissed Himmler's fantasy that he could negotiate a peaceful settlement of the war with the Allies and have the SS absolved of all its crimes. Bormann knew that was impossible. He was convinced that the SS would be classified criminals because they had liquidated 2,500,000 Poles, 500,000 gypsies, 450,000 Russian POWs, and 4 to 6 million Jews. Being a realist, he threw his lot in with Skorzeny, the rough-and-ready commando chief, who had no direct connection with the SS atrocities, but who was a fearless, intelligent, and greedy officer who welcomed a chance to cut himself in for a share of the treasure. Skorzeny and his commandos shepherded numerous shipments across Europe to the U-boats which took the hoard to South America or other hiding spots to await Bormann after the war. When the U-boat bases became inaccessible by the land route, air shipments from Germany to Spain were inaugurated.

Where did all the money and other valuables come from that Bormann shipped out of Nazi Germany? Certainly, much of it came from industrialists who were eager to get their funds, materials, and other assets into a neutral country for use after the war. But because of Hitler's edict that this was strictly prohibited and punishable by death, most of those industrialists were reluctant to take too many chances, and limited the sums they shipped in order to reduce their exposure. Bormann made certain that these shipments were accurately recorded and forced the industrialists to give him power of attorney over the assets shipped out of Germany. Purportedly the power of attorney was given to the Nazi Party, but this was only a ruse. Bormann intended to collect his share at a later date. Yet these shipments account for a mere fraction of the so-called Bormann treasure. With financial acumen comparable to that of Schacht himself, Bormann devised several schemes that resulted in windfall profits for himself. One was the secret "Max Heiliger" fund.

This was a secret special account at the Reichsbank in Berlin, held under the fictitious name "Max Heiliger." Bormann was completely unaware of the existence of the fund until late 1943, when Skorzeny tipped him off that numerous mysterious shipments were being made in automobiles and vans to the Reichsbank. Skorzeny's commandos had been asked to protect the shipments, many of which were coming from concentration camps all over Europe. Bormann, his curiosity aroused, investigated. He discovered that only five men had access to the account. They were Reichsbank President Walther Funk; Emil Puhl, a vice-president of the Reichsbank; the cashier of the bank; one director; and the man who handled the secret shipments, Albert Thoms. That the account was so restricted suggested to Bormann that something was going on that he, as Hitler's chief of the Party Chancellery, should know about. Pressing Funk for an explanation—this was not too difficult; Schacht called him a "harmless homosexual and alcoholic"—Bormann learned that the shipments consisted of gold, jewels, and currency taken from Jews killed in the extermination camps.

This was a jackpot that Bormann hadn't expected. Nor did he have any reservations about making the agreement between Himmler and Funk a three-way affair by forcing his own way into the secret arrangement. Before long Bormann had complete access to the Max Heiliger fund and he made good use of it—for himself. When he learned that there were so many shipments that Thoms required 30 men just to help him unload the automobiles and vans, he decided on a unique plan to help Thoms save manpower. He ordered Funk, through Bormann's own staff member Dr. Helmut von Hummel, to divert some of the shipments to the Party Chancellery. Funk didn't protest and before long the shipments were nearly equally divided between the bank and Bormann's headquarters. This was no small operation. From Poland alone came gold coins weighing more than 100,000 kilograms and 180 million reichsmarks. Crate after crate contained gold teeth, dentures with gold fillings, jewelry, watches—anything of value that the Jews possessed when they were taken to the extermination camps. In 1944 the Max Heiliger account contained millions in marks, pounds sterling, dollars, and Swiss francs, nearly 4,000 ounces of platinum, half a million ounces of gold, and 5,000 boxes of diamonds among other valuables.

Eventually the shipments obtained by Bormann from the Max Heiliger account became such a large operation that he gave it the code name *Aktion Feurerland.* Skorzeny, of course, was in charge of the physical transfer of the treasure out of the country. Since Skorzeny's assignments were made by Bormann, Hitler never suspected what was going on behind his back during these closing months of the war. Funk and Himmler, both afraid of Bormann, didn't dare mention Bormann's dipping into the secret fund. Juan Perón, the Argentine strongman who eventually became president, cooperated fully with Bormann and made certain that the shipments sent to South America were handled efficiently and secretly. Most of the money from the Max Heiliger fund sent to Argentina was deposited in the name of Evita Duarte, who was Perón's mistress until their marriage in October 1945.

Besides the fee he exacted from the industrialists for helping them ship assets out of Germany, and his personal share of the Max Heiliger fund, Bormann had other sources of wealth. One was a blackmail operation through which he obtained enormous additional contributions from German industry. Known to have great influence with Hitler over which firms got what war contracts, the ambitious and money-hungry industrialists were willing to bribe Bormann to favor their corporations. Only he knew how much was funneled into his pockets in this manner and where it was sent as the twilight of the Third Reich approached—he and the man who helped get the lucre out of Germany, Otto Skorzeny.

Two of Germany's best-known industrialists learned just how costly it was to deal with Bormann. Dr. Fritz Thyssen, heir to the Thyssen steel fortune, was an early Hitler supporter. He contributed large sums to the Nazi party, money which was instrumental in Hitler's rise to power. Thyssen thought, as did many others who aided Hitler during the early period, that his financial contributions would give him the right to tell Hitler what he should and should not do. In 1940, after receiving an especially critical letter from Thyssen, Hitler decided that he had been patient long enough. He ordered Thyssen arrested and confined to a concentration camp. Bormann grabbed the opportunity to make himself some extra money. He arranged for Thyssen to be released from the concentration camp and escorted to Switzerland—for a fee rumored to be over a million dollars payable in Swiss francs. As luck would have it, good for Bormann and bad for Thyssen, in 1942 the German industrialist, living along the Riviera in a luxurious villa, was arrested by the SS again when German troops overran the area. This time he was sentenced to death and once again Bormann came to his rescue. Bormann was able to do this by persuading Hitler that it was in the best interests of the party and of the Führer himself to keep on the good side of the German industrialists and that he could do so by being lenient with Thyssen. He never mentioned the fortune that he was accumulating by acting in Thyssen's behalf.

The deal he made with the Krupp family was also financially rewarding for Bormann. This agreement came about because the Krupps wanted to keep their industrial dynasty in the family but a law that had been passed in 1920 made this impossible. The holdings were considered a public heritage and could not be willed to the next Krupp in the line of succession as the family desired. Gustav Krupp von Bohlen und Halbach was in charge of the Krupp operations in 1942. A heavy financial supporter of Hitler, he decided to try to get the law changed, and he concluded that Bormann had enough power and influence with the Führer to bring it about. Bormann was first approached about the scheme in August 1942 and again Bormann heard opportunity knock. He agreed that he would guide the legislation Krupp desired if Krupp agreed to accept the Party Chancellery chief as a silent partner in the Krupp real estate holdings in South America. Krupp agreed without hesitation and on November 23, 1943, Hitler's directive concerning the Krupp holdings became law. The Krupp company was exclusively a family holding once again. Bormann had convinced the Führer that such a move would win favor with the other industrialists.

So by the time of the siege of the bunker in April 1945, Bormann had much of his treasure safely out of the country. All he had to be concerned about was getting safely out of Berlin himself. It is at this point that the ongoing Bormann controversy begins. It has been verified that Bormann left the bunker area with Artur Axmann, Werner Naumann, and Hans Baur at approximately 11:30 on the night of May 1. Altogether there were 15 in the breakout group but these four plus Günther Weltzin, Axmann's aide, became separated from the others soon after the escape attempt started. Axmann had succeeded von Schirach as Hitler Youth Leader in 1941; Naumann was Goebbel's state secretary; and Baur was Hitler's longtime personal pilot. By 2:20 A.M. the small group had reached the Lehrter railway station but as they tried to move further toward the outskirts of Berlin they found themselves blocked by a tank battle. While one eyewitness, Hitler's chauffeur Erich Kempka, swears that Bormann was killed by a shell from one of the Russian tanks, Baur contradicts him. Hitler's pilot states that he and Bormann were together *after* the tank battle, as do Naumann and Axmann. They took shelter in a damaged tenement house for a few minutes and when there was a break in the fighting moved down to the river Spree and followed it. It was here that Baur says he lost track of Bormann during a Soviet infantry attack in which he was severely wounded and captured. He spent the next ten years in a Soviet prisoner-of-war camp.

Weltzin was also captured and died in a Soviet prisoner-of-war camp. Axmann, who eventually was captured by

American counter-intelligence agents, states that he was with Bormann after Baur was captured.

> We reached the bridge over the Friedrich-List-Ufer just west of the Humboldt Harbor. The bridge leads to the Lehrter Bahnhof S-Bahn station. We jumped from the bridge and found, to our chagrin, that there was a whole Russian infantry platoon bivouaced under it. They promptly surrounded us. But to our amazement and joy they simply kept announcing in a boisterous chorus, "Hitler kaput, Krieg aus!"

In light of information turned up during the three decades since the Berlin breakout, this strange encounter with the Russian troops is significant. After this encounter Bormann dropped completely out of sight. Where did he go? Axmann vows that Bormann was killed near the bridge that passed over the railway lines in the area, that he saw his body in the moonlight. Yet, the body has not been found and officially identified to the world's satisfaction. Did Bormann slip away from the Russian troops and escape to South America? It has been reported that he lives in Paraguay today and at eighty years of age is still in good health. Yet there is no official verification of this report. Nor has anyone proved that he is living in the Matto Grosso jungle of Brazil as Pascuale Donazio, an Italian fascist, vowed. In 1966 Simon Weisenthal, the famed Nazi-hunter, stated that in all probability Bormann was alive and living near the frontier of Argentina and Chile but admitted he could not prove it. No one yet has provided evidence of Bormann's whereabouts, dead or alive, convincing enough to collect the $25,000 reward that the prosecutor's office in Frankfurt-am-Main has offered.

There is one other possibility, and that grows out of the revelations of Reinhard Gehlen in 1971, 26 years after Bormann's disappearance. Gehlen, who went from a position as Hitler's wartime chief of intelligence against Russia; to top CIA strategist during the Cold War; to head of the BND (West Germany's intelligence service), was considered one of the most knowledgeable intelligence officers in the world. His word carried great weight, and when he stated that Bormann escaped to the Soviet Union in 1945 his testimony could not be ignored. If Bormann *did* escape to the Soviet Union at that time, how did he do it? Indications are that the best opportunity he had was when he and Axmann leaped from the bridge into the midst of a Russian infantry platoon, just as Axmann testified. Did Bormann know that the Russians were waiting for him there to take him to the Soviet sector? Did he go with them in a pre-planned escape operation? Gehlen's statement added to the already worldwide controversy over Bormann's fate, but if one is looking for a probability, Gehlen's theory is as substantial as any other.

What about the Bormann treasure after the war? If he did escape to the Soviet Union or, for that matter, to South America or elsewhere, wouldn't he have tried to recover the secreted funds? There is no solid evidence that Bormann himself tried but it is known that Skorzeny, his SS associate in the operation, did obtain a large portion of the treasure in Spain and Argentina. Skorzeny spent large sums on the protection of former SS officers and men after the war, provided funds for a legal organization to defend them if and when they were arrested, and financed an elaborate escape route for Nazis from Germany to South America. At the same time he accumulated a postwar fortune of his own, probably from the secret funds. No one knows if he passed any of the treasure on to Bormann. Through a firm he used as a "front," the H.S. Lucht Company, with headquarters in Düsseldorf, Skorzeny carried on activities throughout the world which would have made it easy for him to transfer funds to Bormann even behind the Iron Curtain. A report from Laverne Baldwin, the American Consul General in Düsseldorf, about Skorzeny's activities with the H.S. Lucht company in 1954, deals with a visit Skorzeny's wife, the Baroness von Finkenstein, made as a representative of the firm to the Madrid offices of the Otto Wolff Company of Cologne:

> The reference dispatch reported that Baroness von Finkenstein, the wife of Otto Skorzeny, visited the Madrid offices of Victor Oswald in the spring of 1954 in the company of one Frank Gallati who is the manager of the Otto Wolff Company. The Otto Wolff Company is part of the same Otto Wolff iron and steel complex which was broken up after the war under the Allied decartelization and deconcentration procedures. The firm has always been extremely interested in trade with the east and Otto Wolff von

> Amerongen, one of the owners, is chairman of the Russian committee of the Ost-Ausschuss [Eastern Committee] of the Federal German Industry Association.

Obviously it would have been very simple for Skorzeny to meet with and deliver to Bormann large sums through his ostensible business activities with the H. S. Lucht firm.

In 1956, when Gamal Abdel Nasser of Egypt became infuriated by the withdrawal of funds for the Aswan Dam by the United States and Great Britain, he turned to the Soviet Union for help. Skorzeny, who was in Egypt training the Egyptian dictator's security police, sided with Nasser despite the SS officers' deep hatred of the Russians. An associate of Skorzeny's in Egypt acted as a go-between with the Soviets, as U.S. Embassy Dispatch No. 2276 reports:

> Dr. [Wilhelm] Voss has been playing a double game since October 1952. Among the group of German military experts closely cooperating with each other are Voss, Skorzeny, Major Mertins, and Colonel Ferchl. The latter was a former member of the German General Staff and curiously enough was liberated by the USSR in 1950. No other members of the German General Staff have been liberated since 1946. Ferchel and Mertins are in touch with two Russian women. Voss has four Czechs working with him. He pretends they are Sudeten Germans and has asked the German embassy to give them passports (refused).

This was another wide-open channel that Skorzeny could have used to get the secret funds to Bormann were the latter in the Soviet Union.

Bormann always sought anonymity while in office and to a large extent he succeeded. Hitler, Goebbels, Göring, and the other top Nazis were easily recognizable throughout the world but Bormann never was well known and his face and features were similar to those of thousands of other Bavarians. Consequently the attempts to trace him since the collapse of the Third Reich have been fruitless. The monies he secreted with the help of the SS were certainly large enough to cover tracks and buy silence wherever he may have gone.

14

The SS and Hitler's Disappearance

In 1945 the disappearance of Adolf Hitler was of much more interest to the world than the disappearance of either Hermann Fegelein or Martin Bormann—not that there was a shortage of different versions of what happened to the Führer. The Russians, of course, controlled the zone in which the bunker was located and refused to permit Allied investigators to search the ruins. The Soviets first reported that they had discovered a body which they thought was Hitler's; dental work, they said, seemed to corroborate that conclusion. Then they backed off and Stalin stated that he believed Hitler was still alive. A detailed investigation into the circumstances surrounding Hitler's disappearance was conducted by Major H. R. Trevor-Roper, acting on behalf of the Counter Intelligence War Room and the British Army of the Rhine. The investigation took three weeks in September-October 1945 and included all evidence available in the United States, British, and French zones of occupation. His conclusion was that Hitler had committed suicide although he admitted that he had been unable to question those persons present in the bunker at the time who were later captured by the Soviets.

At about the same time that the Trevor-Roper report was issued, Detachment 1369 of the Allied Expeditionary Force Military Government received a statement from Dr. Karlheinz Spaeth vowing that he was the physician in attendance when Hitler died of wounds on May 1, 1945. According to Spaeth, he was the battalion doctor with the 2nd Battalion,

23rd Regiment, 9th Parachute Division. His unit was engaged in battle in and around Berlin. On the 1st day of May he established a collection station for wounded in a cellar of the Landswehrkasino across from the bunker at the zoo. About 3:00 P.M. he was informed that Hitler was in the area so he left the cellar to get a look at the Führer.

"The commander of the battalion, Oberstleutnant Graf von Raiffenstein, received the report from Lt. Kurt Uhlik, who was leading Company 5," Spaeth said. "I was watching as the commander and Hitler approached the tank barricade and heard him warn the Führer that they were in the line of fire of the Russian troops nearby. Hitler ignored the warning, kept walking toward the tank barricade, and was wounded."

At the time he was with a number of SS men. Spaeth was called within a few minutes back to the collecting station, where Hitler had been taken.

"A shell fragment about 10 cm long and 8-10 mm wide had pierced the uniform and went through his chest," the doctor testified in his deposition. "The fragment had damaged both lungs. I took a few first aid bandages and bandaged him. During this time Hitler groaned continuously. He was not fully conscious. To relieve his pain I got some morphine and gave him a double strength injection. A half an hour later I examined his pulse and respiration and found that his breath had stopped. Hearbeats continued for about three minutes then ceased. I pronounced the Führer dead and informed the SS leaders of this fact."

Spaeth further stated that the SS "blew Hitler's body into the air" with two three-kg. charges. Later the doctor was wounded and captured by the Russians. While in a Soviet hospital he was questioned by a Russian officer and he made a sketch of the area where, according to him, Hitler died of his wound.

This report further confused the situation. The doctor was investigated and found to be trustworthy, yet his story certainly didn't jibe with Trevor-Roper's report. When both reports were examined closely it began to dawn on the Allied officials that much of the key evidence in each was provided by SS personnel. Could the SS men be trusted? Or were they trying to glorify Hitler's death in the Spaeth report, indicating that the Führer had died a hero, fighting to the last? Or had

Hitler really escaped from Berlin with the SS covering his trail in both reports: that his body was burned or had been blown to bits? Evidence gathered during the more than three decades since the end of the war reveals that one of the last missions of the SS was to cover up what really happened to Hitler. The SS was to keep the Führer's image alive and glorified so that a new Nazi movement could be started when the time was opportune. One tack was to have reports, letters, and news items appear in various parts of the world indicating that Hitler was alive and well. For several years these accounts kept Allied investigators, German Nazi-hunters, reward-seekers, and the just plain curious busy. And the fact that there has never been any hard evidence (such as a body) presented to the world verifying Hitler's death has only accented the mystery. Even the Russian autopsy report of 1968, the supposed confirmation, has been riddled by experts.

Some of the accounts contained enough confirmable portions of what is known to have happened during those last days to require further investigation. Some were ridiculous, others puzzling, a few intriguing. When one SS officer stated during interrogation at a POW camp that he watched Hitler board an Me-109 fighter in Berlin to fly to Spain, Allied investigators didn't check with U.S. Army Air Force personnel to see if this was possible. Instead, they immediately hurried to Nuremberg to question Otto Skorzeny, Hitler's commando chief and one of the most prominent of the SS leaders captured alive. When they read the statement to him, the big German just laughed.

"That would be impossible. If our Messerschmitt planes had that long a range we would not have lost the war."

Nor could an Me-109 to which the SS prisoner was referring carry a passenger. It was a single-engine fighter that carried only the pilot.

At the same time that the Trevor-Roper and Spaeth reports were presented to the U.S. government, George Albrecht, a German prisoner of war at the POW camp at Ruston, Louisiana, decided he knew where Hitler was hiding. His deposition to the commanding officer of the camp was considered important enough to forward to the War Crimes Branch, Theater Judge Advocate, in Europe. He stated:

> Due to the fact that my home is situated between Neumünster and Kiel in Schleswig-Holstein and because I know the environs very well I want to give the following statement on Adolf Hitler's possible hiding place.
>
> On Christmas 1941 I was sitting in an inn of my hometown in Rodenbeck. A man I knew to be a well-known Nazi sat down beside me at the table. I overheard his conversation with another party member. He told his friend that his two sons were in Hitler's elite guard and that a secret radio station was located in a nearby farm. He hinted that it was a secret gathering place for high-ranking Nazis who used the radio. I think these two SS officers might have brought Hitler to this farm after the war ended.

Since it was suspected that the German prisoner who gave the deposition was a former SS member, his statement was ignored at first. However, a few days later, an article in a British newspaper explained that those officers in the British military who believed that Hitler was still alive were of the opinion that he was probably hiding in the Schleswig-Holstein area as a farm worker. Immediately U.S. intelligence agents searched the entire area for some sign of the Führer. They even checked the numerous caves in the area but they found no indication that Hitler was in that section of Germany. The search did add one more bit of confusion for the Allied investigators.

As the weeks passed in 1945, memos and telegrams were transmitted by the score as the Americans, British, French, and Russians tried to make up their minds whether Hitler was dead or alive. With Admiral Dönitz announcing Hitler's death at every opportunity, it was decided that a statement from Eisenhower should be issued to clarify the matter. A memo from Major General Clayton Bissell, assistant chief of staff of the U.S. Army, explained the predicament:

> Late Tuesday afternoon General Marshall telephoned me that he thought it might be necessary and appropriate to counter the announcements being made by Dönitz of Hitler's death in order that the Hitler martyr myth would be destroyed and to destroy any hope of the German people that there might be a split between the Russians and the Anglo-Americans. It was agreed that the best action was to prepare a message to Eisenhower to be cleared by

the President calling Eisenhower's attention to Dönitz's statements and proposing that he issue a release designed to nullify them.

Prior to receiving word from General Marshall that he should try to counter Dönitz's claims that Hitler was dead, Eisenhower had publicly stated that he believed the Führer had died in the bunker. This initial statement was based on the fact that the Russians announced they had found Hitler's charred body. When he received the memo giving him Marshall's view that Dönitz was trying to make a martyr of Hitler by proclaiming that the Führer had died a hero in the bunker, Eisenhower promptly reversed himself and stated "there is reason to believe that Hitler may still be alive." This, of course, caused a sensation when it appeared in the October 8, 1945, issue of *Stars and Stripes*. Enhancing the possibility that Hitler might have escaped from the bunker alive was a new Soviet announcement that Stalin did not think there was enough evidence to verify that the burned corpse found in the bunker area was that of Adolf Hitler.

One of those known to have been at the bunker within a few days of the end was Hanna Reitsch, the well-known female German test pilot and a close friend of Adolf Hitler. Agents from the Air Interrogation Unit of the U.S. Forces in Austria decided that she should be questioned again. They went to Leopold's Krone Castle in Salzburg to get her eyewitness account of her days in the bunker and to ask her, "Is he dead or is he not?" At the time they didn't realize that she was also a close associate of Otto Skorzeny, the SS commando chief, who was as determined as other SS members to keep the Allies in doubt about Hitler's fate. After a lengthy interrogation during which she gave the details of her adventurous flight into and out of Berlin in late April and a description of the condition of those still in the bunker at that time, she stated that the claimed possibility that Hitler was still alive was completely absurd. She maintained that the Hitler she left in the shelter was physically unable to have gotten away. "Had a path been cleared for him from the bunker to freedom he would not have had the strength to use it," she said. When she was confronted with the rumor that Hitler might still be alive in Tyrol and that her own flight to that area after she left the bunker might be more than coincidental, she was deeply upset. "Hitler is dead!" she repeated. "The man I saw in the bunker could not have lived. He had no reason to live and the tragedy was that he knew it well, knew it perhaps better than anyone else." (In 1953 she denied the validity of the information obtained from her by the interrogators.)

Shortly after the interrogation she was in contact with Skorzeny at the camp where he was prisoner. United States agents tailed her but were unable to overhear their conversation. If Skorzeny was curious about the Allied evaluation of her testimony concerning Hitler, he would have been pleased to note that the agents reported that they believed Reitsch was sincere and conscientious and had told the truth. Later, they reversed their conclusion. There were too many contradictions in her story based on evidence gathered during further investigation.

Of course, the SS had a great deal of unsolicited help in placing Hitler in various parts of the world during this postwar period, all of which aided their cause. A letter was intercepted by the Miami, Florida, District Postal Censor in 1945 that stated that Hitler was living in Argentina and gave many details about his hiding place. Norman M. Stineman of Washington, D.C., wrote to reporter Vincent de Pascal of the *Chicago Daily Times* that Hitler and hundreds of other leading Nazis were in Argentina preparing for their next onslaught against civilization. "Through the cooperation of the government officials of Argentina, these Nazis are directing the construction of great industrial plants in that country, disguised as steel mills but designed and equipped to be converted quickly to the manufacture of long-range robot bombs for the destruction of cities in the U.S. and Brazil," Stineman wrote. "Hitler is hiding in a luxurious underground retreat, built underneath a German-owned hacienda. Two doubles are with him. The body found in Berlin by the Russians is that of another double who was murdered and planted there to deceive the Allies. The hiding place is located about 675 miles west of the Brazilian port of Florianopolis and 450 miles northwest of Buenos Aires.

"The western entrance to the elevators that lead to the retreat consists of a stone wall operated by photo-electric cells that in turn are activated by code signals flashed from ordinary flashlights. The wall promptly slides to the left, permitting automobiles to enter after which the wall slides back in place."

The information in Stineman's letter was so detailed and he seemed so confident of his facts that the Federal Bureau of Investigation was asked to check. Two months later the War Department received a memo from J. Edgar Hoover, Director of the FBI, which stated, in part:

> Mr. Stineman declined to furnish the identity of the individual from whom he received the report as to Hitler's whereabouts. It has now been learned that the source was Dr. Brown Landowne, of Orlando, Florida. Dr. Landowne is a 97 year old spiritualist leader of a cult and is a spiritualist prophet. To date no serious indication has been received that Adolf Hitler is in Argentina.

That ended that investigation!

The French authorities were duped by a former SS member posing as an informant in the French zone of occupation and this incident caused ill feelings between the French and U.S. intelligence agents. In January 1946 an American counterintelligence unit received a French report stating that a resistance movement was afoot in the city of Weinheim, that propaganda posters had been posted in the city, and that Hitler was in hiding in the vicinity of Heidelberg. It was alleged that Hitler was in communication with the resistance leader in Weinheim and had visited the city disguised as an American soldier riding in a U.S. military vehicle. The French went so far as to name the resistance leader: Professor Stein, first name unknown. They stated that the meetings of the resistance movement were held in the Deutsches House on Friedrichstrasse in the city. A member of the resistance group, Friedrich Menz, supposedly knew exactly where Hitler was located. The propaganda posters mentioned by the French report advertised that Hitler was alive and would be heard shortly.

United States intelligence agents hurried to Weinheim and went directly to the Deutsches House. Kenneth L. Rosenthal and Edgar V. Thomas, the two agents in charge of the Weinheim investigation, were not happy with the results.

> Deutsches Haus and its owner, Emil Bressler, who was not a member of the Nazi party, enjoy the reputation of an honest establishment whose owner would report any illegal activities to the German police chief with whom he is personally acquainted. Surveillance of this man did not reveal him to be engaged in any activity that could be regarded as even faintly suspicious. No person fitting the alleged disguise of Hitler frequented the place.

The agents became more irritated at the French when they were unable to discover any professor by the name of Stein living in Weinheim. A dentist by that name had been a resident but was in a POW camp because he was a former SA leader and associate of Goebbels. Obviously he was in no position to lead a resistance group. When it came to Friedrich Menz, who was supposed to know Hitler's exact whereabouts, the agents realized that the French report was entirely inaccurate. Menz was anti-Nazi and had been arrested twice for criticizing the local Nazi leaders during the Third Reich. Rosenthal and Thomas were furious.

> We request that French authorities be asked to bring their informants into the open with the assurance of absolute secrecy maintained so that they can be questioned about the basis for their claims. Investigations of this type tax to the maximum the time of the limited personnel available.

When the agents' memo was brought to the attention of the French intelligence authorities, they were insulted and refused to cooperate with American intelligence any further. It was later discovered that the dentist named Stein who was in a POW camp had instigated the plot by contacting a former SS member hiding in Baden Baden who then posed as an informant and gave the "information" to the French.

Many anonymous letters were received and forwarded to the headquarters of the U.S. Forces, Europe, where it was decided whether further investigation was warranted. One such letter came from Sweden and it, too, was later traced to a former SS officer who had escaped from Germany in May 1945. This same officer went to South America the following year and helped establish a neo-Nazi organization in Argentina. In his 1946 letter from Stockholm, he wrote that if the

American authorities looked in the Bavarian mountains they would find a long cave approximately 466 meters long with more than 90 camouflaged entrances. According to the ex-SS member, Hitler was living there in a room 30 by 30 meters furnished with an electric stove and all the other comforts he had had at his Obersalzberg retreat, the Berghof. A long pipe from the top of the mountain was used to drop food and other supplies to Hitler. In addition, the Nazi treasure was supposedly hidden in the cave and the writer of the letter only wanted one sixth of this treasure when the Americans recovered it! Needless to say, this report was ignored.

Another letter, shorter and to the point, was addressed to the Commanding General, U.S. Army, Mediterranean Theater of Operations, and came from a man named Vianello (no first named listed) who resided at Via Panfilo Castaldi 19, Milan, Italy. He simply asked:

> I should like to inquire as to what reward you would give to the person who can lead you to Hitler. Write Vianello.

This short notice aroused the curiosity of U.S. intelligence agents in Italy and they visited Vianello only to discover he was only interested in whether the amount of reward offered would warrant his searching for Hitler. He knew nothing of Hitler's whereabouts.

A report by an informant to the headquarters of the CIC on October 25, 1946, concerning the disappearance of Hitler explained one of the most important reasons the SS went to such great lengths to confuse the facts about the whereabouts of the Führer. This report stated that Hitler was alive and living in the vicinity of Munich. A former member of the *Liebstandarte Adolf Hitler* supposedly was hiding Hitler and had furnished the Führer with false papers of a man killed during the war. The last paragraph of the report explained further:

> The informant stated that Hitler is very ill and is expected to die very soon. Their purpose of hiding Hitler until burial time is to show the people that Hitler was alive after the Allies had claimed him dead. In this manner, the population would become skeptical of any statements made by the Allied powers.

In 1946 the Germans, occupied by four different powers, had doubts about the veracity of each. Any confusion the SS could add would only make the task of governing the conquered nation more complex. In the case above, the CIC agents were able to refute the report, but once again a great deal of time and effort was expended in doing so.

One of the strangest postwar SS efforts on Hitler's behalf occurred in April 1947 when a letter from an SS officer named Werner Eckers was received by General Clay, Military Governor of the U.S. Zone of Occupation. Enclosed with Eckers' was a 17-page second letter purportedly written by Hitler on March 2, 1947, to President Truman. Eckers, realizing that a letter from the Führer would require additional verification, offered to personally provide further information if a notice was published in the Munich newspaper *Neue Zeitung* telling him where to meet American authorities and on the condition that he be guaranteed safe conduct.

The 17-page enclosure, according to Eckers, was dictated to him by Hitler, who lost his right arm in the battle for the Reich Chancellery. In the letter Hitler stated that after recuperating in a friendly country he had returned to Germany to help reconstruct his nation but had decided to remain silent. He stated that he felt that any active intervention by him in the affairs of occupied Germany would only drive the country into the arms of the Russians. However, he made twelve specific proposals to President Truman for German-American cooperation. United States authorities, discounting the possibility that the letter was actually written by Hitler, were nevertheless interested in the proposals since it was obvious they were being put forward by SS survivors. The list included:

1. Immediate suspension of all trials of leading National Socialist personalities.
2. Immediate amnesty for members of the corps of political NSDAP leaders and of the SA, SS, Gestapo, etc., if these men and women were members prior to April 1, 1933, or had an SS membership number below 150,000.
3. Cancellation of all verdicts and suspension of all proceedings against members of the army, the SS, the Luftwaffe, the Navy, the police force, the Security Service, etc.

4. Assurance that the Oder-Neisse line will not become the final boundary in the east and rejection of all other territorial claims.
5. Continued supply of the German people with sufficient food and raw materials until the time when it will have become able to supply itself so that the Germans will not be compelled to surrender to Bolshevism.
6. Formation of a volunteer corps composed of all old and young combatants against Bolshevism, in particular the members of the SA and SS.
7. Immediate suspension of internment and labor camps and release of those inmates who belonged previously to the NSDAP and all its branches.
8. Removal of all émigrés and all persons guilty of treason and high treason and also of all former inmates, political and criminal, of concentration camps from public positions as well as then prosecution before a new people's court.
9. Establishing of special courts to pass judgment on high officials of the National Socialistic government, of the NSDAP, armed forces, etc. who are guilty of treason against their own people, as for instance von Papen, Schacht, von Seydlitz, etc., or who used their influence to obtain benefits for themselves.
10. Quick removal of all foreigners and Jews from Germany.
11. Speedy release of all German POWs by all enemy countries.
12. Return of former German colonies, these territories to be settled by German colonists, and unrestrained emigration allowed for German men and women with their families to other European and overseas countries.

After further investigation it was recommended to the White House that no action be taken on the proposals. The information in the letter and the manner in which it was presented precluded it being from Hitler. However, the proposals in the letter were kept in mind by the American authorities as an outline of the desires of the surviving SS. The document allowed the authorities to prepare defenses against many of the subsequent actions taken by these fanatics. Yet the American government did, in practice, accede to several of the proposals, for reasons deemed to be in America's interest, before the occupation of Germany ended. It is ironic, for instance, that many former SS officers and men either avoided trial or were later released from their war crimes prison sentences because they could be useful to the United States in its containment policy against the Soviet Union. The results were those requested in the bogus-Hitler letter of 1947!

The search for Hitler, alive or dead, continued throughout the postwar years without positive results. The Germans who had been in the bunker with Hitler during the final days and who were captured by the Russians were considered the key to the puzzle, but their testimony, when it was finally obtained, did little to help. Immediately after the capture of these Nazis the Western Allies were unable to question them because the Russians refused to cooperate. Finally the U.S. Army's 7707 European Command Intelligence Center gained access to General Walter Paul Schreiber who had been appointed chief surgeon for Berlin on April 29, 1945, and who was later captured by the Soviets in the underground field hospital near the Reichstag building. Schreiber had talked with Otto Günsche, Hitler's SS adjutant, who supposedly had seen Hitler's corpse and had helped burn it. Both Günsche and Schreiber were prisoners in May 1945 at the Russian camp at Strausberg. When Schreiber asked Günsche what he knew about Hitler's suicide, the SS adjutant replied: "I did not see the dead Führer. Those things were all done without us."

Schreiber also talked with Hans Baur, Hitler's personal pilot, at Strausberg. Baur, who had been with Hitler in the bunker, said that he believed Hitler was dead but that he had not seen the body either. On May 9, in a fenced-in barracks of a POW camp near Posen, Schreiber saw Heinz Linge, Hitler's personal servant, who supposedly helped burn Hitler's body and that of Eva Braun after they committed suicide. Linge was held in the barracks next to the one occupied by Schreiber. The barbed wire fence separating the two barracks ran close to the general's window and he was able to ask questions when Linge passed by. Linge said that he did not see the dead Führer but that he did see two bodies, wrapped in carpets, being carried up the narrow winding staircase leading out of the bunker. He was later told that they were the bodies of Hitler and Eva Braun. When Linge, Günsche, and others who had been in the bunker with Hitler were finally released from Moscow's Lubianka Prison in 1956, they told substantially the same stories they had told Schreiber eleven years earlier. Their testimony did not clear up the mystery.

In an indirect way, the SS became responsible for greater use of the polygraph (lie detector). One of the first lie detectors was made in 1921 by John Larson and an improved model was put into use in 1926 by Leonarde Keeler. But it wasn't until 1945, when John Reid developed a polygraph which recorded not only blood pressure, pulse, respiration, and skin reflexes, but also muscular pressure and other changes, that the U.S. military began using it. A secret memorandum from the Office of the Provost Marshal General to the War Department Director of Intelligence, about the fate of Adolf Hitler recommended the use of the newly developed lie detector. Paragraph three of the memo states:

> There is available to the Army a means whereby the reliability of the testimony of witnesses can be tested with a high degree of accuracy. The polygraph, under the hands of a competent, trained operator, has been used with astonishingly good results in the criminal investigation activities of the Army not only in the Zone of the Interior but in Europe and the Far East. It has been utilized to screen thousands of prisoners of war to determine the extent of their Nazi tendencies. Should it be desired to determine the reliability of the testimony of witnesses in the Hitler enigma it can be done simply and expeditiously by requiring them to submit to a polygraph examination.

How many witnesses were given lie detector tests is unknown but it is undoubtedly a large number. Many were subjected to the test against their will. Even this new instrument, however, didn't settle the question of what happened to Adolf Hitler. In 1953, eight years after the respected Trevor-Roper report was "accepted" as the official version of Hitler's last days, Hitler still had not been declared officially dead. On February 24, 1953, the German Foreign Office addressed a letter to the Secretary General of the Allied High Commission stating:

> Sir:
> I have the honor to inform you as follows: upon application the local court in Berchtesgaden has instituted public proceedings for the purpose of issuing a declaration certifying the death of Adolf

> Hitler. Investigations made so far show that the death of Adolf Hitler had not been registered with either the Registrar's Office of Greater Berlin, Berlin N 54 Ruckerstrasse 9 or the Registrar's Office in Berlin-Halensee. Albrecht-Achillesstrasse 65/66. Furthermore, there is no entry in the records kept on declarations of death.

The German Foreign Office requested all Allied records pertaining to the death of Adolf Hitler. Then, in 1968, 23 years after the end of the Third Reich, the Soviets suddenly decided that their first version of Hitler's death, announced in 1945 and then repudiated shortly afterwards, was correct. To prove it they published an autopsy report. The body that had been first identified as Hitler's and then dismissed as the body of an SS soldier who had been in the bunker at the time was once again designated in the official Soviet record as that of the Führer. There was no way the Russian report could be verified since they had cremated the remains on May 15, 1945, and scattered the ashes across the countryside. Western records, however, varied greatly from the findings of the Soviets: U.S. and British investigations indicated that Hitler had taken poison *and* shot himself but the Soviets said that the corpse had no bullet hole in it; the German medical records found by the Allies indicated that Hitler had normal testicles; the Soviets said one testicle was missing. The Soviets based their decision primarily on Hitler's dental record but those records, prepared by Dr. Hugo Blaschke, had been available for years. So the 1968 Soviet report only added to the confusion.

Is Hitler dead or alive? Did he escape from Berlin to live out his life in South America? Did he die in the bunker in April 1945 with his mistress Eva Braun at his side? Since there is no body, no grave, and no verification of his death except statements from witnesses who don't agree with each other, there will always be doubt that he committed suicide. Since he's not been seen alive since 1945, there is also doubt that he survived the bunker. If anybody knows the truth it is likely to be some of the surviving members of the SS—and they aren't talking.

15

American Secret Alliance with the SS

The end of the war and the collapse of the Third Reich revealed the horror wrought by the SS under Hitler. The world was shocked as reports of the Holocaust became known and photographs were published of the victims found in the concentration and death camps of Europe. The entire SS organization became a target for Allied investigators seeking war criminals and at Nuremberg, where the war crimes tribunal met, the SS was officially declared a criminal organization. SS members were even shunned by many German citizens who had helplessly observed their actions during the years of Nazi power but who had been unable to interfere without jeopardizing their own lives. Everywhere the SS was undoubtedly the most hated of Nazi organizations, and public feeling in the United States was no exception. There was an outcry for their "heads." In a freedom-loving country, the deeds of the SS were considered so horrendous that death to the perpetrators seemed the only answer. American government officials agreed—at least publicly.

Eisenhower's proclamation to the Germans set the tone for the Americans in their occupation zone: "We shall obliterate Nazism and German militarism. We shall overthrow the Nazi rule, dissolve the Nazi party, and abolish the cruel, oppressive, and discriminatory laws and institutions which the party has created." To follow these guidelines, the Americans, through the U.S. military government, decided that they would denazify the 13 million surviving German adults in their zone. Under the watchful eye of Colonel Orlando Wilson, commander of the Public Safety Branch of the Office of Military Government, the Germans were ordered to complete a detailed questionnaire disclosing all aspects of their life during the Third Reich. Long prison terms were threatened to those Germans who didn't fill out the questionnaire fully and truthfully. The American counterintelligence corps, using the Nazi files found in the Brown House in Munich, checked the questionnaires to make certain that the answers were correct. Five major categories were defined and each German was placed in one of the five. They were: major offenders, offenders, lesser offenders, followers, and exonerated.

The plan seemed simple and workable. It proved complex and unworkable. After the questionnaires were scrutinized, it was discovered that there were nearly 4 million Germans in the American zone alone in the categories requiring trials! There were not nearly enough American personnel in Germany to handle that many cases. A rough estimate indicated that it would take more than eight years to complete the trials. American officials also came to conclude that the denazification program had many failings, and that if zealously pushed could do more harm to American interests than was at first understood. They began to realize that all Nazi party members did not join for the same reason. Some joined under pressure to keep their jobs, others because they believed in the party's aims. Many wealthy persons contributed large sums to the party and helped it grow, but never became members. And as the relationship between the United States and the Soviet Union deteriorated during the postwar years, many of the "war criminals" identified under the American denazification program became more and more valuable to the U.S. facing all these problems, American officials decided that they would solve the sticky problem by turning the entire denazification program over to the Germans.

On June 1, 1946, all denazification trials became the responsibility of the Germans. Immediately there were two important results: The United States was relieved of the responsibility for passing judgment on the indicted Germans, and it became very obvious that the German judges were not going to be as severe as the Americans had first intended to be when the program began. Enough time had already passed that the average German citizen felt safe in deciding not to testify against other Germans; they preferred not to be seen as traitors. In fact, most of the Germans considered admitting that they had played a minor role in the Nazi party, proof that they had been loyal to their country! By right, the American officials should have been angry and disillusioned by the debasement of the process and should perhaps have reclaimed the denazification program from the Germans. But the world situation was such at the time that they were more pleased than disappointed. There was not a word of criticism when the Germans freed General Franz Halder, Hitler's army chief of staff; Edward Jadamczik, former Gestapo chief in East Prussia; Gunther Reinecke, chief SS judge; and Hugo Stinnes, the Ruhr steel and coal industrialist; and when the courts classified Karol Baron von Eberstein, an SS general, a minor offender. Others who received light or no sentences were Heinrich Morgan, deputy SS judge (exonerated); SS General Felix Steiner (minor offender); SS General Wilhelm Brückner (three-year sentences); SS Brigadier Alexander von Dornberg (exonerated); and Kurt Schmitt (minor offender).

Why didn't the United States complain about the verdicts of the German denazification courts? The ever-growing conflict between the United States and Russia was causing great concern in Washington. The huge American military force that had played an important role in the defeat of Nazi Germany had been demobilized and only a small U.S. military establishment remained in Germany. Washington had believed that Russia, too, intended to demobilize. Instead, Stalin had enlarged his military force in eastern Europe and gave evidence of intending to move into western Europe if the Western Allies showed any weakness. With their military strength at a minimum, American officials realized that the situation was critical. It was at this time that a subtle change in the official U.S. attitude toward the SS "war criminals" took place. It was decided that the SS members who had been active on the eastern front and were knowledgeable about the Soviets and their tactics could be of help. When the Soviets seized Czechoslovakia and established the Berlin blockade, the public outcry against the SS acts during the Third Reich was ignored by the American officials and a secret alliance between the United States and the SS was instigated.

One of the first high-ranking SS officers contacted was Otto Skorzeny, who was in a detention camp at Dachau. Skorzeny had been cleared by an American tribunal of any war crimes, but the German denazification court wanted to try him. United States officials were confident that the Germans would free him, too, but when the denazification trial was postponed seven times under pressure from Communist groups in the American zone so that Czechoslovakia could prepare a request to have Skorzeny extradited to their country for trial, the matter came to a head. The American counterintelligence agency tipped off Skorzeny that they could delay the extradition request for a few weeks with paperwork; after that, if he was still in the camp, there was little hope of keeping him from Soviet-dominated authorities in Czechoslovakia. The Americans arranged for him to be transferred to Darmstadt where, with the help of some SS comrades who had still not been arrested, Skorzeny escaped on July 27, 1948. The escape was well planned. An automobile with American military license plates and carrying three men wearing U.S. military police uniforms arrived at the Darmstadt prison main gate early in the afternoon. One of the occupants, disguised as a captain, announced to the guards at the camp that they had arrived to take Otto Skorzeny to Nuremberg for a scheduled hearing. Showing forged documents to the guard, the "captain" insisted he must get the prisoner immediately so that he could get back to Nuremberg before nightfall. The guard, convinced he was doing his duty, turned Skorzeny over to the trio and they got into the car. That was the last time Skorzeny was in prison.

Did the Americans help Skorzeny's escape? The Soviet authorities were convinced that they did and were furious. One Russian report stated that Skorzeny had been flown to the United States, where he was being interrogated about his knowledge of Russian military forces. Washington vehemently denied the report and stated that American investigators were searching throughout Europe for the elusive Skorzeny. Questioned in later years about the escape, Skorzeny just laughed. "The uniforms were provided by the Americans," was all he would say, referring to the military police uniforms worn by the trio that picked him up at the Darmstadt prison camp.

If the Americans help Skorzeny escape as the Soviets charged, what was the reason? Even among U.S. military authorities in Europe at the time there was confusion and mistrust. When the G-2 section of the U.S. Army in Europe heard rumors that Skorzeny was working very closely with U.S. counterintelligence in thwarting Soviet aggression, the assistant chief of staff immediately sent a query to the 66th Counter Intelligence Corps Group. The reply was "double-talk" at a high level. One paragraph stated: "In view of his past as well as the notoriety received by Skorzeny in the press during past years, it is felt that any open sponsorship or support by the U.S. government on behalf of Skorzeny would probably expose the U.S. government to extreme international embarrassment. However, the possibility exists that Skorzeny has been and is being utilized by U.S. intelligence."

In a later letter, the 66th CIC reported that Skorzeny was not a source or contact for their organization but admitted that they knew his whereabouts. There is no question that Skorzeny was used by various U.S. agencies and military units during this period. The confusion arises because of lack of communication and the adherence to strict secrecy by each of the U.S. organizations hiring Skorzeny. Each was fearful that if the American public discovered that they were collaborating with a former SS officer, the resultant publicity would be detrimental to their organization. CIC agents, for example, still suspected that he had aided several high-ranking Nazis to escape from Germany during the last days of the Third Reich, perhaps even Hitler as had been rumored. They wanted Skorzeny out of prison so they could follow him in hopes he could lead them to Bormann, Fegelein, Hitler, or others of prominence. He didn't.

They did discover, however, that Skorzeny and his SS comrades had an efficient escape route out of Germany and an organization to administer it. *Die Spinne* (The Spider) was organized by Skorzeny and other SS members long before he escaped from Darmstadt. As one U.S. intelligence report stated: "The leader of this movement is Otto Skorzeny, who is directing this movement out of Dachau. The Polish guards are helping the men that receive orders from Skorzeny." *Die Spinne* established a route of "safe houses" between Germany and Italy, starting from Stuttgart, Munich, Frankfurt, or Bremen. From any of these cities the SS members traveled to Memmingen in the Algäu section of Bavaria. From there two routes took the men south to Italy, one going through Bergenz, Austria, and the other through Switzerland. Rome and Genoa were the destinations. It took the CIC considerably longer to learn, however, that most of the drivers of the trucks delivering the popular American army newspaper *The Stars and Stripes* were *Spinne* members and that behind the bundles of newspapers were one or more other SS members en route to Italy. The U.S. military police never checked these trucks. Working with Skorzeny in *Die Spinne* were SS Captain Franz Röstel, Hermann Lauterbacher of Himmler's staff, Hasso von Manteuffel, and Helmut Beck, among others.

Despite their knowledge of *Die Spinne* and the escape route, American authorities did nothing to stop the exodus of SS members. By this time the Korean conflict was under way and the United States was concerned about what other action the Communists might take in other parts of the world. Many political and military officials thought that Korea was merely a ploy to attract attention while lulling the U.S. asleep in western Europe and to draw further troops from the already weak American occupation forces in Germany. The ultimate aim of the Communists, according to these analysts, was to move into western Europe and control all of Germany. Skorzeny, understanding the situation clearly, made an offer to the Americans. He was in contact with most of the German generals who had survived the war, knew where the SS officers who escaped the Allies were located, and had a long list of ex-Wehrmacht and SS soldiers, including his former commandos, who were ready and willing to help the United States against the Russians. He vowed that he could organize four or five divisions of veterans who had fought against the Soviets during World War II and have them ready to defend western Europe or to be transferred to Korea within a short time, if the U.S. agreed and provided the necessary funds. It was a tempting offer and one that the American authorities seriously considered during the critical period of the Korean conflict.

By this time Skorzeny had set up an "engineering" office in Madrid under the protection of dictator Generalissimo Francisco Franco, whose brother-in-law Skorzeny had saved during the Nazi period. Actually he was coordinating *Die Spinne* activities from the office as well as handling illegal arms sales. He also managed to close a deal between Germany and Spain for the delivery of railway stock and machine tools, a deal made possible through his SS and German industrialist connections. His commission earned Skorzeny additional wealth beyond his share of the booty he'd gotten out of Germany at the end of the war. When it became obvious that the Communists were not going to use direct military force to take over all of Germany during the Korean conflict, Skorzeny's proposal to gather a new SS army was refused. But the United States government still had use for Skorzeny and his SS comrades.

As the Korean War continued it became evident to American strategists that Germany's industrial might, especially its steel-producing potential, could be vitally important to the Allies. The United States had limited West Germany to no more than 11 million tons of steel production annually, but as Peking entered the Korean War this limit was immediately rescinded. But the question of how to *quickly* increase that steel production for weapons to defend Western Europe puzzled American officials until it was suggested by Skorzeny and other Germans that the industrial barons who had been sentenced to jail as war criminals were needed. The most prominent of these was Alfried Krupp, of the Krupp arms dynasty. Krupp had joined the SS in the summer of 1931 while still a civil engineering student at Aachen Technical College, and eventually reached the rank of colonel. During these years the Krupp factories perfected the Panzers and designed and built other weapons for Hitler. During the Third Reich the Krupps controlled one hundred thirty-eight private concentration camps where slave labor was kept. At Nuremberg in 1948 Alfried Krupp was found guilty of war crimes and sentenced to 12 years in prison. All his property, including the factories, was ordered confiscated. This was the man that Hitler's commando chief suggested should be released from prison, given back his industrial and personal property, and permitted to rebuild his armaments dynasty. To the American public this would have seemed heresy—but the public was not aware of what was going on at the office of the new high commissioner of the U.S. zone of occupation.

John J. McCloy, the new high commissioner, was concerned about two matters: the Korean conflict and the possibility of Soviet aggression in Western Europe; and, second, the fate of the Germans sentenced to prison by the tribunal at Nuremberg. In an effort to arrange German help for the defense of Western Europe, he permitted Krupp to hold meetings in prison with his former board of directors and legal staff in order to discuss the reopening of the Krupp plants if permission to do so was granted. McCloy then established a panel under the chairmanship of David W. Peck, presiding justice of the New York Supreme Court, to review the sentences of the Nazis sentenced by U.S. tribunals. The two initiatives merged on January 31, 1951, when McCloy signed two documents: one releasing Krupp from prison, the other restoring his property to him. The SS had won another battle, a postwar battle where the odds had appeared unbeatable. Krupp soon had his dynasty back in operation and within a matter of months was producing 18 million tons of steel. This steel was of great value to the United States during the Korean crisis since the nation's mills could not provide enough steel for the defense of both western Europe and Korea.

Skorzeny was later revealed to be Krupp's representative in Argentina, verification that the SS influence had certainly not died with the end of the Third Reich. Far from it. After the United States "suggested" that West Germany rearm and join NATO, many German generals resumed important positions in the new military force. However, because of fear of public reaction both in Germany and in the U.S., prominent SS officers played a minor role at the beginning, seeking positions outside Germany. Men such as former SS Lieutenant General Wilhelm Farmbacher; Leopold Gleim, chief of Hitler's personal guard; Joachim Daemling, former chief of the Gestapo in Düsseldorf; Dr. Hans Eisele, Buchenwald's chief physician; and Heinrich Willermann, the SS doctor at Dachau; went to Egypt at the request of the U.S. to help build up Gamal Abdel Nasser's security forces. Skorzeny spent time in Argentina as well as Egypt helping organize pseudo-SS forces for these countries. By 1953, 101 prisoners had been released from prison under the McCloy-Peck sentence review procedure, so many that Eleanor Roosevelt, the ex-president's wife, demanded an explanation from the high commissioner. McCloy merely said that he considered it a fundamental principle of American justice that accused persons have a final right to be heard. He didn't mention that his predecessor, General Lucius Clay, had already had each case reviewed. Nor did he mention the real reason that Krupp and a host of other Nazis were being released—to work with and for the United States.

Germans not as well known to the public as Krupp were released from prison for a reason which was even more secret. Wilhelm Hoettl, an SS officer who worked with Ernst Kaltenbrunner, chief of the SD who was sentenced to hang at Nuremberg: Gerhard Pinckert, a member of a terrorist group commanded by Skorzeny; Alfred Benzinger of the Secret Field Police; Fritz Schmidt, Gestapo chief at Kiel; and other SS officers were quietly discharged from Landsberg and other prisons or the indictments pending against them were dropped. Most of them disappeared from sight under assumed names but they definitely did not go into hiding. They became secret intelligence agents for the U.S., first for the military forces, later for the newly formed Central Intelligence Agency. Of all the strange alliances between the Nazis and the U.S. during the postwar years, this was the most secret.

The idea for the alliance actually began in 1944 when Hitler's chief intelligence officer on the eastern front, Reinhard Gehlen, came into disfavor with the Führer. At the time Gehlen was chief of Foreign Armies East and greatly respected by General Heinz Guderian, his superior officer. When Gehlen reported to Guderian that the Russians were planning a huge winter offensive and warned that the attack would crush the Nazi armies in the east, Guderian had him repeat the prediction to Hitler personally. The Führer raged that Gehlen's report was wrong and that he should be sent to a lunatic asylum. Guderian, angry, vowed that he, too, would go. Both men were subsequently relieved of duty by Hitler but not before Gehlen had decided that the war was lost. Convinced of this, he made plans to protect himself and his staff after the surrender he knew would come. At the same time, he planned to lay the groundwork for the rebuilding of Germany. His plan was simple. He made copies of all his important documents dealing with intelligence work on the eastern front, put the copies into 50 steel cases, and buried them in the Bavarian mountains. He was aware that the U.S. had no intelligence organization operating behind Russian lines because the Soviet Union was an ally. He was convinced, just as Hitler was, that the United States and the Soviet Union would not remain allies long after the end of World War II, that the two nations would eventually fight each other over the control of Europe.

Gehlen and a skeleton staff of his Foreign Armies East hid out in the Bavarian mountains after the war ended until they could surrender to the American troops in the area. When Gehlen walked into the U.S. Army headquarters in Fischausen in May 1945 and announced who he was, he expected to be treated as a VIP prisoner. Instead he was sent to a prison at Miesbach and ignored. It wasn't until Soviet agents came to the American zone asking for him by name that the American officials paid any attention to Gehlen. It was then that they discovered that Gehlen knew a great deal about the Soviet forces, and that he had voluminous files detailing their disposition, organization, and leadership. By this time it was becoming more and more evident to the Americans that the Russians, instead of cooperating with the Western Allies in the difficult problem of governing the large areas of Europe that had been liberated from the Nazis, were determined to seize control of as much of that territory as possible. Not only did the United States find itself vulnerable because of its military demobilization but because it had no intelligence operation. The Office of Strategic Services (OSS) had been disbanded under orders from President Truman and as yet no other organization had been established to replace it.

So when the Russians showed an interest in Gehlen and demanded that he be turned over to them, General Edwin Luther Sibert, G-2 of 12th Army Group, interrogated Gehlen. When the German general offered to place himself, his Foreign Armies East staff, and his intelligence files at the disposal of the United States under certain conditions, Sibert immediately notified General Walter Bedell Smith, Eisenhower's chief of staff. The offer was tempting, but once again the thought of collaborating with Nazi officers so soon after the end of the war and the realization of the public outcry that would provoke if such a collaboration were discovered, made the two men hesitate. Finally Smith decided that Washington should make the decision. Gehlen and three of his officers were flown to the United States in Smith's plane.

Even in Washington the decision was not quick. It took nearly a year before Allen Dulles, formerly the station agent for the OSS in Switzerland; Loftus Becker; Dr. Sherman Kent; General Lucius Clay; J. Edgar Hoover; and the others decided that it would be in the best interests of the United States to take Gehlen up on his offer. Moral considerations would have to take a back seat, and they so advised the Pentagon.

One of the restrictions placed on the German general, however, was that he would not use SS men in his operation. Gehlen was based at Pullach, a small town south of Munich, and he immediately began rebuilding his intelligence organization by reestablishing his network of agents in the Soviet zone of occupation and in the Soviet Union itself. Without the knowledge of Sibert and Smith initially, Gehlen combed the American prison camps for former German intelligence agents and managed to have them released so they could join his organization. Among these agents were many SS men. By the time the Americans discovered that Gehlen had duped them it was too late. The American intelligence chiefs had become too dependent upon his organization for information about the Soviets to disown it. After the CIA was formed in 1947, the Gehlen group joined it as the Soviet intelligence arm and worked with the CIA until 1956 when the organization transferred to the new West German government as its intelligence section.

So within months after the public learned about the SS atrocities and the worldwide condemnation of that hated organization, the United States was actively collaborating with surviving SS members in a number of ways. This was one of the most closely guarded secrets shared by the SS and the United States government following the war.

16

South American Reich

When the prominent Chilean exile, Orlando Letelier, was brutally assassinated in Washington, D.C., in September 1976, few investigators of the crime gave a thought to Hitler's SS at the time. When the American expatriate Michael Vernon Townley testified that he had wired Letelier's car with explosives on orders from the chief of Chile's secret police, General Juan Manuel Contreras, the assassination became a political bombshell in the United States. President Carter demanded that Contreras be extradited to the United States to stand trial and when Chilean President Augusto Pinochet refused, the U.S. ambassador to Chile was recalled, pushing relations with Chile nearly to the breaking point. However, the CIA, FBI, and investigative agencies of other countries, as they delved deeper into the murder of Letelier, traced the plot back to a secret organization in South America called Operation Condor.

Operation Condor, they discovered, is an intelligence gathering organization that concentrates on leftists around the world and especially those who are exiled from any of Condor's member countries—Argentina, Brazil, Bolivia, Uruguay, and Paraguay. According to a top secret report issued by the Senate Foreign Relations Committee, Condor has special teams assigned to travel anywhere in the world to assassinate persons on the Condor "hit list." It was then learned through further investigation that the headquarters of Condor was in Chile and the organization worked very closely with the DINA, the Chilean secret police headed by Contreras. The trial then led to an enclave deep in the foothills of the Chilean Andes south of Santiago, an enclave known only as "the Colony" to outsiders but officially named Colonia Dignidad (Noble Colony) by the Chilean government. Regardless of what name it is called, the secret colony is actually a Nazi stronghold that is protected by the Chilean government and which works very closely with the DINA. Informed sources within the Chilean government state that one of the responsibilities of the ex-Gestapo and ex-SS officers at Colonia Dignidad is to demonstrate Nazi torture methods for the Chilean secret police and to instruct the DINA in such brutality. These sources verified that there is a detention camp for Chilean political prisoners within the colony.

Colonia Dignidad was established in Chile in 1961 by German ex-Luftwaffe officer Paul Shaeffer. He began his organization shortly after World War II in Holporf, Germany, then moved it to Sieburg, a town near Bonn. Shaeffer guaranteed the defeated German citizens both the spiritual and material needs they craved during these harsh postwar years. He also promised anonymity to those Germans who joined his group. This was a powerful lure for many of the SS men on the run from Allied investigators. They quickly joined Shaeffer and when he moved the entire organization from Germany to Chile in 1961, his SS membership was pleased since South America was known to be a safe haven for unreconstructed Nazis. The reason for the move to Chile has never been verified but it is thought that Shaeffer was guaranteed complete independence for his colony by the Chilean government. In return Schaeffer's SS men were to train the Chilean secret police. During this same period ex-SS officers and German military personnel were being hired by Argentina, Egypt, and many other countries for the same purpose. Whether or not Skorzeny had a hand in the Colonia Dignidad affair remains a secret. His other such activities elsewhere, however, suggest that he probably did help Shaeffer set up the deal with the Chilean government.

According to one investigator, Charles A. Krause, it is not even permissible to take a photograph of the front gate of the enclave. "I was threatened with arrest by police who finally took from me an undeveloped roll of film with pictures of

Dignidad's entrance, taken from outside its gates. The police, who wore no identification badges, would only say that they were from Parral, about 20 miles to the west, and that they were acting on orders from Santiago."

He did learn that the colony has its own airstrip, its own fleet of aircraft, and a private communications system. The elaborate communications system permits Shaeffer and his colleagues to keep in radio contact with a "mother house" in Sieburg and with a mansion in Santiago that is filled with modern electronic communications equipment. The entire 15,000-acre enclave is enclosed by a high barbed wire fence and citizens of the area say it is the place where "nobody comes and nobody goes." The proximity of the Argentine border and the private airstrip and fleet of planes makes it easy for inhabitants of the colony to leave and return without any normal customs formalities. It makes an ideal secret hideout for Nazis on the run. Both the CIA and Simon Wiesenthal, the famed Nazi-hunter, state they have evidence that such fugitives as Dr. Josef Mengele, the Third Reich's "Angel of Death," have spent time at Colonia Dignidad. There is also evidence that Shaeffer is in contact with pro-Nazi groups around the world and that large amounts of money are sent to Colonia Dignidad each year by such groups.

The saying that "nobody comes and nobody goes" at Colonia Dignidad applies only to the regular members of the enclave, not the leaders. When called upon, the ex-SS men of the colony are not reluctant to go any place in the world to help their former SS and Nazi comrades. One such mission in 1977 nearly brought down the government of Italy. Herbert Kappler, a former SS colonel who was serving a life sentence for ordering the execution of 335 Italian civilians in German-occupied Rome in 1944, appealed for release from prison thirty-three years later for humanitarian reasons. He had been hospitalized for several months for the treatment of stomach cancer. His appeal, however, was turned down by the highest court in Italy, so the fraternity of ex-SS men decided to take matters into their own hands. According to the periodical *Bild am Sonntag* of Bonn, there is no doubt about who was involved. "The flight was planned and prepared by former members of the SS. One of them was an officer of the SS Security Service in Rome during the war." Three of the ex-SS officers involved in the escape came from Colonia Dignidad.

It was a bizarre plan, one that reminded the Italians of Skorzeny's commando missions during the war. This one couldn't be blamed on him, however, since he had died of cancer two years earlier. Kappler's wife, Anneliese, visited his room on August 15 as she did almost every day. Kappler was on the fourth floor of the military hospital in Rome and Anneliese explained to the guards that she had a large suitcase with her to take home Kappler's dirty clothes. She stayed with her husband until 1:00 A.M. and when she left the hospital room she was dragging the heavy suitcase. One of the guards offered to help her but she refused, saying that a friend would meet her on the first floor to carry the suitcase. When she stepped from the elevator on the ground floor, two men were waiting. One seized the suitcase and hurried toward the red Fiat waiting outside. The other took Kappler's wife's arm and led her to the car. A third man was behind the wheel. As soon as the suitcase was placed in the trunk of the Fiat and everyone was in the car, the driver raced the engine and drove out of the hospital parking lot. Upstairs on the fourth floor, the guards kept checking through a peephole in the door of Kappler's hospital room to make certain he was in bed. They didn't realize until morning that they were watching a dummy made from pillows. Kappler, shriveled to less than 100 pounds by his long illness, had been carried from the hospital in the suitcase!

Kappler was never taken back into custody. It was believed he was hiding in Soltau in north Germany where Anneliese Kappler's father had been a prominent Nazi leader, but Kappler was never located. The ex-SS members who aided in Kappler's escape knew that the federal constitution of West Germany bars any extradition of Germans to foreign nations so that even if Kappler had been found he would not have been sent back to Italy. The uproar over Kappler's escape created so much criticism that it appeared for a time that the Italian government would fall. Fully 32 years after the end of the war Hitler's elite SS had put a democratically elected European government in jeopardy.

The charge by Simon Wiesenthal that Josef Mengele had spent time at Shaeffer's Colonia Dignidad in Chile in 1979 is another indication of the powerful protection afforded this Nazi enclave by the Chilean government. Mengele earned the title of "Angel of Death" because he was the doctor who decided who would die in the gas chambers at Auschwitz. Standing inside the main gate of the death camp in his elegant parade uniform, he would await the trains bringing the victims. With a quick little move of his hand he conducted the selections—to one side for immediate death or to the other side for slow death by torture, malnutrition, or disease. Mengele also conducted hideous medical experiments on death camp inmates. He would quite often visit the children's barracks, for instance, and test various poisons on selected victims. Sometimes he would perform bizarre operations. Witnesses testified after the war that they saw him throw newborn Jewish infants into a fire, split the skulls of teenagers with a cleaver, torture women through their genitals, inject blinding drugs into gypsies in an effort to change their dark eyes to blue, use hunchbacks and midgets for brutal research. When the war ended, Mengele slipped away to Günzburg in Bavaria where his wealthy family owns a farm equipment plant. He stayed there until 1949, when legal authorities learned of his whereabouts, but before they could arrest him he was gone. Skorzeny made certain of that. He led the SS doctor from one safe house to another along the *Spinne* escape route until he was safely established in Argentina.

Since that time Mengele has been sought by Nazi-hunters from all over the world. When the Israelis kidnapped Adolf Eichmann in Argentina in 1960, they tried to get Mengele, too, but he was forewarned and slipped out of their net. For years he has been reported living in Paraguay. Wiesenthal says Mengele has a villa in San Antonio and a home in Puerto Stroessner, a town located at the confluence of the Paraná and Igaçu rivers. He travels throughout Paraguay in a black Mercedes 280SL accompanied by four ex-SS men who act as his bodyguards. Persons who knew him in Germany during the Third Reich have seen him in the German club in Asunción and other local bars. Yet no one can bring him back to Germany to stand trial for his atrocities. Why? Mainly because of *Die Spinne* protection and money. Paraguay's President Alfredo Stroessner, a man of German descent and totalitarian sympathies, refuses to extradite Mengele and prohibits foreigners from entering his country seeking Mengele. His official position is that Mengele "formerly lived in Paraguay but left the country years ago." In 1979 a group of 57 members of the U.S. House of Representatives wrote to President Stroessner that if he did not extradite Mengele they would vote to end all American economic aid to Paraguay. At about the same time Wiesenthal announced a $50,000 reward for information leading to Mengele's arrest.

These two actions forced Mengele to find a safer haven for a few months, so he was picked up by one of the aircraft from Colonia Dignidad in Chile and flown back to the colony. While the SS doctor was at the Nazi enclave in Chile, Paraguay, under pressure from the United States, revoked his citizenship. Yet this made very little difference in his status. Stroessner still protects Mengele as always and the United States still gives economic aid to Paraguay. In fact, this aid was increased by nearly $6 million in 1979 over 1978. So far *Die Spinne* has proven much more powerful than the United States, Israel, or any other country seeking Mengele. And instead of feeling contrite over his past actions, reports indicate that Mengele today is serving as an advisor to the Paraguayan police who are reducing the Aché Indians of the remote Chaco region to slave labor. As one high Paraguayan police officer remarked: "We are using German methods in dealing with the Indians."

In contrast to the secrecy of Colonia Dignidad, other Nazi activities in Chile are much more public. A political party headed by Franz Pfeiffer openly featured swastikas, stormtroopers in uniform, and Nazi banners. In 1968 they selected a "Miss Nazi World" and the pageant was publicized throughout South America. There is also a Chilean organization known as *Das Reich*, which is composed of German ex-military men who served in World War II. According to Dr. Michael Bar-Zohar, an expert on Nazi war criminals, *Das Reich* has a definite aim. "It is a group for mutual aid and defense against the Nuremberg convictions. Its members include all the war criminals sentenced in their absence, not only leading Nazis and those who have become powerful in their countries of refuge, but also the little men: hotelkeepers, tradesmen, farmers, and the like. All have in common the determination never to serve the sentences awaiting them in Europe."

Because of *Das Reich*, Simon Wiesenthal gave up hope of ever getting Walter Rauff, one of the innovators of Hitler's gas chambers, extradited from Chile. He had located Rauff living in Punta Arenas running a thriving import-export business. When Salvador Allende, an extreme leftist, was elected president of the country, he vowed to wipe out the right-wing Nazi-Fascist elements within Chile, but he discovered even as the highest official in the country, he didn't have that power. As Oswaldo Pascual Gonzales of the Alien Police of Chile said: "The Germans are the best organized, closest knit, most efficient colony of foreign-born citizens and aliens in this country. They have a finger in every pie. We have to treat them with kid gloves. They are the untouchables."

After a short time in office, Allende answered Wiesenthal's request to have Rauff extradited by saying he could not get the law changed that prohibited such an extradition and he did not intend to break the law. Rauff's expensive defense costs were paid by *Das Reich.*

Chile was an excellent haven for Nazis on the run but Argentina, while the Peróns were in power, was the real headquarters for the prominent Third Reich criminals. Juan Domingo Perón was a forty-six-year-old colonel in the Argentine army in 1941 when he met the beautiful actress Eva Duarte, who promptly became his mistress. She was ambitious and intelligent; he was adventurous and influential with a group of reactionary army officers. He was also very sympathetic to the Nazi regime, provided security for Hitler's spies in neutral Argentina, and as Bormann discovered, Perón was willing to conceal for him millions in Nazi party funds. When the Third Reich was crushed in 1945, Perón's view did not change. As a U.S. report stated in 1945:

> Nazi leaders, groups, and organizations have combined with Argentine totalitarian groups to create a Nazi-Fascist state. By its brutal use of force and terrorist methods to strike down all opposition from the Argentine people, the military regime has made a mockery of its pledge to the United Nations to reaffirm faith in human rights, and in the dignity and worth of the human person.

Despite this criticism, Juan Perón became president of Argentina in 1946 and the Nazis in the country heaved a sigh of relief. Within the next few years *Die Spinne* guided hundreds of Nazi fugitives to safe haven in Argentina. Among those reported in Argentina at various times during this Perón period were Bormann, Fegelein, Eichmann, Heinrich Müller, Mengele and, of course, even Hitler himself. Since Nazi-hunters were harassed and thrown out of the country when discovered, hard proof of their presence in Argentina was impossible to obtain. However, in 1960, the world was shocked to learn that Adolf Eichmann, the top administrator of the Final Solution, had been living in Argentina since 1952 protected by Perón and his successors. After eight years of trying to get him out of the country and to Israel for trial, the Israelis had recourse to a James Bond-style kidnapping. Eichmann at the time was working at the Mercedes-Benz plant at Suarez on the outskirts of Buenos Aires and living in an apartment. Later he moved his family to a house in the suburb called San Fernando and it was from this residence on Calle Garibaldi that he was seized and taken to Israel.

The apprehension of Eichmann in Argentina was a success, but despite the fact that he had sent millions to their deaths, the kidnapping caused worldwide controversy. Eichmann was the model SS officer: loyal, ruthless, unemotional. He had been directly responsible for more deaths than any other officer of the Reich although, of course, his orders came down the line from Hitler and Himmler. Yet many persons, including the respected historian Hannah Arendt, did not believe that Eichmann should be tried. After all, they felt, he was taking orders from his superiors. Judge Musmanno, who had tried the *Einsatzgruppen* killers at Nuremberg, favored the trial and was one of the main witnesses against Eichmann when the mass murderer was brought before the Israeli court in 1961. Even Musmanno's testimony was objected to by Dr. Robert Servatius, Eichmann's defense attorney, because the respected jurist was an Italian, not a Jew. *Die Spinne*, *Das Reich*, and other pro-Nazi organizations and individuals did their best to save Eichmann but this time they were defeated. He was found guilty on all 15 counts which included crimes against humanity, crimes against the Jewish people, war crimes, and membership in Nazi organizations, and he was sentenced to death by hanging. During the trial the judges had followed Musmanno's "Penguin Rule" of the earlier *Einsatzgruppen* trial (Musmanno had said the defense can introduce any evidence short of describing the lives of penguins in the Antarctic) but the 1,350,000 words of testimony couldn't save Eichmann. He went to his death in 1962 proclaiming: "Long live Germany. Long live Argentina. Long live Austria. I had to obey the rules of war and my flag. I am ready."

Judge Musmanno saw the Eichmann trial and its verdict as likely to have an important influence on future international law. "Law is built upon precedent. This is the first trial on the crime of genocide since the United Nations outlawed genocide and proclaimed it an offense against humanity and an offense against the law of all nations. This case will establish that a person charged with genocide can be tried anywhere, regardless of the manner in which he was taken into custody. This precedent will have, I think, a salubrious effect on contemporary events. We know that there are those who have attempted and would still attempt to destroy whole populations. The Eichmann trial is a warning as to what can happen to those who attempt genocide."

Unfortunately, the controversy over the Eichmann trial still continues as does genocide in various parts of the world. Yet the Eichmann case clearly spotlights to men of conscience everywhere that some regimes, such as that of Argentina, are willing to harbor the most inhuman of criminals, no matter how heinous their deeds.

After Eichmann's kidnapping many of the Nazis hiding in Argentina moved temporarily or permanently to other countries. Brazil was a country that welcomed them and two SS officers who were delighted to take advantage of the safe haven were Franz Paul Stangl and Gustav Wagner. Stangl was commandant of Treblinka but he was very careful during the Third Reich that his accomplishments at the camp should be kept quiet. That was an accomplishment in itself since Treblinka was second only to Auschwitz in numbers of persons gassed to death. Himmler was aware that Treblinka was operating very efficiently but he failed to give his SS camp commandant the praise he deserved because of Stangl's reluctance for publicity. This reluctance paid off, however, when the war ended. Stangl's name was omitted from the list of wanted war criminals. He was held for a while in an Austrian prison because he was an SS member but he slipped away from the prison after a few weeks, traveled to the Middle East with the help of Skorzeny and other *Spinne* members, and finally made his way to Brazil and a fine job, with the Volkswagen factory in São Paulo.

Life was calm for Stangl for many years until Wiesenthal checked his records and discovered that the "modest" SS officer had been one of Hitler's most ruthless murderers. As verified in the records, he was responsible for at least 400,000 deaths at the Polish death camp between August 1942 and August 1943. For 16 years Stangl lived in Brazil with his wife and four daughters thinking that he had been overlooked by the Nazi-hunters. In 1967, however, he discovered that Wiesenthal had not forgotten him. A cousin who did not like him notified Wiesenthal where Stangl was living and a former Gestapo man gave him the exact address. Stangl's dossier was complete by this time and a change in Brazilian politics gave Wiesenthal the chance he was waiting for. Roberto Abreu Sodré, an anti-Nazi and a friend of the prominent Brazilian-Jewish Klabin family, became the new governor of the State of São Paulo. Wiesenthal presented the Stangl dossier to him and at the same time convinced the Austrian government to request Stangl's extradition. Sodré, much to the shock of the Germans in Brazil, had Stangl arrested on the afternoon of February 28. *Die Spinne* and *Das Reich* immediately came to Stangl's defense, convincing the federal government of Brazil that honoring such a request for extradition was illegal. Stangl was flown to the capital, Brasilia, and kept there while the battle raged among the Brazilian authorities, the pro-Nazis, and the anti-Nazis. The legal arm of *Die Spinne* proved to the Brazilian authorities that Austria had no extradition treaty with Brazil. Wiesenthal immediately convinced West Germany to ask for his extradition because they did have such a treaty. It became obvious from the evidence included in the German request, however, that the Brazilian courts would let Stangl go free rather than extradite him. West Germany was hoping not to get embroiled in a trial controversy such as had resulted from the Eichmann case. Wiesenthal obtained further evidence from the Berlin Document Center, however, to strengthen the West German request. While it was still under consideration by the Brazilian courts, Poland, too, submitted a request for Stangl's extradition. And Israel, fearing that Brazil would refuse to extradite Stangl to any of the countries making such requests, started a rumor that their secret police were in Brazil ready to kidnap Stangl just as they had kidnapped Eichmann from Argentina. Finally, the turmoil was ended when on June 22 Stangl was handed over to German authorities and immediately flown to West Germany. It was a success for the Nazi-hunters because Franz Stangl was the first Nazi war criminal extradited from Brazil. His trial in Germany three years later where he was found guilty and sentenced to life in prison was anti-climactic.

But if Wiesenthal or any other Nazi-hunter thought that the Stangl case would open the way for wholesale extradition of war criminals from Brazil, they were mistaken. Instead there was an upsurge of pro-Nazi sympathy in the country. Synagogues were burned, swastikas were painted on Jewish homes and community centers, and Jews were harassed constantly. Death squads using Gestapo and SS methods of murder and torture were formed by rightists and fascists. Consequently when Gustav Wagner, the former deputy commander of the Sobibor death camp, was discovered living in Brazil the efforts to get him back to Germany met with a complete lack of cooperation from Brazilian authorities.

Wagner was first seen in Brazil in 1967 when efforts were being made to arrest Franz Stangl but by the time the Stangl case was closed, Wagner had disappeared from sight. For ten years Wiesenthal and other Nazi-hunters waited, never mentioning the SS officer's name on their wanted lists. Then on April 20, 1978, a group of Nazis gave a party commemorating Hitler's birthday and photographs of those attending were made. One of those present resembled Wagner. Wiesenthal recognized his oversized ears. Knowing that he would need more pressure on the Brazilian police than his own statement that the man looked like the sought-after war criminal, Wiesenthal asked the Israeli correspondent of the largest Brazilian newspaper *Jornal do Brasil* to come to his headquarters in Vienna. He gave the reporter the complete information on Wagner: his crimes, his escape to South America via the Middle East, and even the number on his Brazilian ID card.

When the article appeared in the newspaper on May 27, the Brazilian public was outraged to learn that such a criminal was living among them.

The Brazilian government wasn't, however. There had been no change in the overall attitude of the government since the court argument over whether or not to extradite Stangl 11 years earlier. Wagner was arrested and taken to Brasilia just as Stangl had been to await the court's decision on the requests of Poland, West Germany, Israel, and Austria for his extradition. The decision came on June 20, 1979. In its ruling the Supreme Court of Brazil turned down the Austrian request on the ground that Wagner had given up his Austrian citizenship and the alleged crimes had not taken place in Austria. The Polish request was rejected on the basis that the country's judicial system was not acceptable to Brazilian law. West Germany was told that the statute of limitations on the crimes had expired. As far as Israel was concerned, the judges stated that since Israel did not exist at the time of the alleged crimes, it had no right to request Wagner's extradition. *Das Reich* and *Die Spinne* had won another battle. ''Brazil is a secure sanctuary for Nazi criminals,'' Weisenthal said after the verdict. The SS veterans already knew that was true. At this writing it is still true.

Gustav Wagner, however, finally met justice, although by his own hand. He stabbed himself to death on October 4, 1980.

17

Missing Nazi Treasure

When Himmler died, two important questions remained unanswered: What happened to the SS treasure? What happened to the SS records? Hundreds of crates of gold teeth, jewelry, watches, and other valuables had been taken from the murdered Jews and shipped to a secret SS fund. A counterfeiting operation had brought huge sums of foreign currency into the SS treasury. Stamp, coin, and art collections had added to the SS booty. Even though Bormann had dipped into the fund and sent large amounts of it out of Germany during the final year of the war, there was still a great deal of wealth remaining. Allied investigators tried to find the missing hoard but Himmler's suicide shortly after the end of hostilities seriously complicated the problem.

One of the first persons questioned by American CIC agents was Erika Lorenz, one of Himmler's secretaries. Lorenz was in Himmler's employ continuously from 1938 until the end of the Third Reich in 1945; she served primarily as "gift secretary," charged with receiving and distributing gifts. For this purpose Lorenz maintained extensive files of high officials, celebrities, Himmler's personal friends, and others, all of whom proved of interest to the American investigators. She had worked at Himmler's three main headquarters: Berlin, Hegewald in East Prussia, and Aigen near Salzburg. They were particularly interested in Aigen since this was the site chosen by Himmler as his last retreat and it was thought that any treasure he intended to take with him after the fall of the Third Reich would be hidden in that area.

Lorenz was interned at CIE (Allied holding camp for suspected war criminals) No. 77 and CIC agents Claude P. Lenart and William Stefen of the 351st CIC Detachment in Berlin were sent to question her.

"Lorenz seemed to be a very naive person, greatly impressed by her boss and his importance, charm, and kindness, and who would have never dared to impose upon Himmler with questions or curiosity," Lenart reported. "She was obedient, a slave-like servant, who performed her duties diligently and competently but never inquired about things not of her immediate concern."

She probably knew that too much curiosity about the activities of the Reichsführer-SS could be fatal. Although the agents obtained very little information from her about the missing SS treasure, she did admit that in March 1945 she went to Aigen to prepare for the later arrival of Himmler.

"Lorenz was in charge of storing baggage that arrived from Berlin and for the purpose she chose a 'Stollen,' a cave in a rock. This cave was located in Hallstein near Salzburg and was part of the salt mine there," Lenart's report stated. "Lorenz visited the cave several times and observed about 40, possibly more, cases and crates of all sizes. Lorenz never opened any of these crates."

The secretary also told the Americans that other crates were stored on Himmler's personal train and in Himmler's house in Gmund on the Tegernsee, but she had no idea what was in them. As to the SS records, Lorenz said she had no idea what happened to them. Under further interrogation, however, she made an additional statement concerning the records.

> In the first days of May—it might have been the 1st, 2nd, or 3rd, I can't remember for certain, I was assigned the task of traveling to Fischhorn and destroying the contents of a steel cabinet which was standing there. I was given the key to the cabinet. I arrived in Fischhorn about 0900 and two SS officers let me into the castle and showed me where the cabinet was standing. I took everything out of the cabinet and laid it on the floor. Then I packed everything into a washbasket and carried it down to the furnace room

> of Fischhorn Castle. There was already a fire burning in the central furnace when I arrived. I do not know whether anything had already been burned there before I arrived. I burned the papers I took from the steel cabinet. I did not leave the furnace room during the entire episode. I did not look at the papers but threw everything into the fire without reading anything. I know nothing of a diary that was supposed to have been in the cabinet.

Interest immediately shifted from Aigen to Fischhorn in the search for the SS treasure and records. The SS Horse Farm was at Fischhorn, near Zell am See, Austria, and was under the overall command of Hermann Fegelein, Himmler's mysterious liaison officer at Hitler's headquarters. Since Fegelein had not been found after the end of the war, Fischhorn became doubly important to the American agents. While it was obvious that if Lorenz were telling the truth, the single steel cabinet could not have contained a fraction of the SS records, it was possible that the remainder of Himmler's personal files were somewhere at the horse farm. The secretary, not nearly as naive as the interrogaters first believed, also admitted that the crates and chests hidden in the cave near Aigen were transferred by truck to Fischhorn later. As an afterthought, she told the investigators that Franz Konrad, a member of Fegelein's staff at Fischhorn, had subsequently removed some of the stored material from Fischhorn but she didn't know how much or where he had taken it.

At Fischhorn Castle it was discovered that Konrad had been administrative officer under the direct command of Erwin Haufler, who was in charge of the horse farm. Neither man was available for questioning so a search was immediately begun for them. It was discovered that Konrad had been arrested by the American military forces near Zell am See but had escaped from custody on May 25, 1945. He was traced to a farm near Aufhausen but by the time the CIC agents arrived he had moved on. Konrad's wife was questioned and she suggested they contact a relative in Kirchberg. She was angry with her husband because of his association with a woman named Barbara; Frau Konrad wanted him apprehended. Through the relatives, Konrad was located residing in St. Johann, where he was taken into custody.

Arresting the SS officer was one thing: getting him to talk

about the SS treasure or records was another. However, while the search had been going on for Konrad, CIC agents had learned a great deal about him and his actions in the days following Germany's collapse. Erwin Haufler had been arrested and interrogated and Robert A. Gutierrez, the CIC special agent handling the questioning, reported:

> This agent suspects Konrad of obtaining possession of part of the correspondence between Hitler and Himmler at Fischhorn. According to Haufler, on or about May 2, 1945, Erika Lorenz of the staff of Himmler was sent from Salzburg to Fischhorn to burn the contents of a steel cabinet which contained documents and papers belonging to Himmler. Konrad helped Lorenz with the burning. Shortly afterward Konrad made the statement to Haufler that he (Konrad) had read very interesting correspondence between Hitler and Himmler. Konrad admits having put aside what he termed a book full of historical documents belonging to Himmler.

The Americans were very interested in the Himmler-Hitler correspondence since documentation of Hitler's orders for the Holocaust had not been found. In addition to Haufler's incriminating statement, the CIC agent had located a roll of undeveloped film. When he had the film processed it showed two mountain sites and Konrad at the sites. The terrain resembled that of the immediate area of Fischhorn. Upon questioning residents of the mountainous area around Fischhorn, several persons stated that they had seen Konrad climbing in the mountains quite often just before the capitulation. The investigators, in reviewing the photographs, came to the conclusion that Konrad had taken the pictures with the idea of having a permanent record of landmarks to enable him to relocate the burial place of any documents of treasure.

Konrad, however, denied everything. He insisted that he had taken no valuables from Fischhorn nor any documents. When he continued to insist on his innocence, the Americans went to Mietzen, Austria, and once again questioned his wife, Frau Agnes Konrad, to no avail. "I was told in Schladming that my husband took some things there. I do not know whether my husband took things to other places, too, or not. I don't know about any of this. I am not responsible for his fate; he himself must arrange to get himself out of this. My relatives, especially the Meiers in Kirchberg, are very angry with me because they had to suffer such unpleasantness on my husband's account. I know nothing."

To the agents Frau Konrad sounded like a woman who had not been taken into her husband's confidence, but on the chance that she might be duping them, they traveled once again to Kirchberg to check with the Meier family with whom Konrad had stayed for a while after escaping from the American internment camp. Rudolf Meier, a distant relative, at first stated that Konrad had brought nothing with him when he arrived in Kirchberg but under intense questioning he finally broke down. His testimony startled even the agents:

> Very well, I will tell you: Konrad brought here 400,000 RM [reichsmarks], some foreign money, and some jewelry. He asked if he might bury it here. The 400,000 RM were in 100 RM notes packaged in bundles. The foreign money consisted of Swiss francs, dollars, and Swedish crowns. As far as I remember there were two rings and some gold dollars. Konrad said I might keep 100,000 of the 400,000 RM. Frau Konrad was here about a week ago. She said that her sister-in-law in Schladming had told her that the writings and gold were still buried there, that the Americans had not yet found them. Konrad told me that in the last days before the capitulation he had large sums of money under his control; I think he spoke of several millions. My wife also told me that an article in the Salzburg newspaper said that a Polish countess had received paintings from the Göring collection valued at 7,000,000 RM.

It was obvious that both Frau Konrad and Meier had not told the truth during their initial interrogations. Altogether the CIC obtained the following monies and jewelry from Rudolf Meier:

1.	German money	365,898	reichsmarks
2.	American money (gold)	140.00	dollars
	(paper)	615.00	dollars
3.	Canadian money (paper)	1.00	dollar
4.	Swiss money	6,500	francs
5.	English money	10	pounds
6.	Swedish money	100	kronen
7.	Postage stamps	17,233	reichsmarks

8. Jewelry:
   a. 1 large gold man's ring with 29 diamonds and a large blue stone
   b. 1 large gold man's ring with three large diamonds

Since these monies and jewelry were found in the French zone, they were turned over to the French authorities after a report dated October 14, 1945, covering their recovery was submitted to the 7th Army CIC. The total value of the items was far below what the Americans were seeking but they were encouraged with the find because it indicated that Konrad definitely knew where large sums of the SS treasure were located. It was also discovered that Konrad had given Haufler, his superior officer, nearly 100,000 RM, three valuable gold rings, four gold watches, and some foreign currency. They were recovered from Frau Haufler at her home in Ammerland am Starnbergersee. But the real question in the minds of the investigators was the source of these monies and jewelry.

The trail led from Konrad to Jurt Schiebel, who formerly was adjutant of office II of the RSHA (Reich Central Security Office). This was the budget administration section of the SS headquarters. Schiebel was located in 7th Army internment camp No. 71 at Ludwigshaven, where he was questioned by CIC agents. He quickly admitted that when he left Berlin on April 21, 1945, he had with him 200,000 gold Napoleons in ten sacks, foreign exchange in American dollars, as well as 5 million RM in 100 RM notes. According to him he distributed the money to the Gestapo and secret police officers who had survived and to Karl Radl, Otto Skorzeny's adjutant. Since there was not enough to satisfy Skorzeny, Schiebel stated that he sent an aide to Weitra, where more SS treasure was hidden. The aide brought back "considerable amounts" of gold and silver and some silverware for Skorzeny. These valuables helped finance *Die Spinne*.

Since Schiebel had very little money on him when arrested and freely admitted that he had distributed the valuables from the SS treasure to others immediately after the end of the war, the American agents decided to follow up on a tip he had given them. Schiebel stated that several trucks—he didn't know how many—had taken valuables from Fischhorn to Taxenbach, Austria. He provided the investigators with four maps with distinctive markings on them which he thought were sites where valuables from the SS treasure might be buried. He suggested they contact Wilhelm Spacil. This was a new name on their list of Nazis to be interrogated and a quick check disclosed that Spacil had headed the SS headquarters budget administration section under Kaltenbrunner. His whereabouts and activities since the end of the war were completely unknown so CIC agent Walter Hirschfeld, who had done considerable undercover work while posing as a former SS officer, was asked to question Konrad again. This time Hirschfeld made no effort to dupe Konrad. He played it "straight" hoping the SS administrative officer would cooperate now that it had been proven that he had hidden a considerable amount of money and valuables. Hirschfeld found Konrad a difficult subject, however, as his report states:

> The interrogation of Hauptsturmführer Franz Konrad took place from 0130 to 0600 hours. It was not an ordinary interrogation because that has been done so frequently by me and other people that there must be whole batches of his statements, but I tried instead to appeal to his conscience and to assure him that he would not be extradited to Warsaw if he would be willing to tell us the whereabouts of the remaining things we are after. He wouldn't accept the offer. In my opinion Konrad is a fanatical Nazi who will not talk despite imprisonment and an impending death sentence.

In the end, however, it was Konrad's involvement in the Warsaw ghetto atrocity and his fear that he would be hanged for his actions at that time that convinced him to talk. He had been transferred to Warsaw in June 1942 with the assignment of taking over the management of all factories in the ghetto. In addition he had the responsibility of collecting every article of value, such as furniture, books, machines, and other items left behind by the inhabitants of the Warsaw ghetto in the course of the deportations to the death camps. Konrad was to take these materials to depots established for the purpose. He had stayed in Warsaw under the jurisdiction of the infamous Jürgen Stroop, who was later hanged for directing the destruction of the ghetto, until the ghetto's final liquidation. When it became evident to Konrad that the Warsaw atrocity was going to be considered a war crime and that those involved would be tried before a war crimes tribunal, he decided to tell what he knew—or, at least, part of what he knew—about the disappearance of the Nazi treasure.

> I met Spacil at Fischhorn at the end of April 1945 and he asked me whether I needed money. He gave me 500,000 RM, 2500 dollars, and 1550 Swiss francs. I got this money near Mittersil at a bath. There was a truck there and several men in civilian clothes. I stopped there for five minutes at the most. Later it was on a Sunday, the end of April or beginning of May, I went again to Mittersil because I had no more money. In the meantime I had received a letter which I was to pass on to Spacil in which was stated that the truck which had been standing at Mittersil contained 29 million RM and 100,000 Swiss francs in gold and this truck was to be added to the other trucks in a side valley from Bischofshofen. I did not find anyone at Mittersil. I therefore drove to Taxenbach, to a mill, and found Spacil. In the court was standing a five-ton truck with steel cabinets in it. It looked like the same truck I had seen at Mittersil. I asked Spacil for more money. He called to an Untersturmführer-SS standing nearby and asked if anything was left. I then got another 500,000 RM, 10,000 Swiss francs, 3000 dollars, 200 Swedish crowns and 40 English pounds.

It was evident that any large sums of SS money were under the control of Spacil but when Spacil, who had been arrested in the meantime, was questioned, he admitted little or nothing. He agreed that he had been visited at Taxenbach on May 5 by Konrad and that he had given him some monies due the SS officers under Konrad's command for back pay. As for the trucks, he stated he knew nothing about them. He was much more explicit about minor matters and obviously was angry that Konrad had told the CIC agent about receiving the money from him. In an effort to get Konrad into more trouble with the American authorities, he reported that Konrad had told him that he had the suit worn by Hitler during the July 20, 1944, assassination attempt, an entire exchange of letters between Eva Braun and the Führer, and Hitler's diary. Spacil said the diary was written on very thin airmail paper and Konrad had buried it with the other items in a tin case. While the mentioned items had little or nothing to do with the missing SS treasure, they were of interest because of their historical value. The official U.S. report on the items later discovered at Schladming because of Spacil's tip lists the following:

1. The suit which was supposed to have been worn by Hitler at the time of the attack on his life on July 20, 1944. This suit had been in Berchtesgaden along with other things belonging to Eva Braun.
2. One chest full of photo albums depicting the private lives of Hitler and Eva Braun, belonging to Eva Braun. Also notes made by Eva Braun from her letters to Hitler and art photos of Hitler and Eva Braun.
3. One chest of silverware with the emblem of the Polish crown. Assumed to have been Polish property taken from Poland by the Germans during the occupation of Poland. Konrad insists that he knows nothing about the silverware.
4. Silverware with monogram of Eva Braun belonging to Eva Braun herself.
5. Part of a postage stamp collection acquired illegally by Konrad while with the SS at the Warsaw ghetto. Konrad estimates that the collection in peacetime is worth 80,000 RM.

All the items were turned over to the 7th Army CIC. Approximately one year later U.S. Army European Command Headquarters authorized the destruction of the coat and trousers worn by Hitler on the day of the assassination attempt. Reason? "Destruction of these items is recommended to prevent possibility of their becoming a future shrine should they ever fall into German hands."

The historical items aside, the CIC investigators continued to question Spacil about the large sums of money purportedly in his possession, but he refused to admit anything. A search was conducted for the trucks supposedly parked in the Taxenbach area but they could not be located. German civilians, however, admitted that countless trucks had been seen on the winding roads in the area, many of them heading for the Alt Aussee region where the looted art treasures had already been located in the salt mines. Other trucks, they reported, climbed the steep slopes near Taxenbach and disappeared. Meanwhile the OSS had discovered that a huge counterfeiting project had been carried out by the Nazis and that the counterfeit currency had been converted into gold in neutral countries. One OSS officer had retrieved $500,000 in gold hidden in Austria.

The hiding place had been revealed by a German informant hoping to escape arrest for his part in the counterfeiting scheme. But no large cache had yet been discovered. All leads seemed to go nowhere. The Polish "countess" to whom Konrad was suspected of giving paintings valued at 7 million RM from the Göring collection was discovered in Kitzbühl, Austria, and turned out to be the wife of an Iranian and a former mistress of Konrad. She was not a countess, she had no paintings. The salt mines of Alt Aussee, while holding a fortune in looted art objects and paintings, did not contain the SS treasure. The CIC agents, busy gathering information about war criminals for the Nuremberg trials and searching for verification of Hitler's death in addition to a great many other assignments, let the matter of the SS treasure drop for a while.

While checking on Eva Braun's jewelry at Fischhorn, however, in hopes of tracing Hitler's mistress on the chances she still might be alive, the subject of the SS trucks came up in a conversation with a German prisoner. The German remarked that if anyone knew where the trucks were in the mountains, it would be Walter Reisinger, a former *Ortsgruppenleiter* and SS member who lived in Taxenbach. According to the informant, Reisinger was a forester and knew every inch of the rugged terrain in that area. Reisinger was traced to the Colling POW camp near Hallstein, where he was questioned. Little information has ever been released about the interrogation of Reisinger or the results, but it is known that a large part of the SS treasure was located due to his testimony. The official report concerning the Reisinger case, released by the Special Investigation Squad, Counter Intelligence Corps Detachment 970, states briefly:

A. RSHA Funds (unknown quantity estimated to be worth 25 million dollars).
   1. Recovered by Lt. Claus K. Nacke and T/3 John E. Alter of MII Team 466-G, 7th Army Headquarters. The above two were accompanied by Lt. Walter Hirschfeld now working for the 7th Army Headquarters CIC.
   2. Taken from an SS man, Reisinger, a forester at Taxenbach, Austria, near Zell am See. Reisinger was arrested by US [Armed Forces] CIC.

3. Ownership—RSHA funds given to Spacil to hide for future operations.
4. Disposition—turned over to the 7th Army CIC by Special Agents Richard C. Cahoon, Robert Blake, and Robert A Gutierrez.
5. The amount of various foreign currencies, gold, and jewelry could not be determined without sorting and a long-drawn-out count. On the advice of G-5 7th Army the entire treasure was turned over to the Military Government.

What was the actual amount found? After it was taken over by the U.S. Military Government, what happened to the millions in currency and the caches of gold, silver, and jewelry accumulated by Himmler and his SS? It is assumed that the booty ended up in the U.S. Treasury but this has never been publicly acknowledged. Some believe its disposition was kept secret to avoid claims by Holocaust victims. Others are convinced that it was used by American intelligence agencies to finance the Gehlen organization, the German spy network that worked with the United States during the postwar years to check Soviet aggression in Europe. Still others are convinced that a considerable portion of the treasure was stolen a second time—by Allied personnel after the war.

The search continues more than three decades after the fall of the Third Reich, not only for additional SS treasure, if any exists, but for the SS records. Experts believe the SS hierarchy may have managed to hide as much as one billion dollars in various parts of the world outside Germany. The list of persons authorized to draw on these funds is still missing, a mystery that the experts believe can be solved if the SS records are found. Wiesenthal, after a great deal of investigation, thinks that the records, including the all-important list of those designated to use the hidden SS funds, are at the bottom of the Töplitzsee, the lake not far from the Alt Aussee region in Austria where the Nazi art objects and paintings were found. He is not the only one who is convinced. Since 1950 several attempts have been made to recover whatever is at the bottom of the lake. In that year several Germans retrieved 12 boxes from the lake and escaped before the authorities could find out what was in the boxes. Five years later a Herr Gerkens, who had once worked in the area for the

Nazis developing underwater rockets, died from a "fall" from a rock near the lake. In the summer of 1959 a research team financed by a well-known German magazine arrived at Töplitzsee with underwater cameras intending to explore the 90-meter-deep waters. All they found was trouble. Their diving platform was badly damaged by unknown attackers, the crew members received threatening letters, and they were kept under constant surveillance by strangers in the nearby hills. They recovered several crates with counterfeiting plates for English pounds and a few documents of no particular value. In 1963 a young German, Alfred Egner, drowned in the Töplitzsee while diving to depths of 200 feet. It was learned that he had been hired by a former German SS intelligence agent and a gold coin dealer from West Germany. Several gold coins were found in Egner's wallet and his family admitted it was not the first time he had searched the lake for treasure.

Were the deaths accidental or are members of *Die Spinne* still guarding that part of the SS treasure and the SS records that have not yet been discovered? Does the money used to defend SS men arrested for war crimes come from these missing SS funds? A CIA agent interested in the treasure recently observed, "With the increase in the price of gold since 1945 just think what that SS fund might be worth now."

Enough money to finance a new Hitler?

18

The SS and Russia

One matter about which the Soviets and Americans agreed at the end of the Third Reich was that the SS was a criminal organization. The Russians had suffered greatly at the hands of the SS troops, especially in the Ukraine. Mass murder on the eastern front, both of civilians and military personnel, was a common SS practice. At Nuremberg where the Soviets often protested actions of the western members of the International Military Tribunal, there was complete agreement on the SS. In fact, Russia had agreed to the war crimes trials even before the British gave their assent. The proceedings had been proposed by the U.S. War Department in a January 1945 report entitled "Memorandum for the President: Trial and Punishment of Nazi War Criminals."

Even the United States government had wavered about the wisdom of such trials and the consequences of the precedent they would set, but an SS action in January 1945 brought the matter to a head. That was the massacre of American prisoners of war at Malmédy, Belgium, by Peiper's SS troops during the Battle of the Bulge. As a result of that action, the United States committed itself to the trials and hoped to get the British and Soviets to agree. Churchill, however, opposed the trials at first, favoring summary execution without trial for the top Nazis accused of war crimes. Stalin agreed with the United States although there was a disagreement over procedure and over just who should be tried. When the British realized that the trials would be held with or without their participation, they, too, signed the agreement as did the French. Article IX of the "Charter of the International Military Tribunal" was aimed directly at the SS and read:

> At the trial of any individual member of any group or organization the Tribunal may declare (in connection with any act of which the individual may be convicted) that the group or organization of which the individual was a member was a criminal organization.

This was such a general article that the Americans made a list of Nazi organizations which they believed most warranted a judgment of guilty. They included the "Leadership Corps" of the Nazi party, the Reich Cabinet, the General Staff and High Command of the armed forces, the SS, and the Gestapo. Later the SA was added to the list. When it came time to vote on these organizations, all four senior judges of the Tribunal agreed that the SS was a criminal organization—one of the few times they voted unanimously throughout the trials. In accordance with Article IX of the charter, Ernst Kaltenbrunner, chief of the SD at the end of the war, was chosen as the representative defendant of the SS.

Kaltenbrunner was indicted on three counts. The evidence supporting the charges of war crimes and crimes against humanity, when presented to the Tribunal, was so horrible that even many of his fellow defendants turned against him. His defense counsel, Dr. Kurt Kaufmann, refused to shake hands with him after he had heard the evidence presented against Kaltenbrunner. The judgment found him guilty of being aware of conditions in the concentration camps, ordering the executions of prisoners in the camps, arranging for the evacuation and liquidation of inmates of concentration camps as the end of the war neared, mistreatment and murder of POWs, ordering the SS not to interfere with attacks on Allied fliers who parachuted from their aircraft, organizing a slave labor program, and playing a leading role in the Holocaust. He was sentenced to die and was hanged on October 16, 1946, at Nuremberg. His guilt was taken as confirmation that the SS was a criminal organization and other SS leaders were tried and sentenced for their crimes.

There was then no question that during 1945 and 1956 both American and Soviet political and military officials felt only revulsion toward the SS. The thought that either country would reverse this attitude within a matter of months was unbelievable—but both did. The American authorities, through their alliance with the Gehlen organization, were the first to exploit the skills of the SS when relations with the Soviets deteriorated shortly after the war. Gehlen kept telling the American authorities who monitored his organization that in principle he rejected using SS men; in fact he was recruiting them as fast as possible. His personal rationale was that the SS men were ideal for undermining the East German security service. When he learned that some SS members could even provide him with the archives of the Wannsee Institute in Berlin, where SS experts on Russia had analyzed during the war every important Soviet book, newspaper, and map, Gehlen couldn't resist. Before long his organization had a large number of SS men at his headquarters in Pullach and in the field, so many that on September 23, 1954, the Soviet high commission lodged a protest with the U.S. The Russian note went unanswered. A year earlier W. S. Semionov, High Commissioner of the USSR in Germany, had demanded from the three western powers a promise to "liquidate the criminal organizations which carry on subversive activity from Berlin against the DDR [German Democratic Republic]." Again, on April 12, 1955, The East German government protested against the "use of Berlin as a center of espionage and subversive activity against the DDR and neighboring countries in connection with the arrest of a great number of espionage and terrorist groups." Many of those arrested were former SS members who had joined Gehlen.

These protests embarrassed the United States. It was obvious that the Soviet government was trying to convince the world that while the Americans had condemned the SS as a criminal organization at Nuremberg, they were now using these same war criminals to spy against the Soviet Union. The Russians would have it appear that they made no such similar use of the SS members under their jurisdiction. The first part of the Soviet charge was absolutely correct. The United States, through the Gehlen organization, *was* using SS members to spy on Russia. However, it soon became more and more evident that the Soviets, too, were willing to use Nazi war criminals to further their own espionage activities.

American intelligence authorities agreed with Gehlen's claim that if he didn't take the SS men into his organization they would promptly cross over and join the East German secret service.

East Germany, with Soviet approval, had established a security service called the *Staats Sicherheits-Dienst* (SSD), the initials of which reminded the Allies of Himmler's infamous SD. At the head of the SSD was Ernst Friedrich Wollweber, one of the Kremlin's most efficient spymasters and saboteurs. Born in Hesse, he had joined the German navy and was one of the leaders of the mutiny in the Third Fleet at Kiel in 1918 that started the fall of the Kaiser. Later he became a leader of the German Communist Party, graduated from Moscow's military-political college, and returned to his homeland to try to help lead the Communist party to power in the 1920s and 30s. When Hitler became Chancellor, however, Wollweber fled the country and didn't return to Germany until 1945 when the Russians set him up in their occupation zone as "Commissioner for Transport and Shipping." Later he was promoted head of the new security service. Wollweber had no love for the SS but he was a realist, as was Gehlen in West Germany, and when it became obvious that some of the SS members could help he was quick to enlist them in the SSD.

Gehlen first discovered that the Soviets were using SS members when the expected archive material from Berlin's Wannsee Institute could not be produced as promised by his own SS men. When these officers went to the former location of the institute to dig up the buried archives they discovered that the valuable documents were gone. The Russians had found the archives. It was obvious that someone in the SS had tipped off the Soviets and just as obvious that SS experts were working with Wollweber. This was true, but Wollweber had his predecessor as chief of the security service, Wilhelm Zaisser, to thank for it. Zaisser, like Wollweber, was born in Germany and in 1918, as a member of the German occupation force in the Ukraine, he had become a Communist. He, too, had been trained in Moscow between the wars, graduating from the Red Army espionage academy. After assignments in China, Manchuria, and Spain for the Soviets he returned to Russia. It was there in 1942 that he discovered the worth of the SS men.

Zaisser was given the responsibility of operating the anti-fascist school in Kragnogorsk where all German prisoners considered possible candidates for Soviet use in postwar Germany were interrogated. Even during this period Stalin coveted control of Germany once the Nazi regime could be destroyed. Zaisser soon learned that the SS officers captured by the Russians were ideally suited for a postwar secret service. They were already experts in counterespionage, counterintelligence, and internal surveillance. With the willing aid of captured German General Rudolf Bamler, a member of the Abwehr and who had been a close friend of Heydrich, Zaisser set up a police and intelligence unit ready to move into Germany as soon as hostilities ended. Thus, the Soviets were enlisting the SS members to their cause while Gehlen was still involved with his wartime intelligence duties on the eastern front.

Immediately after the war Stalin insisted that the Soviet secret service should operate in Germany—that a German staffed and controlled secret service was unnecessary. Zaisser bided his time with his SS-staffed unit, convinced that the NKVD (People's Commissariart for Internal Affairs) and the GRU (Central Administration for Intelligence) would not be able to handle the myriad details that would be involved. He was correct. In order to hunt Nazi criminals, maintain surveillance on German anti-Communist citizens and groups, track down spies, and to carry out many other duties, the NKVD and GRU needed help. Late in 1945 a German auxiliary was organized to work with the two Soviet agencies and, as confidence in this unit increased, the SSD was finally established. At that time Zaisser took over with his German secret service unit. Bamler had the overall responsibility of keeping the SS members in line and he served as an advisor to Zaisser. Louis Hagemeister, formerly a member of the Reich Central Security Office counterintelligence section, became a member of the SSD station at Schwerin; SS member Reinhold Tappert, who had been a valuable member of the SS security police headquarters detachment, became a part of the SSD Berlin station unit; and SS officer Johann Sanitzer, a former Gestapo official in Vienna, went to the SSD office in Erfurt. The Soviets, like the U.S. Army officials who discovered that Gehlen was recruiting so many SS men for his organization, had serious reservations about Zaisser's German security service. It wasn't moral principles nor a fear of public protest from Soviet citizens that motivated the Russian authorities, but an innate distrust of the SS members. However, they didn't interfere with Zaisser's organization as long as it delivered and, unfortunately for the Americans, British, and French, it delivered very well.

The Americans found out how efficient the Zaisser secret service was during the KgU affair. This *Kampfgruppe gegen Unmenschlichkeit* [Battlegroup against Inhumanity] was founded by a West German named Rainer Hildebrandt to protest the Soviet concentration camps in the Soviet zone and to trace missing Germans in the Soviet occupied area. When the American CIC discovered that the KgU had recruited a large number of members, the CIC station chief in Berlin approached Hildebrandt about the two agencies working toward a common purpose. Hildebrandt agreed. From then on the organization was financed and aided in many other ways by the CIC and later by the CIA. The latter organization wasn't satisfied with the aims of the KgU, however, and insisted on the members performing acts of sabotage in East Berlin. Zaisser, meanwhile, had placed an SSD member, a former SS man, in KgU's headquarters. After he had gained all the information required, he gave the order to close in on the organization and on the night of September 8, 1951, most of the KgU network was arrested and the documents stored in their headquarters were confiscated by the SSD. The aftermath of the East German coup, made possible in large measure by SS members of the SSD, was serious for the CIA, CIC, and the Gehlen organization, the three American intelligence-gathering organizations.

In 1953 when Lavrenti Beria, chief of the Soviet Secret Service, fell from favor in Moscow and was executed, Zaisser, who was a close ally of his, lost his position in East Germany. Wollweber took over. Wollweber was determined to neutralize the Gehlen organization and he let no opportunity pass by to do so. One method he used was to infiltrate SSD agents into Gehlen's organization; the most suited to this role were the SS men. For quite a while many Americans had been worrying that Gehlen's group had been infiltrated by Soviet agents and this worry increased as the CIA worked more and more closely with the Germans. One such critic was the ardently anti-Soviet Arthur G. Trudeau, who had headed the 1st Constabulary Brigade in Germany during the Berlin blockade and airlift. During the Berlin blockade he had formed Task Force Trudeau to force a ground entry to the city, but U.S. officials had refused to give the order to go ahead. In 1953, although he was stationed in the Far East, he warned Washington during his visits to the capital that with Gehlen becoming privy to CIA secrets and slated to know NATO confidential plans in the future, his organization should be checked very closely for Soviet infiltrators. Trudeau was ignored and two years later, after he repeatedly made his warning while chief of army intelligence, he was relieved from this post and sent back to the Far East.

Ignoring Trudeau was a serious error. The Gehlen group *was* penetrated by Soviet agents in 1953 and had been for some time. One such agent was Victor Schneider, a former SS officer in the section commanded by Heinrich Müller, who had helped investigate and destroy the ''Red Orchestra'' Soviet spy network in Germany during World War II. Late in the war, however, he ended up in the Sachsenhausen concentration camp for ignoring Müller's orders. After the war, the KGB leaders forgave him his part in the destruction of the ''Red Orchestra'' when they concluded that he could help them in his position as a bookkeeper in Konrad Adenauer's Christian Democratic party. The Soviets by this time were convinced that Adenauer would lead the new West German government when it was formally established, and they wanted contacts within his organization. Unfortunately for the western powers, Gehlen had also hired Schneider to work for his own organization and had recommended him to Adenauer. Moreover, through Gehlen's influence, Schneider's wife Erika had obtained a position in the Ministry of Defense. The two were sending packets of copies of important documents to East Germany every week.

Another SS officer, Freidrich Panzinger, whom Himmler had entrusted to investigate anti-Hitler conspiracies during the Third Reich, was recruited by Gehlen to work at his organization's headquarters at Pullach. When Gehlen switched from working with the CIA to become head of intelligence for the new West German government, he had been forced to get rid of Panzinger because of his notorious SS record. Panzinger was already in the employ of the KGB at the time, having been compromised by the Russians while their prisoner during the last months of the war. Gehlen, completely ignorant that Panzinger was playing a double role, re-hired the SS officer when he needed an agent to act as a defector to the East. This was an ideal assignment for Panzinger. The Soviets provided him with "important" information to give Gehlen while at the same time the SS officer was copying Gehlen's files and giving the material to the Soviets.

When an East German SSD officer defected to the West in 1961 it was discovered that Karl Feuchtinger, a former SS officer who held a position in the West German Ministry of Defense, was a Soviet agent. And so it went. Weekly the Soviets in East Germany were arresting Gehlen agents and putting them on public trial and almost as often Gehlen and the CIA were discovering Soviet agents in their midst, a great many of them SS officers.

What really puzzled both Gehlen and his American counterparts was the source of the leaks that enabled the Soviets and East Germans to round up hundreds of Gehlen's agents. Even after the Schneiders were denounced by the investigative work of Gehlen's trusted Heinz Felfe, chief of counterespionage at Pullach, the leaks continued. Panzinger was also reported by the same Felfe to the West German prosecutor investigating war crimes. Panzinger was arrested and committed suicide in his cell, and Feuchtinger's double-agent career was eventually ended. Still the leaks continued. Gehlen pressed his counterintelligence chief to find the guilty persons but even then he was convinced that the leaks were not coming from his own headquarters. The forty-three-year-old Felfe, who had been head of an RSHA section under Walter Schellenberg, the SS chief of *Amt VI* (Foreign Intelligence), worked day and night on the problem but was unable to come up with the culprit or culprits. This was understandable since Heinz Felfe, Gehlen's trusted associate at Pullach, was the double agent everyone was seeking.

A close look at his background should have made Gehlen and the CIA agents searching for the Soviet "mole" suspicious of him. His entire life except for a few years of his early childhood had been spent in the SA, SS, or the Gehlen organization. He was an active participant in the 1938 pogroms against the Jews, had been a member of the SS bodyguard units during the Third Reich, and had been in charge of an SS section that concerned itself with watching Allen Dulles, the American OSS chief in Switzerland. During the last months of the war, Felfe was one of the SS officers who helped Skorzeny hide the Nazi treasure, art objects, and paintings. Even his postwar prisoner record indicated that he was a man who should have been kept under close surveillance by the West. Captured while still wearing his SS uniform, he was imprisoned first in England and later in Canada. By 1946, however, he was back in Germany and for reasons still a mystery but thought to be the result of influence by British intelligence officers, Felfe was completely cleared of any war crimes by a German denazification court. He was immediately hired by the British as an informer to help them arrest other SS officers and Gestapo agents. During this period he visited his family in Soviet-occupied East Germany where he was approached by the Russians to work for them as a double agent. He didn't make up his mind at that time although on his return to the West he joined several leftist organizations.

In 1948 he was reunited with two good friends of his SS days, Erwin Tiebel and Hans Clemens. Tiebel had worked at RSHA headquarters under Felfe while Clemens had been head of the Gestapo office in Dresden. After the war Tiebel had prospered in the building materials business but Clemens had not been so fortunate. His wife had left him and he was unable to obtain the type of position he desired—high pay, influence and power, and adventure. He couldn't, that is, until his estranged wife put him in touch with Soviet secret service officials in Dresden, where she was living with a Soviet army officer. The KGB made him an offer that was financially appealing but the deciding factor was his hatred of the Americans and British. He agreed to become a Soviet agent in the West.

Back in West Germany, Clemens called upon the SS brotherhood for help. First he contacted his two friends, Felfe and Tiebel, and offered them the opportunity to work for the Russians. Felfe agreed immediately, Tiebel went along reluctantly just to remain in the good graces of his buddies. In order to obtain positions which would permit them to obtain secret information to give to the Soviets, the trio again relied on the SS network. Clemens asked Willi Krichbaum, an SS officer who was Gehlen's station agent in Bad Reichenhall, for a job with Gehlen. Krichbaum, unaware Clemens was a Soviet agent, was seeking SS officers for the organization at the time and quickly agreed. Five months later Clemens had gained enough influence in the Gehlen organization to induce Krichbaum to hire Felfe. Tiebel was hired as a courier. So by the end of 1951 the three SS officers were inside Gehlen's operation working for the Soviet secret service.

It is amazing that Felfe, who turned out to be the most valuable of the three to the Soviets, could have remained in his position so long without detection. It wasn't until 1961 that he was arrested. During the intervening ten years Felfe worked his way up to a key position at Pullach with help from the Russians. The Soviets fed him information to relay to Gehlen, much of it top-secret material that they were willing to sacrifice in return for getting Felfe into a responsible slot in the German spy unit. In 1954, after Felfe had delighted Gehlen by pretending to have set up a circuit of informers in Moscow, Gehlen said, "That Felfe fellow is outstanding. He can produce what others cannot." Gehlen didn't stop to wonder why Felfe succeeded so well where other agents failed.

In 1958 he was appointed to the Soviet desk in Gehlen's counterespionage section. This was an ideal position for Felfe. He was able to copy documents at will and forward them to the KGB's East German headquarters at Karlhorst. He photographed the names and background information of West German agents, warned Soviet officials when it appeared certain that Soviet agents were going to be arrested, sent the Russians copies of all interrogations of their people who had defected to the West, and undermined Gehlen in every possible manner. Yet he did it with such panache that Gehlen never suspected him. Felfe also completely duped the CIA liaison officers who had worked with the Gehlen organization until it was absorbed into the new West German secret service, the *Bundesnachrichtendienst* or BND, in 1956.

The defection of the East German SSD officer to the West in 1961 was Felfe's downfall. Not only did this defector provide evidence that Feuchtinger, who was working in the West German Ministry of Defense, was a Soviet agent, but he insisted that there was a Soviet agent at BND headquarters. After a long investigation suspicions centered on Felfe, but Gehlen refused to believe the evidence. He ordered the investigation to continue and concentrate on others at the headquarters more likely to be the "mole" than his trusted associate. There was no other suspect. Wolfgang Langkau, who headed security at Pullach, bluntly told Gehlen that Felfe was their man, but it wasn't until October 27, 1961, when a radio message from the KGB to Felfe was intercepted by the BND monitoring section that Gehlen finally admitted that Felfe had completely outwitted him. On November 6 he ordered Felfe arrested. At the time of his apprehension Felfe had fourteen microfilms of secret BND documents in his briefcase and a tape intended for Karlhorst. At his home the BND investigators discovered several radio transmitters used to contact the KGB, a cache of microfilms, and a large file of secret documents from BND files.

Felfe, Clemens, and Tiebel were tried in July 1963, and all three were found guilty. Felfe received a prison sentence of fourteen years, Clemens ten years, and courier Tiebel three years. It was a severe blow to Gehlen's reputation as a spymaster and detrimental to the West German government. A partial estimate of the damage inflicted by Felfe during his association with Gehlen included the loss of at least 100 agents, numerous codes and rendezvous sites, over 15,000 restricted photographs, and 350 Minox films. There had also been innumerable radio messages conveying information from Felfe to Russians at Karlhorst. It was the beginning of the downfall of Reinhard Gehlen and had a serious effect on NATO secrecy for several years after Felfe's arrest. The CIA escaped public criticism over the Felfe affair because it was not widely known that the Gehlen organization had been financed by the United States from 1946 until 1956. Still, the CIA had been seriously compromised by the SS veterans at Pullach.

We know how well many of Himmler's SS men have adjusted to working for new masters; let us now see how well some of them still work for their old.

19

The Brotherhood Today

More than thirty-five years after Hitler disappeared and Himmler died, the SS is still a subject of controversy. Despite the irrefutable documentation that has been uncovered to verify its brutality, there are those who defend the record of the SS and its surviving members. *Die Spinne* and similar secret organizations made up of SS veterans spend millions of dollars defending their ''Death's Head'' comrades when they are caught and brought to trial. The defense techniques are often amazingly effective. In 1977, for example, 32 years after the end of the Third Reich, a Dutch journalist asked Simon Wiesenthal to help him find Siert Bruins, a Dutchman who had been sentenced to death in absentia in 1949 for the murder of several Jews hidden on Dutch farms during the German occupation. A check with Dutch police resulted in the information that while Bruins certainly was on their wanted list, very little effort had been made to find him. The Nazi-hunter, using his contacts, did in a few months what the Dutch police had not done in nearly 30 years—he located Bruins living in Breckerfeld, a small German town 68 miles east of Düsseldorf. All Bruins had done was to drop the ''i'' from his name; he called himself ''Bruns.'' It appeared that justice finally was going to be victorious. But not quite. His lawyers promptly claimed that during the years between 1949 when he was sentenced to death and 1977 when he was finally arrested, Bruins had become a German citizen and as such could not be extradited to stand trial in Holland. He was released from jail.

One indirect benefit of the Bruins case was that it alerted the Dutch public that many of their countrymen who had collaborated and committed crimes while in the service of the SS were still alive and well and untouched by the law. It is estimated that there are at least 350 such Dutch Nazi criminals still free after 35 years. As a result of the Bruins publicity, the police have begun to track down some of the criminals, but they have already run into trouble from *Die Spinne*'s well-paid lawyers. Johannes Hendricks was a member of the Waffen-SS and had been sentenced in absentia for crimes he committed together with German occupation forces. He was found but he, too, had become a German citizen and could not be extradited. Two Dutchmen who had been sentenced to life imprisonment for murder, Gerald Weimar and Anton Soetebier, were located living in Altea, Spain. Auke W. Pattist, a concentration camp guard with a life sentence over his head, was also located in Spain. The legal battle to extradite them has begun but the chances of success are not promising.

Spain is a safe haven for the SS men. Skorzeny lived there in peace until his death in 1975. Leon Degrelle, Belgium's leading Nazi collaborator, to whom Hitler once referred as an ideal example of a man whom he would have liked as a son, settled in Spain after the war and made a fortune in real estate. On a television program, when asked whether he didn't regret his actions during the Third Reich, Degrelle replied: "I am only sorry that I didn't succeed. If I had the chance I would do it all over again but much more forcefully."

SS veterans, many of whom have already been found guilty in absentia of war crimes, live in freedom today throughout Europe and the United States as well as South America. What is most amazing is the attitude of the countries in which they reside; it is as if justice is not to be done at this late date. Although their whereabouts are often known and have been known for many years, little or no action has been taken. Only now are questions being asked about the slowness of justice. In Düsseldorf, during a recent trial of concentration camp guards, German teenagers caused a turmoil with their flood of questions. Why dig up the past? Why did it take so long to bring them to trial? Why pick on old, frail persons who have been hard workers, good parents, and churchgoers ever since the end of the Third Reich? Are the trials hurting the image of present-day West Germany and its citizens? Isn't it inhumane to ask former concentration camp inmates to testify about incidents they have been trying to forget for years? The SS-veterans and their organizations thrive on such turmoil and profit from the public's indecision. Judges who are assigned the trials in West Germany are also aware of the controversy and their critics claim that these judges go out of their way to accept defense excuses to postpone trials, sometimes for years.

Dr. Werner Best, a Nazi legal expert and Reich Commissioner for occupied Denmark from 1942 until 1945, was, prior to that appointment, the man Hitler depended upon to explain the many "accidents" in Gestapo prison camps. Best served under Heydrich before going to Denmark. Immediately after the war he was tried in Denmark for war crimes, sentenced to death in a 1948 verdict, and released from prison in 1951 because of pressure put on the Danes by *Die Spinne*. Later, however, he was arrested in West Germany for alleged complicity in the murder of 8,723 Poles while serving under Heydrich. The case was postponed time and time again for various minor reasons and finally the case was dropped entirely because of Best's "old age."

Horst Schumann, one of the medical experimenters at Auschwitz, was finally extradited from Ghana in 1966. Yet, six years later he had still not been brought to trial; his lawyers had cited his high blood pressure. Johannes Thümmler, Gestapo chief at Katowice, wasn't brought to trial because the West German prosecutors insisted that they could not get enough evidence from Poland to present a case. While the prosecutors were making this claim, a German writer successfully gathered enough material in Poland to script a two-hour television documentary. Georg Fleischmann, accused of executing Jews at Smolensk, was arrested in 1965 but died in 1970 prior to being brought to trial. There are many more similar cases.

The case of Aribert Heim defies belief. For years Wiesenthal searched for Heim, a former camp doctor at the Matthausen concentration camp, in Germany and other European [illegible]. While he has not located the doctor, he has dis-[illegible] (in 1978) that Heim is the owner of a large building in Be[illegible]n which rents for $3,500 per month. The rent money is paid to his sister, who promptly forwards it to the doctor. When the German internal revenue service tried to get the sister to pay the income taxes on the rent money, a lawyer appeared at their offices with a tape recording of Dr. Heim stating that the money is his alone and he pays the taxes. Yet the German police have made no effort to trace Heim or to arrest him.

The United States, a country dedicated to human rights, has been an offender when it comes to prosecuting Nazi war criminals. The Displaced Persons Act of 1948 provided that:

> No person shall be eligible to receive the benefits of the Act who advocated or assisted in the persecution of any person because of race, religion, or national origin.

In spite of this provision it became obvious that a number of displaced persons who entered the U.S. after World War II had participated in one way or another in Nazi war crimes in the Soviet Union, eastern Europe, or the Baltic States. In the 1950s and 1960s newspaper articles and radio commentaries publicized the allegations against some of these individuals and in recent years television programs covered the subject. Many of these articles and programs criticized the Immigration and Naturalization Service (INS) for its lack of progress in investigating the alleged war criminals and charges of misconduct in its investigations were made. In the early 1970s an INS employee complained that his investigation of alleged Nazi war criminals was hampered by INS officials. It was also charged by critics that the INS was infiltrated by an organization dedicated to protect Nazi war criminals who escaped prosecution for their crimes. *Die Spinne*? In all probability it was this group, although the SS organization was not officially named.

Evidence gathered over the years by Nazi-hunters in the United States revealed that many of the war criminals managed to enter the country after the fall of the Third Reich through "Operation Paperclip," a program intended to recruit German scientists and technicians before the Soviet

Union lured them to Russia. Supposedly strict background checks were made on each German refugee before he was permitted to enter the U.S., but in reality few if any such checks were made. Among those who entered the country in this manner were many SS medical men who performed inhuman experiments in concentration camps. Other SS men, posing as scientists or skilled technicians, found the U.S. a safe haven after the war.

In 1977, when it appeared that the INS was making no headway at all in its investigation and prosecution of Nazi war criminals in the United States, Joshua Eilberg, chairman of a congressional committee appointed to put pressure on the INS, asked the Comptroller General of the United States, Elmer B. Staats, for help. In part his letter to Staats stated:

> The Immigration and Naturalization Service, with the cooperation of the Department of State is presently compiling evidence on alleged Nazi war criminals who entered the United States fraudulently. Three cases are in the process of being heard by judicial authorities and it is expected that proceedings in a number of other cases will be instituted in the near future.
>
> For the past two years I have been following closely the action being taken by the Service in these cases. Certain allegations have emerged which lead me and some of my colleagues to believe that the existence and backgrounds of these individuals were known to the Service for a long time without any action having been taken.
>
> These people entered the United States and acquired benefits under the Immigration and Nationality Act in contravention of United States law. No adequate explanation has been forthcoming from the Service as to why they did not proceed against these individuals until Congress brought the matter to their attention.
>
> I would like to enlist the cooperation of the General Accounting Office in conducting a thorough investigation of this situation, especially to determine if Immigration personnel deliberately obstructed active prosecution of these cases or engaged in a conspiracy to withhold or quash any information in its possession.

A year later the Comptroller's report was issued, stating that the GAO investigation indicated that it was "unlikely that any widespread conspiracy has existed in federal agencies—especially in the Immigration and Naturalization Service—to obstruct investigations of allegations that individuals, now residents of the United States, committed atrocities before or during World War II while serving the Nazi government of Germany." However, the report went on to state that the GAO could not absolutely rule out the possibility of undetected, isolated instances of deliberate obstruction of investigations of some alleged war criminals because of the passage of time and the GAO's limited access to agencies' records. The cases of 94 individuals were investigated. Of these 94 two were expelled from the country, one by deportation and one by extradition. In the remainder of the cases the individuals were allowed to remain in the country. Some of the individuals were not even questioned by INS.

The principal observations of the GAO investigators made it clear that very little concentrated effort was expended to prosecute the Nazi war criminals in the U.S. The report bluntly stated that investigations of most war criminal cases by the INS prior to 1973 were deficient or perfunctory and in many cases no investigation was even conducted. The INS didn't even know in 1973 how many alleged Nazi war criminals were in the country and it wasn't until five years later that it had compiled a list of 252. After 1973 the quality of investigations improved but, the report stated, further improvements still are needed. The role of other U.S. agencies in tracking down Nazi war criminals were controversial according to the GAO.

> The CIA said it had contacted 22 as sources of information. One decided not to be involved; of the other 21, 7 were paid for information or services provided. The CIA said its contacts with some of them came at a time when there was an acute shortage of intelligence on Soviet intentions and on developments in eastern Europe.

These were Nazis working with Gehlen and the CIA.

> The FBI had information on 47 of the 111 individuals on the GAO list. It had a confidential relationship with two of them; they were not paid.

> In the past the Department of State did not cooperate with investigations of war criminals because it was reluctant to pursue leads overseas or to seek information from Soviet sources. The Department expressed concern that the Communist countries would use its actions for propaganda. In the 1960s the Soviet Union had done so to embarrass the West, particularly the Federal Republic of Germany. The Department had information on 46 individuals, one of whom was employed as a consultant.
>
> The Department of Defense had information on 33 of the 111 individuals, one of whom was provided employment.

After the Comptroller's report was published congressional criticism of the INS progress forced the Department of Justice to step up its hunt for Nazi war criminals. In May 1979 the Office of Special Investigations was established "to coordinate the government's efforts to locate, denaturalize, and deport Nazi war criminals in the United States." Racked with internal dissension over procedures and personnel, the new unit began proceedings against several alleged war criminals by the beginning of 1980. Karlis Detlavs, accused of being involved in the 1941 mass murder of thousands of Latvian Jews in the Riga ghetto, was found living in suburban Baltimore. Frank Walus, who came to the United States in 1959, was faced by 12 witnesses who vowed he was the baby-faced Jew killer involved in murder and torture in the ghettos of Kielce and Czestochowa while he was a Gestapo agent. He was located living in Chicago where he was once Democratic precinct captain. The Justice Department investigators located Serge Kowalchuk living in a Jewish neighborhood of Philadelphia; he is now accused of participating in the murder of 5,000 Jews in Lyuboml, Poland. One Jew who survived the 1942 massacre traveled from Israel to testify against him. In Cleveland, Ohio, the man called "Ivan the Terrible" by the inmates, John Demjanjuk, was charged with involvement in the death of 500,000 Jews. Demjanjuk, according to the charges, was the man who ran the large diesel-powered gas chambers at Treblinka. Deportation proceedings were commenced against Mecys Paskevicius of Santa Monica, California, after he was accused of "participating in persecutions, including arrests, beatings, hangings, shootings, and killings of persons because of their race, religion, national origin, or political opinion'' between 1941 and 1944.

Will they be deported to stand trial in Europe for their alleged crimes? It may take five years or more before any decision is made in the cases now under way but the odds favor the defendants. Witnesses die, *Die Spinne* lawyers seem to have unlimited funds to delay the cases for numerous reasons, and the complexity of the cases and lengthy appeal procedures all add to the chances that few if any of the 200 suspects will ever be forced to leave the country. The decision of a federal judge in Fort Lauderdale, Florida, in another case indicates that the judicial process against Nazi war criminals at this late date is largely symbolic. The judge ruled that the government failed to prove that Feodor Fedorenko, who had been a guard at a Ukrainian concentration camp, had committed war crimes. He stated that the aged and emotional witnesses against Fedorenko, some who had come from Israel to give their testimony, were not credible. Furthermore, the judge declared that Fedorenko ''has been a responsible citizen and resident for 29 years and the record as to his conduct 35 years ago is inconclusive.'' It was an alert to the Holocaust survivors and victims' families that they should not be deluded into thinking that justice shall finally be done.

Ironically, it was learned that while the Justice Department was trying to round up Nazi war criminals, Ladislaus Nizansky, a former SS officer who allegedly took part in a number of crimes during the Third Reich, was found by Wiesenthal to be working for the U.S.-financed Radio Free Europe in Munich. Wiesenthal suggested that the United States should be more careful about how it spends its money.

The SS brotherhood spends a great deal of money, time, and effort protecting its members around the world and does so very successfully, but it has other interests. Politics is one. As a group their opinions can be influential, and they can elect or appoint candidates who think as they do. This is true in both East and West Germany. A report issued in Berlin some years ago estimated that 2,000 ex-Nazis had government positions in East Germany. Max Hartwig, an SS officer who served at Buchenwald and Oranienburg concentration camps, was then State Secretary for Church affairs under Walter Ulbricht; Franz Noble, former SS officer and a Nazi since 1937, was in the cultural section of the government; Werner Gast, a former stormtrooper, was a member of the local security police; and Professor Johannes F. Gellert, who headed the Geographic Society of East Germany, was an SS member during the Third Reich and a staunch supporter of Adolf Hitler. The list went on and on. Not all the East German functionaries on the list were SS officers but all were Nazis.

The situation is not all that different in West Germany. Candidates for the presidency in 1979 suddenly discovered that their Third Reich backgrounds were under close scrutiny. The incumbent president at the time, Walter Scheel, was forced to admit that he had joined the Nazi party in 1942 while another candidate, Karl Carstens, couldn't deny that he had been a member of the party from 1940 until the end of the war. Hans Filbinger, a state governor who planned to run for the presidency, was discovered to have such a tarnished background as a military judge during the Nazi era that he was forced to resign from office. The fortieth anniversary of the outbreak of World War II and the SS "September Conspiracy" in Poland saw many of the SS veterans and other Nazis running for public office in their homeland just as though the Holocaust had never occurred.

According to a 1979 West German interior ministry report on terrorism there were 24 Nazi groups in the country plus 52 more extreme right-wing organizations supporting many of the same principles. These neo-Nazi groups have names like "Viking Youth" or "Hanna Recreation Club" and meet to hear speeches attacking the "worldwide Jewish-Bolshevist conspiracy." They even have a newspaper, the *NS-Kampfruf (National Socialist Warcry*—the newspaper is published in the United States). In Frankfurt pro-Nazi stickers were posted around the city and a Nazi flag was raised over a building to commemorate the anniversary of "Crystal Night" of November 9, 1938, when Nazi terrorists roamed German cities to smash the windows of Jewish businesses. In Mannheim there was a rally of extreme right-wing organizations at which more than 800 of those attending wore Nazi identification. The rally was in memory of the Nazi war dead and to dedicate a stone memorial to Joachim Peiper, the SS officer who was their hero during the war and postwar years.

In other parts of the world neo-Nazism is even more active. In France a confessed bank robber claimed that some of the money from a $10 million Nice bank burglary was channeled to SS officers all over the world. In Madrid members of the Jewish community receive death threats periodically from a terrorist organization calling itself "The Adolf Hitler 6th Commando of the New Order." Wiesenthal states that he has on file over a hundred right-wing groups in the United States that preach hatred against blacks and Jews. A West Virginia printer and a Chicago street fighter have been trying for some time to unite all such Nazi factions under the single banner of "white power," and while they have not yet succeeded, they have not given up the attempt either.

Albert Speer states that Himmler and Hitler had plans for the SS to lock up 14 million prisoners after Germany won the war. Speer was given construction plans for barracks and camps large enough to hold this many men. The plan was for Himmler to become a great entrepreneur in postwar Germany, using the 14 million prisoners as slave laborers to rebuild the country and establish the new Germany as the strongest, most productive nation in the world. Under the supervision of the SS, the slave laborers would have had no freedoms and would have faced the same brutality as they did during the war.

Terrorism, in America or anywhere in the world, should be a reminder of the SS and what happened during the Third Reich. Skorzeny and other SS survivors instructed many of the leaders of terrorist groups all over the world in Nazi techniques during the postwar years on assignments in Egypt, Argentina, Brazil, Spain, and other countries. The aftermath of Himmler and the SS still has a devastating effect on the world today and will for generations to come. The SS war criminals must be hunted down because they committed crimes, and they must be punished, but it is those who will try to emulate the black-shirted murderers in the future who are the real threat. The SS must never be forgotten so that a new Holocaust can never take place.

Bibliography

Baille, Hugh. *High Tension*. New York: Harper, 1959.
Bleuel, Hans Peter. *Sex and Society in Nazi Germany*. New York: J. B. Lippincott, 1973.
Bormann, Martin. *The Bormann Letters*. London: Weidenfeld and Nicolson, 1954.
Bracher, Karl, and Sauer, Wolfgang. *Die Nationalsozialistische Machtergreifung*. Cologne: Westdeutscher Verlag, 1960.
Burgess, Alan. *Seven Men at Daybreak*. New York: E. P. Dutton, 1960.
Cole, Hugh M. *The Ardennes: Battle of the Bulge*. Washington, D.C.:Department of the Army, 1965.
Farago, Ladislas. *Aftermath*. New York: Simon and Schuster, 1974.
Ferencz, Benjamin B. *Less Than Slaves*. Cambridge: Harvard University Press, 1979.
Fest, Joachim C. *The Face of the Third Reich*. New York: Ace, 1980.
Gilbert, G. M. *Nuremberg Diary*. New York: Farrar, Straus and Giroux, 1947.
Gilbert, Martin. *Final Journey*. New York: Mayflower Books, 1979.
Henderson, Sir Nevile. *Failure of a Mission*. New York: G. P. Putnam's Sons, 1940.
Hitler, Adolf. *Hitler's Secret Conversations 1941-1944*. New York: Octagon Books, 1972.

Höhne, Heinz. *Order of the Death's Head*. London: Secker and Warburg, 1969.
——. *Canaris*. New York: Doubleday and Co., 1979.
——, and Zollung, Hermann. *The General Was a Spy*. New York: Coward, McCann and Geoghegan, 1972.
Infield, Glenn B. *Disaster at Bari*. New York: Macmillan, 1971.
Irving, David. *The Destruction of Dresden*. London: William Kimber and Co., 1963.
——. *The War Path*. London: Michael Joseph, 1978.
——. *Hitler's War*. New York: Viking Press, 1977.
Knierien, August von. *The Nuremberg Trials*. New York: Regnery, 1959.
Knoebel, Edgar Erwin. *Racial Illusions and Military Necessity*. Boulder: University of Colorado Graduate School, 1965.
Kogon, Eugen. *The Theory and Practice of Hell*. New York: Farrar, Straus and Cudahy, 1950.
Mader, Julius. *Jagd nach den Narbengesichte*. Berlin: Deutscher Militärverlag, 1962.
——. *Die Graue Hand*. Berlin: Kongress Verlag, 1961.
Manvell, Roger, and Fraenkel, Heinrich. *Himmler*. New York: G. P. Putnam's Sons, 1965.
Montgomery, Paul L. *Eva, Evita*. New York: Pocket Books, 1979.
Musmanno, Michael A. *The Eichmann Kommandos*. Philadelphia: Macrae Smith, 1961.
O'Donnell, James P. *The Bunker*. Boston: Houghton Mifflin, 1978.
Papen, Franz von. *Der Wahrheit eine Gasse*. Munich: Paul List Verlag, 1952.
Payne, Robert. *The Life and Death of Adolf Hitler*. New York: Praeger, 1973.
Puttkamer, Jesco von. *Von Stalingrad zur Volkspolizei*. Wiesbaden, 1951.
Reitlinger, Gerald. *The SS: Alibi of a Nation*. London: William Heinemann, 1956.
Roxan, David, and Wanstall, Ken. *The Jackdaw of Linz*. London: White Lion, 1976.
Russell, Lord, of Liverpool. *The Scourge of the Swastika*. New York: Philosophical Library, 1954.

Shirer, William L. *The Rise and Fall of the Third Reich*. London: Secker and Warburg, 1961.

Smith, Bradley F. *Reaching Judgment at Nuremberg*. New York: Basic Books, 1977.

Snyder, Louis L. *Encyclopedia of the Third Reich*. New York: McGraw-Hill, 1976.

Stipp, John L. (editor). *The Hitler Conspiracy*. New York: Manor Books, 1955.

Trunk, Isaiah, *Jewish Responses to Nazi Persecution*. New York: Stein and Day, 1979.

——. *Judenrat: The Jewish Councils in Eastern Europe Under Nazi Occupation*. New York: Macmillan, 1972; Stein and Day, 1977.

Von Lang, Jochen. *The Secretary*. New York: Random House, 1979.

Warlimont, Walter. *Inside Hitler's Headquarters*. London: Weidenfeld and Nicolson, 1964.

Notes

p. ix "Never has there been": Musmanno, p. 27.

p. 1 "I need chicken wire": *New York Times Magazine*, November 7, 1976, p. 102.

p. 2 "Basically it may be stated": Memorandum from Streckenbach to Himmler, March 9, 1942. RFSS Microfilm 140 Group T-175. National Archives, Washington, D.C.

p. 3 "Joachim was apprehensive": Author interview with Ernst Ruthe, Munich, June 14, 1978. Ruthe lived in Argentina for several years after World War II but returned to Germany in 1968. Retired today, he now lives in Munich. He was not tried for war crimes.

p. 5 "Close your hearts": Shirer, p. 532.

p. 5 "The damned enemies": Cole, p. 10.

p. 6 "A blow there will strike": ibid., p. 17.

p. 8 "He was only following": Author interview with Peiper on June 8, 1976, at Traves. I was seeking information for a biography of Otto Skorzeny and was not aware of *l'affaire* Peiper until later.

p. 9 "If Peiper dies": Mader, p. 214.

p. 11 "Moral principles are not": Author interview with Peiper.

p. 11 "We're coming for you": *New York Times Magazine*, November 7, 1976, p. 108.

p. 12 "Joachim would take": Author interview with Ernst Ruthe.

p. 13 ''The bodies of hundreds'': Author interview with Bruce Jacobs, Pittsburgh, December 7, 1979.
p. 13 ''Deaths were averaging'': Martin Gilbert, p. 212.
p. 15 ''I do not doubt'': Hitler, p. 87.
p. 16 ''I told myself'': Reitlinger, p. 13.
p. 16 ''Protection of meetings'': Rosenwink Address, Central Archives Microfilm 17. Hoover Institute.
p. 17 ''The SS is an organization'': Schreck letter to Nazi party headquarters, September 27, 1925. Microfilm 87. Berlin Document Center.
p. 18 ''The SS will never'': September 13, 1927, order from SS headquarters. Microfilm 87. Berlin Document Center.
p. 19 ''We went about it'': Himmler address of January 18, 1943. Microfilm 155, Group T-175. National Archives.
p. 19 ''Pure Nordic'': Knoebel, pp. 15–17.
p. 20 ''The task of the SS'': Order from NSDAP headquarters, November 7, 1930. Central Archives Microfilm 17. Hoover Institute.
p. 23 ''On the last day of February'': Bracher, Sauer, p. 943.
p. 24 ''The characterless arrogance'': Papen, p. 346.
p. 27 ''Grandmama dead'': *Der Spiegel*, November 13, 1963, p. 74.
p. 30 ''The fact that Heydrich'': Höohne, Canaris, p. 177.
p. 31 ''Maintained treasonable relationships'': Höhne, *Order of the Death's Head*, p. 231.
p. 31 ''Why in heaven'': Puttkamer, p. 106.
p. 32 ''Hitler had bluntly told Beck'': Document TC-73, No. 48, dated January 5, 1939. Polish White Book.
p. 32 ''Preparations must be made'': Stipp, p. 121.
p. 33 ''Say you don't'': Keitel testimony, IMT, Volume X, p. 579.
p. 34 ''Green leather jerkin'': Irving, p. 241 (1978).
p. 34 ''It was clear to me'': Stipp, pp 136–137.
p. 34 ''I shall give'': ibid., p. 143.
p. 35 ''I met with von Ribbentrop'': Author meeting with Hamilton Fish, February 11, 1972, at the Harvard Club, New York.
p. 36 ''The unconditional assurance'': Henderson, p. 317.

p. 37 "Stop everything at once": Shirer, p. 557.
p. 38 "Hitler was once again friendly": Henderson, p. 275.
p. 38 "I immediately sensed": ibid., p. 275.
p. 40 "The Polish government unwilling": Stipp, p. 170.
p. 40 "Yes, that's how the war started": Höohne, *Order of the Death's Head*, p. 301.
p. 41 "There is nothing worse": Musmanno, p. 1109.
p. 42 "I am shattered": American Military Tribunal, Book 1A, Ohlendorf Documents.
p. 43 "Of the Polish upper classes": Schellenberg Report dated September 27, 1940. RFSS Microfilm 239, Group T-175. National Archives.
p. 46 "Yank, I will give you": Author interview with Musmanno, January 31, 1962.
p. 48 "The *Einsatzgruppen* are authorized": Warlimont, pp. 158–159.
p. 49 "Communists, Jews, gypsies": Höohne, *Order of the Death's Head*, p. 406.
p. 49 "I felt it was my duty": IMT, Volume IV, pp. 29–30.
p. 51 "Most of you know": N.C.A. IV, pp. 558–578 (text of the entire speech). The documents of the Nuremberg trial that appear in *Nazi Conspiracy and Aggression.* Library of Congress, Washington, D.C., 8 vol., 1947ff.
p. 53 "Dear Herr Reich Minister": Manvell and Fraenkel, p. 252.
p. 55 "The most remarkable person": Author interview with Musmanno.
p. 55 "Count One. Common Plan or Conspiracy": Musmanno, pp. 49–50.
p. 56 "On what basis": Musmanno, p. 110.
p. 57 "I asked him if the question": Author interview with Musmanno.
p. 59 "The fact that individual men": Musmanno, p. 124.
p. 59 "I cannot imagine": ibid., p. 123.
p. 60 "A total of 135,000 persons": Irving, p. 262 (1963).
p. 61 "Many of the Jews listed": Musmanno, p. 126.

p. 61 "I know that it was of the greatest importance": Musmanno, p. 216.
p. 62 "The defense can introduce": Author interview with Musmanno.
p. 62 "Otto Ohlendorf, you have been found guilty": Musmanno, pp. 260–261.
p. 65 "I should like to take": Musmanno, p. 224.
p. 67 "I followed the van": Eichmann: Record of Interrogation, Volume 1, pp. 175–177, National Archives.
p. 68 "For a number of men": ibid.
p. 70 "The Führer has ordered the Final Solution": G. M. Gilbert, p. 230.
p. 71 "The killing itself": ibid., p. 229.
p. 72 "I remember one incident": Russell, p. 160.
p. 73 "Which was festive": Trial of War Criminals before Nuremberg. M. I. Tracy, Tribunals. Oct. 1946–April 1949. 15 Vols. Washington, D.C., 1949–53.: NI-15253, p. 410.
p. 73 "That the Jewish race": ibid., NI-838, pp. 1322–1323.
p. 73 "The mere view of the tightly drawn": Russell, p. 162.
p. 75 "I must confess": Snyder, p. 167.
p. 75 "We were all so trained": G. M. Gilbert, p. 238.
p. 78 "From time to time": Infield, p. 15.
p. 79 "We'll just put the cargo": ibid., p. 18.
p. 82 "Subject: N.Y.D. Dermatitis": Report sent to the commanding officer of the Ninety-eighth British General Hospital by A.L. d'Abreu, Surgical Division. National Archives.
p. 84 "It was easy": Author interview with Dieter Gollob in Madrid, 1973. Gollob was one of Skorzeny's commandos. After the war he moved to Spain, where he was associated with Skorzeny in business for several years. He died in 1976.
p. 85 "The type of death": Final Report of Bari Mustard Casualties by Stewart F. Alexander, dated June 20, 1944. Edgewood Arsenal Archives, U.S. Army.
p. 92 "In 1945 during the interrogation": Testimony of Gottlieb Berger at Nuremberg on September 19, 1945. National Archives.

p. 95 "This morning on the twenty-seventh": Burgess, p. 160.

p. 100 "Talk freedom at home": "Death of a Hangman" by Roy Kohler, *Pittsburgh Press*, November 20, 1955.

p. 102 "The Reichsmarshal gave me this": British Broadcasting Company Program, "The Vermeer Forgeries," by Michael Warton.

p. 103 "The following gentlemen performed": Payne, p. 77

p. 104 "On behalf of the Führer": Consolidated interrogation Report No. 4. National Archives.

p. 105 "Eventually Buemming informed me": ibid.

p. 106 "Considering we have 20,000 items": ibid.

p. 106 "I have only just learned": ibid.

p. 108 "The Führer, on receiving the report": ibid.

p. 109 "I have promised to support": ibid.

p. 110 "The Führer wishes that": ibid.

p. 112 "Based on the Führer's orders": Roxan and Wanstall, pp. 148–149.

p. 115 "The field office of the Todt Organization": Kogon, p. 118.

p. 116 "We even were asked to contribute": Author interview with Karl Becker, Munich, June 1978. Becker was a prisoner at Dachau for three years.

p. 117 "Daily farming-out wage": RFSS Microfilm, Group T-175, "Files of the Personal Staff of the Reichsführer-SS." National Archives.

p. 119 "It is a fact, however": Interrogation of Gottlob Berger, October 30, 1947, at Nuremberg. Interrogation Summary No. 3913. National Archives.

p. 121 "Himmler's herbs didn't save": Author interview with Charles Bruegge, Munich, July 1978. Bruegge survived Dachau but not, he insists, because of any nutritional value of Himmler's herbs.

p. 124 "By order of the supreme command": RFSS Microfilm, Group T-175. National Archives.

p. 125 "How can we be so cruel": *Time*, October 28, 1974, p. 36.

p. 127 "Beyond the bounds of civil laws": MA 330/B.4112. Institut für Zeitgeschichte, Munich.

p. 129 "She attracted me immensely": Bormann, p. 39.
p. 130 "Himmler's first marriage": Manvell and Fraenkel, p. 105.
p. 131 "As the Führer stressed": Memorandum 1-29-44 "Re: Safeguarding the Future of the German People." National Archives.
p. 131 "The fact that a man": Manvell and Fraenkel, p. 191.
p. 132 "Who will ask in 300": Bleuel, p. 172.
p. 134 "If any such idiot": Hitler's Secret Conversations, p. 477.
p. 139 "General Burgdorff and Fegelein came": Bormann, p. 85.
p. 139 Fegelein and Burgdorff invade": ibid., p. 140.
p. 140 "The longer the war lasts": Von Lang, p. 277.
p. 142 "Did you happen to hear": "Whereabouts of Hitler, Eva Braun and Hermann Fegelein," dated September 21, 1945. U.S. Army Intelligence and Security Command (USAISC).
p. 147 "Treason and treachery by Himmler": Irving, p. 818 (3).
p. 147 "I think I can say with certainty": USAISC Report.
p. 151 "Whenever I visited Hess": Fest, p. 193.
p. 160 "We reached the bridge": O'Donnell, p. 305.
p. 161 "The reference dispatch reported": American Embassy Dispatch No. 154, dated September 9, 1954. U.S. Department of State.
p. 162 "Dr. [Wilhelm] Voss has been playing": Memorandum of Conversation, by G. Lewis Jones, Cairo, Egypt. Document 774.5214-2853. U.S. Department of State.
p. 164 "The commander of the battalion": "Hitler's Death," dated September 10, 1945. Document 338–346. USAISC.
p. 165 "That would be impossible": Report 491. USAISC.
p. 166 "Due to the fact": File Memo to Theater Judge Advocate, dated October 19, 1945. Document 316. USAISC.
p. 166 "Late Tuesday afternoon": Memorandum for Colonel Buttles, from Major General Clayton Bissel. Document 497. USAISC.

p. 167 "Had a path been cleared": Interrogation Summary: Hanna Reitsch, dated October 8, 1945. Documents 237–250. USAISC.

p. 168 "Through the cooperation": Letter Proclaiming Knowledge of Hitler's Whereabouts, dated July 26, 1945. Documents 422–443. Also 386. USAISC.

p. 169 "Mr. Stineman declined to furnish": "Report that Adolf Hitler is in Argentina," from J. Edgar Hoover to War Department, dated September 6, 1945. Document 386. USAISC.

p. 170 "Deutsches Haus and its owner": "French Report on Alleged Resistance Movement," dated January 22, 1946. Documents 229–232. USAISC.

p. 170 "We request that": Memorandum from Rosenthal to C.I.C., Region II Headquarters, February 6, 1946.

p. 171 "I should like to inquire": "Letter from one Vianello, Milan, Italy," dated June 11, 1947. Documents 118–121. USAISC.

p. 171 "The informant stated": "Possible Lead on Adolf Hitler." Documents 165–166. USAISC.

p. 172 "Immediate suspension of all trials": "Document Allegedly Written by Hitler," dated June 12, 1947. File No. 350.09. Documents 095–097. USAISC.

p. 174 "I did not see the dead Führer": "Last Days of Hitler," a report by R. M. Thoroughman about the interrogation of Walter Paul Schreiber, dated November 15, 1948. Documents 033–034. USAISC.

p. 175 "There is available to the army": "The Fate of Adolf Hitler," a memorandum for the Director of Intelligence, dated May 6, 1947. Documents 122–123. USAISC.

p. 180 "The uniforms were provided": Author interview with Skorzeny.

p. 181 "In view of his past": Report about Skorzeny from 66th CIC. Document 439. USAISC.

p. 181 "The leader of this movement": Confidential Intelligence Report, by Agent Fritz Fischer, CIC. Document 214. USAISC.

p. 189 "I was threatened with arrest": "Colonia Dignidad: Nobody Comes, Nobody Goes," by Charles A. Krause. *Washington Post*, February 11, 1980.

p. 190 "The flight was planned and prepared": *Bild am Sonntag*, Bonn. August 21, 1977.

p. 193 "We are using German Methods": *Time*, September 26, 1977,

p. 193 "It is a group": Farago, p. 388.

p. 194 "The Germans are the best organized": ibid., p. 387.

p. 194 "Nazi leaders, groups, and organizations": Montgomery, p. 54.

p. 196 "Law is built upon precedent": "Musmanno on Eichmann," by Trude E. Feldman, *The National Jewish Monthly* (date and volume not available).

p. 201 "Lorenz seemed to be": "Operation Globetrotter—Re: Lorenz, Erika," dated November 18, 1946. Document 156. USAISC.

p. 201 "In the first days of May": ibid.

p. 203 "I was told in Schladming": Interrogation of Frau Agnes Konrad. Document 306-C. USAISC.

p. 204 "Very well, I will tell you": Interrogation of Rudolf Meier. Document 306-MM. USAISC.

p. 206 "The interrogation of Hauptsturmführer Franz Konrad": "Fanz Konrad—Interrogation at Regensburg," dated July 4, 1946. Document 185-A thorough G. USAISC.

p. 208 "The suit which was supposed": "Ownership and Disposal of Effects Recovered as a Result of the Interrogation of Wilhelm Spacil." Documents 208–209 USAISC.

p. 208 "Destruction of these items": "Hitler-Eva Braun Material Report," dated July 23, 1947. Document 092. USAISC.

p. 209 "RSHA Funds": "Ownership and Disposal of Effects Recovered as a Result of the Interrogation of Wilhelm Spacil." Documents 208–209. USAISC.

p. 213 "At the trial of any individual": Smith, p. 61.

p. 214 "Liquidate the criminal organizations": Mader, p. 103.

p. 214 "Use of Berlin as a center": ibid., p. 107.

p. 221 "That Felfe fellow is outstanding": Höhne and Zolling, p. 232.

p. 224 "I am only sorry": *Time*, April 2, 1973, p. 37.

p. 226 "No person shall be eligible": Report by the Comptroller General of the U.S., dated May 15, 1978, p. 2.

p. 227 "The Immigration and Naturalization Service": ibid., p. 44.

p. 228 "The CIA said it had contacted": ibid., p. iii.

p. 228 "The FBI had information": ibid., p. iii.

Index